Mathcad
A Tool for Engineering Problem Solving

MCGRAW-HILL'S BEST

Mathcad
A Tool for Engineering Problem Solving

Philip J. Pritchard
Manhattan College

WCB
McGraw-Hill

Boston   Burr Ridge, IL   Dubuque, IA   Madison, WI   New York   San Francisco   St. Louis
Bangkok   Bogotá   Caracas   Lisbon   London   Madrid
Mexico City   Milan   New Delhi   Seoul   Singapore   Sydney   Taipei   Toronto

WCB/McGraw-Hill

A Division of The **McGraw·Hill** Companies

MathSoft and Mathcad are registered trademarks of MathSoft, Inc.

MATHCAD: A TOOL FOR ENGINEERING PROBLEM SOLVING

This book is printed on acid-free paper.

5 6 7 8 9 0 DOC/DOC 0 9 8 7 6 5 4 3

ISBN 0–07–012189–3

Vice president and editorial director: *Kevin T. Kane*
Executive editor: *Eric Munson*
Developmental editor: *Holly Stark*
Marketing manager: *John T. Wannemacher*
Project manager: *Alisa Watson*
Production supervisor: *Lori Koetters*
Compositor: *Shepherd, Inc.*
Typeface: *10 / 12 Century Schoolbook*
Printer: *R. R. Donnelly & Sons Company*

Library of Congress Cataloging-in-Publication Data

Pritchard, Philip J.
    Mathcad : a tool for engineering problem solving / Philip
Pritchard.
      p. cm.
    Includes index.
    ISBN 0–07–012189–3
     1. Engineering—Data processing.   2. MathCAD.   I. Title.
TA345.P765   1999
620'.00285'5369—dc21   97–47318

Contents

Preface

This book was written as part of the McGraw-Hill *BEST* series (Basic Engineering Series and Tools). The intended audience for all of the books in this series is the introductory engineering class. However, as I was writing the book, it became apparent that, due to the nature of Mathcad itself, even a text covering only its main features would end up covering some material to which a beginning engineering student might not yet have been introduced. Hence, although the primary market for this text is still the introductory engineering class, in truth engineering students from freshmen through seniors, and even graduate students, will find it helpful in learning Mathcad. Practicing engineers who want a compact guide to using Mathcad for solving their engineering problems will probably find it useful as well.

Many colleges in the United States are now using a one- or two-semester course designed to introduce students to the basics of what it means to be an engineer. These courses invariably include exposing the students to use of the personal computer as a communication and analysis tool. For example, they may be taught how to use a spreadsheet, a technical calculation package such as Mathcad, and how to use a programming language such as *C* for doing engineering work. This book is suitable for use in such a course.

Each chapter introduces features of Mathcad by immediately doing engineering examples, so that the student can see that the features being described do have a real-world, practical engineering application. The chapters should be read while at the computer, so that the student can replicate each of the examples. In doing so, they will not only learn how to use Mathcad, but also get exposure to some typical engineering problem-solving methodologies.

Some of the chapters have exercises at the end of each chapter section. These are intended as practice exercises on the specific material covered in that section. It's probably a good idea that the student do all of these. Exercises at the end of each chapter are intended for further practice, and would make good homework questions.

Sophomores, Juniors, and Seniors will also find the book useful in learning Mathcad. Depending on their previous experience with Mathcad, they should be able to move fairly quickly through practically all of the material, except for perhaps one or two sections (for example, Laplace transforms, covered in Chapter 9). These students will include people who have never used Mathcad and those who have some knowledge of it. The former will be able to self-teach by reading the book from the beginning. The latter will be able to pick and choose those topics they wish to learn more about. In fact, the Mathcad 7 Student Edition has a number of important changes from the previous version, not least of which are the equation-editing techniques and the additional built-in symbolic features such as Laplace transforms.

Graduate students and engineers in industry should have no difficulty in reading this book from cover to cover (while using the computer) in a relatively brief period of time. After doing so, they will have a good grounding in the basic features of Mathcad and a sense of its power in solving the engineering problems they encounter.

What is Mathcad, anyway? We'll discuss this in detail in Chapter 1, but here let's just say it's one of several technical calculation applications that are available today. Although it is always difficult to make such predictions, it seems likely that in the next few years it may become the dominant application of this kind. In my opinion, if it does so, it will be well deserved. It has done especially well in its migration from the DOS world to the graphic world of Windows (in its various incarnations of Windows 3.x, Windows 95, etc.). You have probably experienced software that is very "clunky," that requires you to work with several windows within the application, that is just plain ugly, or that has a very odd menu structure or icon system. That software will probably be one that existed before Windows and has never completely migrated to the fully graphic interface. This description certainly does not apply to Mathcad because it has, again in my opinion, more successfully taken to the Windows environment than any other mathematics application. It has a completely graphic interface and is truly WYSIWYG (what-you-see-is-what-you-get).

This is one of the reasons it is my most-used and best-liked computer application (with the runner-up spot going to the spreadsheet). There are lots of other reasons. For example, it is especially good at handling units. My experience with engineering students (including graduate students) over the years has taught me that even the best of them have a somewhat casual attitude to units. (Question: "What's the acceleration of gravity?" Answer: "32.2"). Mathcad will automatically work with the units for you and give you the answer in any units you wish. It might appear that this is a bad thing, similar to giving a calculator to someone who is innumerate, but actually it's not. In my experience with teaching Mathcad, students get a better understanding for units. This is because, if a student tries to do something using units that is improper, Mathcad will "flag" that error, forcing the student to check their own use of units. For example, if a student inadvertently defines a mass in, say *lbf* rather than *lb,* sooner or later Mathcad will compute something that will have units that the student will recognize to be incorrect. In this way Mathcad will reinforce correct units usage, while at the same time eliminating all of the drudgery of unit conversions (from, for example, a density expressed in *lb/ft*^{3} to one in *kg/m*^{3}).

To their credit, the people at Mathsoft have continued to develop Mathcad at a healthy pace. They seem to release a new version about once every twelve to eighteen months, and each new version genuinely has major improvements. For example, the much-improved equation editing of version seven is a major change. There also seems to be a pattern: as each new version comes along, it seems that what was only in the more expensive professional edition in a previous version pretty much gets inserted into the new inexpensive student edition, and a lot of new features are put in both editions. This is true with the Mathcad 7 Student Edition: it has most of the capability of Mathcad 6 Professional Edition (for instance it now has symbolic transforms such as Laplace, Fourier and Z), and Mathcad 7 Professional Edition has new extensive programming capabilities. Mathcad is also kept very current. For example, in the last few years the explosion in attention given to the World Wide Web is reflected in the fact that version seven has built-in web connectivity (and in fact, so did version six). Hence, users of Mathcad have one more avenue for remaining up to date on developments in the world of computing.

I'd like to thank a number of people for their help as I prepared this book. Professors Dan Haines, Bahman Litkouhi, Mohammad Naraghi, and Graham Walker, my students Steve Rutgerson and Suzanne Wright, all of Manhattan College, and Professor Byron Gottfried of the University of Pittsburgh offered many suggestions for improvements. Edward Adams of Adams Technologies gave me many good ideas for exercise questions. The people at Mathsoft, especially Paul Lorczak and Clay Stone, have been very helpful, and are to be thanked for producing a marvelous piece of software. Finally, David Shapiro (who initially contacted me about writing such a book) and especially Eric Munson and Holly Stark (both of whom have a remarkable ability to be simultaneously informal and professional), and all of McGraw-Hill, have earned my respect and thanks for their support. Of course, any praise this book earns should be directed at them, and any errors are mine and mine alone.

Dedication

To my mother, Elaine, for all her tea over the years, and my wife, Penelope, for her sympathy during the struggle to complete this book on schedule.

About the Author

Philip J. Pritchard received his Ph.D. in engineering mechanics from Columbia University in 1987. He has been a faculty member of mechanical engineering at Manhattan College since 1981, where he teaches undergraduate and graduate courses in thermodynamics, fluid mechanics, and analysis and numerical methods, and has twice been the recipient of the teacher of the year award from the Manhattan College student section of Pi Tau Sigma. He publishes and presents papers in the area of engineering education, specifically in the use of the PC (personal computer) for doing engineering analysis. Dr. Pritchard is a member of Sigma Xi and the American Society for Engineering Education.

What Is Mathcad and Why Use It?

What tools do engineers and scientists need to do their job? To answer this question, we need to consider what it is that engineers and scientists do.

Engineers and scientists typically apply the concepts and laws of engineering science and physics to physical phenomena and, based on these, develop mathematical models to simulate (or represent) the phenomena. These models can take many mathematical forms: at their simplest, the model results in an algebraic equation, but sometimes the analysis results in a differential equation or an integral equation. Very often an analysis can lead to not one equation but a set of equations.

As an illustration of this, let's consider an example from electrical engineering. Suppose you have the DC circuit shown in Figure 1.1. *If you're not familiar with DC circuits, don't worry, because the focus of this text is not engineering theory but how to use Mathcad to solve the engineering mathematics problems that result from doing engineering analyses.*

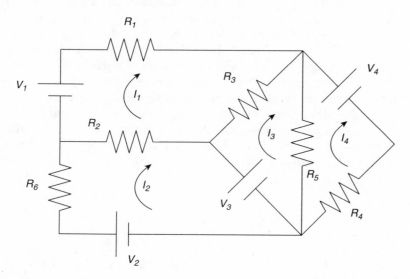

Figure 1.1

Suppose the resistors R_1 through R_6 and applied voltages V_1, V_2, V_3, and V_4 are all known. This fairly complicated circuit must be analyzed to find the currents I_1, I_2, I_3, and I_4 in each loop. In Figure 1.1 we have *assumed* that all four currents are clockwise, so if we find after solving the problem that one of them is negative, it will mean that that particular current runs counterclockwise. Note also that the current in a particular part of the circuit can be deduced from these currents. For example, the current through R_3 will be $I_1 - I_3$.

How do we solve such a problem? To solve it, the engineer uses the appropriate concepts or ideas from electrical engineering to *mathematically* model the circuit. In this case, we can use the idea that the total voltage change around a closed loop is zero. Here we have four unknowns, so we will need four equations. It can be shown that these equations are:

$$V_1 - I_1(R_1 + R_2 + R_3) + I_2 R_2 + I_3 R_3 = 0$$
$$V_2 - I_2(R_2 + R_6) + I_1 R_2 - V_3 = 0$$
$$V_3 - I_3(R_3 + R_5) + I_1 R_3 + I_4 R_5 = 0 \qquad (1.1)$$
$$-V_4 - I_4(R_4 + R_5) + I_3 R_5 = 0$$

How would you go about solving these equations? Well, you could manipulate the equations to try and eliminate all the unknowns except, say, I_1, and then continue on to find the other three unknowns. However, this would be extremely tedious to do, and also it would be easy to make an arithmetical error at some point. Imagine if you had a more complex circuit, with, for example, 100 current loops. You'd end up with 100 equations for these 100 unknowns. We obviously need a better method than manipulating these equations by hand. The approach used is called *linear algebra* (and we'll see how to use Mathcad to do this in Chapter 6). To implement this approach, we will need *mathematical tools*.

This example demonstrates, and is typical of, the situation engineers and scientists almost always face: after using engineering or physics concepts to develop a mathematical model of a phenomenon, mathematical tools are needed to get a solution to the problem. Today these tools invariably involve using a computer.

On the other hand, engineers sometimes need to deal not with an *equation* or *set of equations* but with *experimental data*, which they need to mathematically manipulate in some way to extract useful information. An example of this might be calibration data for a pressure gage:

Reading	1	2	3	4	5	6	7	8	9	10
p_{act} (Pa)	0	5	10	15	20	30	40	50	60	70
p_{ind} (Pa)	0	6	11	13	24	32	38	56	61	73

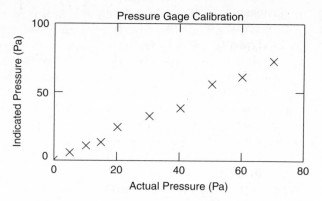

Pressure Gage Calibration

Figure 1.2

The table shows data for the pressure *indicated* by a pressure gage and the *actual* pressure. If we plot this data we get the graph shown in Figure 1.2. (This graph, by the way, was made using Mathcad.) The goal here would be to use this data to find, among other things, how accurate the pressure gage is. You can see, for instance, that it reads an actual pressure of 40 Pa as 38 Pa. Engineers would take such data and do a *statistical analysis* on it to see how good the gage is over the range of pressures measured. This involves computations that are not difficult, but are time-consuming and tedious to do by hand (and we'll see in Chapter 8 that Mathcad will do these calculations for us).

For mathematical manipulations of experimental data, engineers and scientists once again need to turn to mathematical tools. The most obvious tools available to engineers and scientists are calculators. *Scientific calculators* can perform many of the tasks described above (including calculus) and are very convenient for quick "scratch-pad" types of calculations. Their main disadvantage is that their small format means that they have limited capabilities for doing large amounts of data analysis.

The next most obvious tool is the *computer*.

We're all familiar with the extraordinary speed with which computer technology is developing. It's become something of a cliché to say that the computational power of a typical notebook computer is greater than that of the best mainframe computer in the best college in the country of 20 years ago; that it costs one-thousandth as much to buy and operate; and that it takes up less space than do the *Manhattan Yellow Pages* rather than using up most of a large room, which is what older computers with the same power as a notebook computer needed. In the United States, at least, personal computers (PCs) with this kind of power are becoming as ubiquitous as the telephone or television.

Corresponding to this exponential rate of growth of the power of hardware, and its general availability, computer software has undergone tremendous development in the last few years. Although it's hard to quantify, the capabilities of current software are so radically different from the software of even a few years ago that it's hard to avoid using the adjective "revolutionary" in descriptions. This applies to typical business software applications such as *word processors* and *spreadsheets*, and even more so to software for doing engineering or scientific computing or analysis.

The first widely used computer tools for doing engineering analysis were programming languages.

Programming Languages

A programming language is a computer language used to write a *program* consisting of *code* (lines of text) that tells the computer specifically what to do to accomplish a task. The most-used such language over the last 30 years in engineering and science is *Fortran* (from *FOR*mula *TRAN*slation). To see what this is about, consider the following simple example. Suppose you want to solve the following quadratic equation:

$$ax^2 + bx + c = 0 \tag{1.2}$$

where a, b, and c are known constants. Of course, we know that the solution to Equation (1.2) is

$$x = \frac{-b \pm \sqrt{b^2 - 4ac}}{2a} \tag{1.3}$$

However, this solution is a little trickier than it seems. You recall that Equation (1.2) can have *two real roots* or *one real double root* or *two complex conjugate* roots, depending on the values of a, b, and c. Let's imagine writing a program to solve Equation (1.3) that will compute the answer regardless of the solution type.

Before writing code it's usually a good idea to draw a *flowchart* describing what the computer should do at every step, allowing for each of the three possible types of answer that could arise in solving the problem. For Equation (1.3) this flowchart should look something like Figure 1.3 (where *sqrt* stands for the square root).

Now that the logic of the solution method is laid out, the Fortran code can be written. It turns out that it should look something like Figure 1.4. We won't go into the details of how to write code in Fortran, but the lines of code are fairly self-explanatory (especially if lots of comment lines are used, which is a good habit for programmers to have).

After writing this code and *compiling* and *executing* the program, it will do its job: give it values for a, b, and c and it will give you the solution to Equation (1.2). Actually, there's a *bug* (an error) in this program: the program should respond to the user regardless of the values of *a, b,* and *c* that are entered. However, if the user enters a value for *a* of zero, the program will *crash* or *lock up* because it will try to divide by zero! To correct this you'd have to put in an extra decision block that checks the value of *a* and, if it's zero, sends you to a path where the answer $x = -c/b$ is computed [check Equation (1.2) with $a = 0$ to see this]. Then you'd also have to modify the program to allow for the possibility that *c and b* might be zero. In this last case the program should tell the user that invalid data was entered (because for $a = 0$ and $b = 0$ there *is* no equation!).

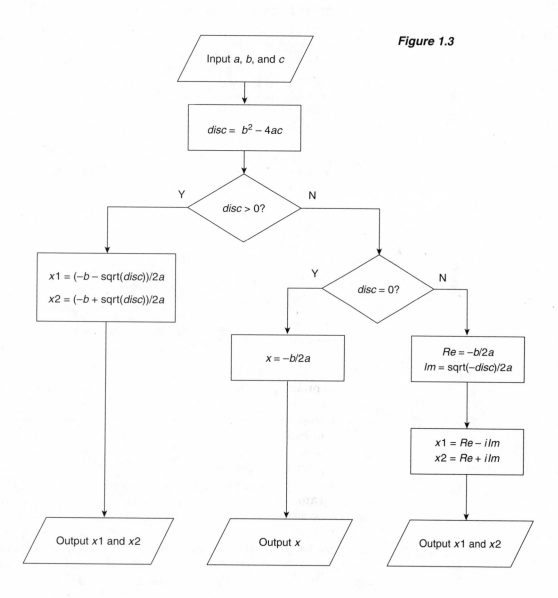

Figure 1.3

```
c                         Program to Solve a Quadratic
c
c       First read the equation coefficients
        real Im
        write(6,*)"Enter the coefficients a, b, and c"
        read(5,*)a,b,c
c
c       Compute the discriminant
            disc = b**2 − 4*a*c
c
c       Determine what kind of roots to expect
        if(disc.gt.0)then
c
c               This is the path for computing two real roots
                x1 = (−b − sqrt(disc))/(2*a)
                x2 = (−b + sqrt(disc))/(2*a)
c               Output the two roots
                write(6,*)"The roots are real, and x1 = ",x1,"and x2 = ",x2
c
c               Come here if we don't have two real roots
        else
                if(disc.eq.0)then
c                   This is the path when we have a double root
                    x = −b/(2*a)
c                   Output the double root
                    write (6,*)"There is a double root, x= ",x
c                   Come here if we don't have a double root
                else
c                   Compute the real part
                    Re = −b/(2*a)
c                   Compute the imaginary part
                    Im = sqrt(−disc)/(2*a)
c                   Assemble and output the complex roots
                    write(6,*)"The roots are complex conjugate,
                        x =",Re,"+/− ",Im
                    end if
        end if
        stop
        end
```

Figure 1.4

As you can imagine, Fortran is a very flexible and powerful high-level programming language, although it does need a bit of effort to learn. It's actually easier to learn now than it was in the 1960s and 1970s, and even the 1980s, because in those times the user would typically interact with the computer using punched cards, so there would be a big time delay between submitting the code to the computer and getting results. These cards were, literally, cards punched with holes, the hole patterns in each card representing one line of code. An engineer would have to sit at a console and punch out these cards, then deliver the batch of cards to the computer operator. (If you ever dropped your batch of cards and got them mixed up, you'd have a serious problem!) The computer operator would physically enter these cards into the computer; the code would be read, compiled, and executed; and the output would be printed out. This cycle would often take a day or more, so if you were a beginning programmer prone to making programming errors, it could take weeks to debug your program. Because part of the learning of any language is using it and getting immediate feedback on any errors, it's easy to see that learning to use Fortran efficiently in its early days was quite an undertaking. Today versions of Fortran are available that will run on a PC, so learning it is a lot quicker and easier.

Fortran is still very popular with engineers and scientists because it is modular: a complicated set of calculations can be broken down into modules handled by *subroutines* that communicate with the main routine or program. Also, it's been around so long that much code has been written with it: most engineers over the age of about 35 will have used Fortran, and so will probably have built up for themselves a useful library of code for solving a variety of problems. Also, much code is commercially available.

Fortran is still being improved and modified and is now at version 90/95. There is also a Visual Fortran, which is much more integrated into the Windows 95 and Windows NT environments.

Fortran has one major disadvantage: it is not inherently graphic. Fortran is happy to give you reams of tabulated data, but if you wish to present your work in a graph, you need to write additional code, or use special library functions that are commercially available. As we've seen in Figure 1.4, it does not have a particularly appealing interface.

In the last 10 years other high-level programming languages have also become common. As a bridge to Fortran, the program called *BASIC* (*B*eginner's *A*ll-purpose *S*ymbolic *I*nstruction *C*ode) was developed. A version of BASIC was supplied with the *disk operating system* (*DOS*) of IBM-compatible computers (even when these systems migrated to Microsoft Windows 3.1). This language, like Fortran developed in the 1960s, used similar syntax to that used by Fortran but was easier to learn and use because it was what is called an *interpreted* language. This means it gave the user immediate feedback on any errors committed, so that the cycle of writing, running, and debugging was immediate, facilitating quick learning. Although not as powerful as Fortran, BASIC was popular with students because of its relative ease of use. It has now pretty much been replaced with a graphically oriented application called *Visual Basic*. This application can be used for solving mathematics problems by creating programs that, when run, present the user with a Windows interface, although it's probably not something you would use for particularly complicated problems.

There are a constellation of other programming languages available, such as Pascal, C, and C++, which are also used by engineers and scientists. All of these come in various "flavors," developed by various companies. All of these languages (except Visual Basic) were developed before the advent of the *graphic user interface* (GUI), and they have remained *command-line* programs (that is, nongraphic).

In the last five years, as an alternative to programming languages, *spreadsheets* have become more and more commonly used by engineers and scientists for their engineering analysis problems.

Spreadsheets

Spreadsheets were initially developed for use in performing *financial* calculations. Because of this they emphasize arranging data in a *tabular* format, so that, for example, columns of data containing costs can be easily added. They have evolved into full-fledged *analysis tools*, with many engineering and scientific capabilities built in, such as comprehensive collections of math functions. In addition they are fully integrated into the GUI interface and have very extensive graphing capabilities.

Although initially there were a large number of different spreadsheets available, there are now three main ones: Microsoft Excel, Lotus 123, and Corel Quattro Pro. The competition between them, and the fact that they have each had many upgraded versions released over the years, has led to all three being extremely feature-rich, powerful applications.

Engineers and scientists have just begun to turn to spreadsheets in the last few years for their computation needs, and their use will certainly increase as knowledge of their advanced capabilities spreads. Several books are available on using a spreadsheet for engineering computations. See, for example, *Spreadsheet Tools for ENGINEERS*, by Gottfried (New York: McGraw-Hill, 1996).

An example of using a spreadsheet is shown in Figure 1.5, which shows the results of computing the temperature distribution in a body.

As you can see, a spreadsheet is an excellent tool for generating and displaying graphical results. It turns out that Figure 1.5 shows the results of solving a *partial differential equation* using a spreadsheet, even though spreadsheets do not have any built-in *calculus* capabilities. Generating the data for the graph involved knowing how to write expressions in the worksheet cells to numerically solve the differential equation.

In general, although spreadsheets are very easy to use and are commonly available, and are also fast and powerful, they do have

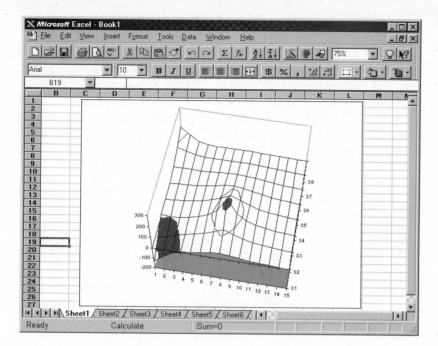

Figure 1.5

some limitations in solving engineering mathematics problems. For example, they do not handle units. Also, if you wish to solve problems involving calculus (for instance, performing an integration or solving a differential equation), you have to write fairly complicated spreadsheet worksheets.

The alternative to using a programming language or a spreadsheet is to use a *mathematics application*.

Mathematics Applications

Mathematics applications are designed from the ground up for performing the kind of mathematics engineers and scientists perform on a daily basis, from simple arithmetical computations to solving a set of differential equations. Because all the well-known ones were originally developed before the advent of the GUI interface, they each have implemented graphical features to differing degrees. Some of them use the command line, similar to that in Figure 1.4, whereas others are now fully graphic. Each has gone through a good number of iterations, adding more features, so that all mathematics applications available today are extremely powerful and versatile. Each one has strengths and weaknesses and, just as with word processors and spreadsheets, each has loyal followings among users.

As in most kinds of PC applications, for example, word processors, a few years ago there were several competing mathematics packages on the market, but these have been gradually reduced to Mathcad and its closest competitors, which include Maple, Mathematica, and MATLAB. Maple and Mathematica are packages commonly used by college mathematics departments because they are powerful in their handling of symbolic calculus. (Actually, Mathcad has a component of Maple's symbolic math built into it.) MATLAB is popular with electrical engineers, because it is adept at analyzing systems, especially when this involves the use of linear algebra.

This text, however, focuses on Mathcad.

1.2

What Is Mathcad?

As we have indicated, Mathcad is one of several state-of-the-art personal computer (PC) *mathematically* oriented applications. We'll see as we proceed through this text that Mathcad is a superb tool for performing engineering analyses. It has many advantages compared to other mathematics packages, with perhaps the five most important and obvious being the following.

1. Mathcad is 100 percent WYSIWYG (**W**hat-**Y**ou-**S**ee-**I**s-**W**hat-**Y**ou-**G**et). This means not only that Mathcad has a completely graphic user interface, but also what you see on the screen is what you get when you print a file. The other applications mentioned above either are not at all *WYSIWYG*, or only partially so. Pretty much *anything* you create in a Mathcad worksheet (its name for a file) not only prints as displayed, but usually makes sense to a person reading the printout, even if they are unfamiliar with Mathcad itself. This is in contrast to other mathematics applications, including to some degree spreadsheets, which usually require you to do quite a bit of work to prepare a document in a way that makes it suitable for presentation to others, or, even worse, require a reader of such a document to be familiar with the application's syntax.

For example, suppose you wanted to evaluate the following unpleasant integral in Mathcad:

$$\int_0^{2\pi} e^{\sin(x)} \cos(x)^2 dx \tag{1.4}$$

We'll see in Chapter 4 that to accomplish this all we need to know is how to type the expression into Mathcad. Following the de facto Windows convention, it turns out that there are always several different ways to accomplish any task in Mathcad, including the task of creating an integral symbol. We will learn how to type such an expression in Mathcad in Chapter 4, so we can end up with something like that shown in Figure 1.6.

The result in Mathcad is: $\int_0^{2\cdot\pi} e^{\sin(x)} \cdot \cos(x)^2 dx = 3.551$

Figure 1.6

This Mathcad output (put into a box to distinguish it from the text of this book) produced the answer for us, in a format that even a nonuser of Mathcad would understand!

2. Mathcad does not require learning special code. This is a corollary of the first point: because Mathcad is *WYSIWYG*, to execute practically any mathematical operation, all you need to do is learn how to type it into Mathcad. As a second example, to solve a quadratic [Equation (1.2)] in Mathcad, you could type the quadratic and then click on a Mathcad icon to ask it to solve the equation symbolically. This is shown in Figure 1.7, where two complex conjugate roots are presented (compare this procedure to that shown in Figure 1.4!).

$$3 \cdot x^2 + 2 \cdot x + 7 = 0 \text{ solve, } x \to \begin{bmatrix} \frac{-1}{3} + \frac{2}{3} \cdot i \cdot \sqrt{5} \\ \frac{-1}{3} - \frac{2}{3} \cdot i \cdot \sqrt{5} \end{bmatrix}$$

Figure 1.7

3. It is live. Once you've created a Mathcad worksheet, if you edit an input (which is easy to do), the subsequent calculations (including graphs) will be immediately updated. This means that one of the most common activities of an engineer, namely performing a "what-if" analysis, becomes very convenient to do. For example, once you've created a worksheet describing the behavior of a steel beam, you could change the length of the beam to see how the deflection of the beam would be changed. Or, as another example, if you want to integrate the expression in Figure 1.6 from $x = 0$ to $x = 4\pi$, all you need to do is edit the expression and Mathcad immediately updates the answer, as shown in Figure 1.8. Using Mathcad, you don't have to do things like recompiling, switching windows, and so forth, to change things.

The result in Mathcad is: $\int_0^{4 \cdot \pi} e^{\sin(x)} \cdot \cos(x)^2 dx = 7.102$

Figure 1.8

4. Mathcad can handle units. It handles *units* beautifully. Although you can even buy calculators with this capability built in, the competing mathematics applications cannot handle units. This is something that's very important for any engineer or scientist. It's common for an engineer to accumulate data from various sources when analyzing a problem. Some data may be in SI units, others in U.S. units, and yet others in nonstandard units. Mathcad has no difficulty in accepting such mixtures and providing you with answers in any units you desire.

As a simple example, imagine computing the mass M, in kilograms, of a rectangular block. The density of the block is $\rho = 5$ lb/ft^3, and its sides are $l = 1$ m, $w = 25$ cm, and $h = 3.5$ in. The formula for the mass is

$M = \rho l w h$. This computation, although not particularly difficult, can be a little messy because the units are mixed U.S. and SI units. Mathcad handles the units calculation easily, as shown in Figure 1.9, where Mathcad computed the mass to be 18.37 kg (and if we want to, we can ask it to give us the answer in, say, lb).

The given data is: $\quad \rho := 5 \cdot \dfrac{lb}{ft^3} \quad l := 1\,m \quad w := 25\,cm \quad h := 3.5 \cdot in$

The mass is then: $\quad M := \rho \cdot l \cdot w \cdot h \qquad M = 1.78 \cdot kg$

Figure 1.9

5. Mathcad is well integrated with the World Wide Web. You can browse live math and HTML files with Mathcad, create hyperlinks on your worksheets, and share files with other Mathcad users via the Internet. From *within* Mathcad (assuming your computer is configured for access to the Web), you can go to the site shown in Figure 1.10.

There is also a free *Collaboratory*, accessible via the Web, which is a kind of users group, with the added benefit that you can exchange Mathcad files with users worldwide. We'll discuss these features in Chapter 9.

Having said all these positive things about Mathcad, we should point out that it has three initial disadvantages:

1. While it's very easy to type equations into Mathcad, until you get used to how it works, *editing* equations can be a little frustrating (the

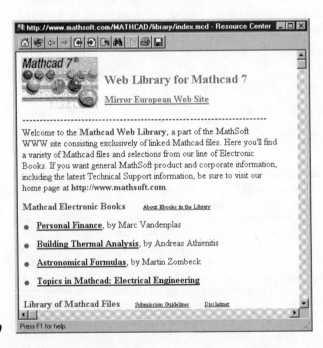

Figure 1.10

editor syntax is not *quite* the same as that for a regular word processor). For beginners it's sometimes easier to just delete an equation and retype it rather than try to edit it.

2. Mathcad requires you to use some keystrokes that, for the beginner, seem a bit odd. For example, we'll see that, to create an equation, instead of using the *equals* sign (=), you must type the *colon* (:). Moreover, when you do this, the screen will produce not the colon, and not even the equals sign (=), but colon-equals (:=)! There are just a handful of such unusual keystrokes, so after a few hours' experience, you'll probably have them memorized.

3. Mathcad has a few *accelerator keys* that are not exactly intuitive or mnemonic. For example, whereas Windows 95 uses the mnemonic **Ctrl + I** (meaning hold down the **Ctrl** key while you press **I**) to invoke italicizing of text (so that **I** reminds you of *italic*), Mathcad uses the non-mnemonic **Shift + /** to create a differential. The slash symbol (/) does not remind anyone of differentiation. Fortunately, the somewhat unusual keystrokes that Mathcad occasionally uses don't need memorizing because, as we have already mentioned, it follows the Windows convention that actions can be accomplished in any one of several ways. For instance, in Mathcad another way to create a differential is by using Mathcad's Calculus palette icon. This means that this disadvantage of Mathcad is not really much of one: after some use, you'll get to know Mathcad's most important accelerator keys, and if you don't, there will always be a menu or icon alternative.

It should be stressed that these three disadvantages of Mathcad are transient, in that after a few hours' experience, you'll probably have become comfortable with Mathcad, and not even notice them. One of the goals of this text is to get you over these initially tricky features, so you can then be confident in solving all kinds of engineering problems using this analysis tool.

Mathcad is now at version 7 so, as you might expect, it is very feature-rich. Just a sampling of these features will give you an idea of how versatile it is:

1. It has many built-in math *functions*, including, of course, such things as the trigonometric functions, but also less common ones such as the Gamma function.

2. It has many built-in *operators* for doing things like curve-fitting, interpolating, complex math, finding the roots of an equation, solving differential equations, and so on.

3. It has extensive *symbolic* capabilities for solving integrals, performing algebraic manipulations, and so forth.

4. It has a gallery of *graph* types available, including such 3-D graphs as surface plots and vector field plots.

Because Mathcad has always been so versatile (it's been referred to as "The Swiss Army knife of math software" by *Windows Sources* magazine), it has in the past sometimes been thought of as a relatively lightweight math package compared to some of its competitors. This presumption once had some basis in fact. For example, an early student edition was severely limited in the size of matrices that could be worked with, and worksheets of only a limited number of pages could be created. In addition, it did not have such practically essential features (for engineers, at least) as differential equation solvers built in. However, in the last few versions, these deficiencies have been remedied (matrices can be any size, limited only by your PC's memory, as can worksheets, and it has, along with other advanced operators, a differential equation solver), so that it's fair to say that Mathcad is a full-fledged, extremely powerful, and versatile mathematics application.

1.3

What's Next

In Chapter 2 we'll cover most of the material you'll need to use Mathcad for any kind of engineering analysis. Chapter 3 will review most of Mathcad's graphing features. It's recommended that you at least read these chapters, while you're at the computer, and at least do all of the section exercises they contain.

The subsequent chapters contain material you can go through either chapter by chapter or on an as-needed basis, as your knowledge of mathematics grows. For example, Chapter 6 (on linear algebra) and Chapter 7 (explaining how to solve differential equations using Mathcad) assume you already have at least some knowledge of the material. If you're a college freshman, the material of some of these chapters may be a little difficult, so you could postpone reading them.

Finally, note that in this text when you see something like **Ctrl + P** it means *hold down the* **Ctrl** *key while you press* **P.**

The Basics
of Mathcad

2

In this chapter we'll look at how to do such rudimentary things with Mathcad as opening and closing it and creating simple Mathcad worksheets (Mathcad's name for files), and then we'll introduce Mathcad specialties such as creating ranges, handling units, and so on. After completion of this chapter you should begin to feel comfortable with using Mathcad, especially as version 7 comes with a new *Help* facility called *Resource Center*, where you'll always be able to find more detailed information.

Once you've mastered the material of this chapter, the rest of the chapters of this book are designed to provide you with more detailed guidance on Mathcad's features, and how to use it for the kinds of things engineers often need to do, such as graphing and analyzing data, solving engineering equations, and so on.

2.1

The Mathcad Interface

To run Mathcad (assuming you followed the default installation method), click on *Start . . . Programs . . . MathSoft Apps . . . Mathcad 7*. This will bring up the Mathcad screen shown in Figure 2.1. The Mathcad interface consists of the *work space,* where you'll do your work; the *menu bar,* the *toolbar,* the *math palette,* and the *format bar,* all for access to various features; and the *title bar* and *status bar,* for giving you feedback on what you're doing at any given instant.

Here we'll assume that you are already familiar with the features that all Windows programs share (e.g., the use of *Scroll Bars*), and focus on those features that are specifically Mathcad's. (If you're a beginner to Windows 95, try using the Windows Start button to find *Help . . .* which will lead you to Windows' Help Topics window. Click on the Contents tab to see several items on using Windows, which you can explore.)

First of all, consider Mathcad's Menu system.

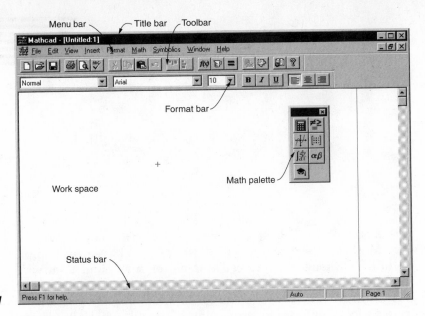

Figure 2.1

The Menu Bar

It's a good idea to click on each menu item in turn (or, if you're not using a mouse, press and release the **Alt** key to get access to the menu bar, then use the arrow keys to navigate around). For example, click on the *Insert* menu item. You now have access to the Graph menu and its options, as shown in Figure 2.2. Notice also that the status bar always tells you what you're in the middle of doing, and usually the menu system tells you what accelerator keys accomplish the same task (Figure 2.2 shows that **Ctrl + 2** can be used for creating a surface plot, not a combination you're likely to memorize!).

Let's now back out of this by pressing **Esc** enough times or by clicking with the mouse anywhere on the blank region (the work space).

Virtually anything you wish to do in Mathcad can be done using a menu item. As you progress through this text we'll discuss menu items as we use them. At the moment, let's point out two: The *File* item gives you access to, among other things, *Exit* to quit Mathcad (to exit you can also click on the cross in the upper right of the Mathcad window or click on the Mathcad icon in the upper left corner); the *Help* item gives you access to several sources of help, including Mathcad's unique *Resource Center*.

The Toolbar

Immediately below the Menu Bar is the toolbar, shown in Figure 2.3. This is a collection of icons assembled for your convenience. Some of these icons, when clicked, accomplish with that one

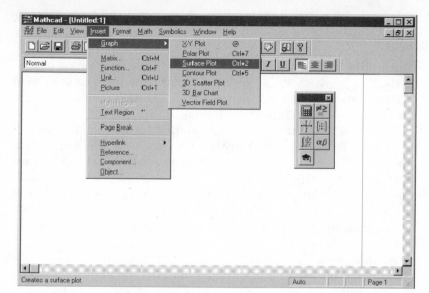

Figure 2.2

Figure 2.3

mouse click what would require several clicks using the menu bar. For example, to insert a function (we'll explain what this means a little later) you would click on the icon labeled $f(x)$. Try moving your mouse over this icon *without* clicking and an explanatory bubble will appear as shown in Figure 2.4. Instead of clicking on this icon you would have to click several times in the menu structure, starting with *Insert*.

Figure 2.4

The icons on the toolbar, beginning with the one on the left, are used for starting a new worksheet, opening an existing worksheet, and so on, through access to the *Resource Center* and access to *Help* (on the right). We will introduce each of these icons as we use them, except for those that are standard in Windows (such as the Copy icon).

The Format Bar

Mathcad has extensive word-processing-level formatting capabilities. This is very briefly described below. If you're not particularly interested in formatting, you can skip to the next section.

The format bar shown in Figure 2.5 is provided for formatting regions of text or mathematics (a *region* is a piece of text or a math expression you've typed in the work space). This is very similar to those you find in many Windows applications (e.g., Microsoft Word) and is basically self-explanatory, except perhaps for the first window.

This is a window for applying pre-designed (by you or by Mathcad) *styles* to a region. Doing this involves the notion of *template* files in which styles are stored. For example, you may wish text regions to be colored red and be in Times New Roman, variables to be blue in Times New Roman Italic, and constants black in Helvetica. To do this you would modify the styles of the default template. To modify *math* styles, first click on the menu item *Format . . . Equation . . .* to give you access to the Equation Format window, where you can then change the format of Variables and so on. Similarly, for modifying *text* styles, you would click on menu item *Format . . . Styles . . .* to give you access to the Text Styles window, where you can then change the format of Heading 1 and so forth.

At this point you would use the menu item *File . . . Save As . . .* to save the file as a new template in the template subdirectory. This template would then be available for you to use with new worksheets. To use it you would start by using the menu item *File . . . New.* A New window would appear listing all the worksheet templates available, including your new one.

Later on, after we've done some work in Mathcad, you might want to practice these template creation techniques. For detailed information on this topic, see Mathcad's *Help.*

The other windows are for changing the font characteristics of words in a paragraph and for aligning text in a paragraph.

Although formatting of worksheets is important for producing professional-looking work (and is in fact one of Mathcad's major strengths), we won't spend a lot of time on it in this text. Suffice it to say that, if you wish, you can apply all the fancy formatting to Mathcad worksheets—pasting of picture files, for example—that you are familiar with in all Windows applications, such as word processors. This is obviously a very useful feature of this mathematics application, and one which other such applications have not implemented as successfully.

In this text, to distinguish Mathcad worksheets from the book text, all regions have been formatted in the Helvetica font. This means that the work shown will often *not* appear in presentation-quality format (Helvetica is best used for things like headlines). When you replicate the examples we'll be doing, feel free to use any fonts, and any other formatting, you wish.

Figure 2.5

The Math Palette

The math palette is a very useful (in fact, essential) component of Mathcad. It consists of a collection of icons for accessing all kinds of mathematical entities. Referring to Figure 2.6, beginning with the top left icon and proceeding clockwise, these icons are for gaining access to the Arithmetic palette, the Evaluation and Boolean palette, the Vector and Matrix palette, the Greek Symbol palette, the Symbolic Keyword palette, the Calculus palette, and the Graph palette. You'll find that each of these palettes contains a very useful collection of icons for accomplishing various tasks. To open a palette just click on its icon. Each of these palettes gives you access to useful features. Figure 2.7 shows all 7 palettes.

Each palette can be dragged to a convenient location, and closed, using standard Windows mouse methods. Obviously, your workspace can easily be consumed by these palettes, so you will not usually leave them all open. Those you do leave open when you exit Mathcad will reappear in the same locations when you start Mathcad again.

As with the toolbar icons, an explanatory bubble explaining each icon's use appears as the mouse is moved over it. Also, as you become more experienced using Mathcad, you will probably end up using the accelerator key alternatives to many icons. This is in conformity with the Windows de facto convention that anything you wish to do can be accomplished in any one of several ways. Whether you prefer to use an accelerator key, an icon, or a menu item is pretty much a matter of personal choice.

Figure 2.6

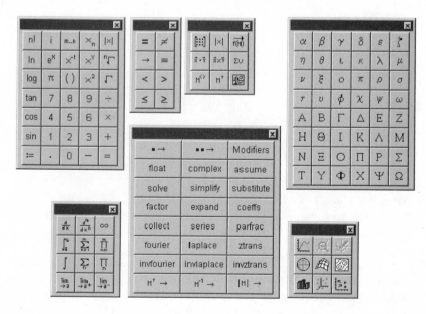

Figure 2.7

One final convenience is that the menu bar, toolbar, format bar, and math palette are all *tear-offs*, meaning that you can drag them around the screen, reorder them across the top of the screen, and so on.

The Worksheet Work Space

The work space is the blank region, representing a sheet of paper, on which you will do all of your work. We're almost ready to actually *do* something in the work space, but first let's see what the default page layout is by clicking the menu item *File . . . Page Setup*. Here you'll find a window for setting page size, orientation, and margin sizes. Let's back out of this by clicking *Cancel*. Next, click the Print Preview icon to see how your (blank!) worksheet would print. Close this window now, so we can learn how to type text and math regions into Mathcad.

Everything you type into the worksheet is either a *text* region or a *math* region. Let's start practicing creating both types of regions now by doing an engineering example. We'll explain the details of exactly what's happening as we go along.

Example 2.1 Uniform acceleration Suppose an object of mass M = 25 lb is accelerating at a constant rate a = 3 ft/s². Its initial speed is Vo = 10 ft/s. We wish to find the distance x (ft) traveled and the speed V (ft/s) after time t = 5 s.

The relevant equations of motion are:

$$x = Vo\,t + \frac{1}{2}at^2 \tag{2.1}$$

$$V = Vo + at \tag{2.2}$$

Don't worry about specifying, but not using, the mass M. We'll use it later to explore some of Mathcad's features.

You can easily solve this problem with a calculator, but let's solve it using Mathcad.

2.2

**Entering and
Editing Text**

First, let's see how we type text into Mathcad. For example, you may wish to give your worksheet a title or add explanatory text as you go along, explaining to a reader of your worksheet what it's about.

Mathcad assumes, when you start typing, that you're typing a *math* expression. If you wish to type a *text* region, you must signal to Mathcad that you're doing so, or it will try to interpret what you're typing as some kind of equation. There are several ways to indicate that you're typing text. To insert text at any point, click at that point to produce the *crosshair* and then use either of the following:

1. Click on the menu item *Insert . . . Text Region.*

2. Before typing any text, type the double quote ("). It appears as an open quote because the double quotes don't actually appear, and you do not type ending quotes.

The second method, using the double quote, is the one you'll find most convenient for starting a text region.

If you start typing at the crosshair *without* either using the menu item or using double quotes, Mathcad will assume you're typing an equation, and you'll quickly end up with something that will either give you an error or just look odd. However, Mathcad version 7 has a new feature where, if you forget to use either method to start a text region, it will assume you're typing an equation *unless* you type a space after the first word, which of course you'll do if you're typing more than a one-word sentence.

To finish typing a text region, do not press **Enter** (this would just start a new line in the current text region), but instead either use the arrow keys to move out of the region or click with the mouse anywhere outside the region.

Try to create the following near the top of the worksheet (see below for detailed guidance if you get stuck):

Uniform Acceleration

By (Your Name)

This worksheet computes the *distance* x traveled and the *speed* V of an accelerating object.

This example consists of three text regions. To create them, click in the approximate location of the first region, use the double quote, and type the text. Then click at the approximate location of the second region and create it. Repeat this for the third region. Now let's format the first as Helvetica 16-point, bold and underlined. In general, to format a region of text, click anywhere on the text region and then use one of the following methods:

1. Click the down arrow on the format bar style window to see a selection of predesigned styles (Normal, Heading 1, etc.), one of which you can select.

2. Use a standard Windows technique to select the text you wish to format (for example, use the arrow keys to move the cursor to the text you're interested in, and then hold the **Shift** key down while you select the text with the left or right arrow keys, as appropriate; or use the mouse to wipe over the text) and use the format bar options to change things such as font, point size, bold, and so on.

Remember that you can always customize the default styles and also create your own if you wish. Which of these two methods should you use? To some degree it's personal preference, but if you wish to generate many worksheets with the same formatting, you should use the first method. The second method has a bit more versatility, because it can be used on a selection of text *within* a region, and the fonts available are not limited to those in the predefined styles. For this example, use the second method. Your regions might not be arranged as you'd like. Let's see how you can rearrange them.

Arranging Regions

You now have three text regions. You may wish to move them around. The method for doing this depends on whether you select one or more regions. If you click anywhere on one region, a *selection box* with *handles* (small black rectangles) appears around it (try this on the first region). To move this region simply move the mouse to one of the box edges. At some point the *small hand* will appear. When this does, press and hold, at which point you can drag the region to a new location. This takes a little practice to get used to. Note that if the mouse arrow is directly over a handle, then instead of the small hand, *small arrows* appear. These are used to *resize* a region.

Sometimes you wish to work with several regions at once. To select several regions, click on some blank point on the worksheet and drag the mouse over an area in such a way that you include (even partially) all those regions you wish to arrange. *Dashed* selection boxes appear around each region. At this point you can cut or copy all enclosed regions using standard Windows methods, including right-clicking, or move them to a new location by dragging (the small hand appears if the mouse is over any of the selected regions). Finally, you can *align* them down or across using the Align Down or Align Across icons on the toolbar (not the left, center, or right icons on the format bar, which are for formatting text in a region). These techniques for cutting, copying, moving, and aligning work for math regions too.

Use these techniques to set up the three regions you've created to look something like those shown above.

Finally, if you wish to *edit* a text region, just click on it and, in addition to the selection box and handles, you'll see a vertical colored line called the *insertion point*. In text regions this insertion point has the same behavior as in a word processor.

For example, make the words "distance" and "speed" in the third region italic. One way to do this is by clicking on the region, then use the arrow keys until you reach the beginning of the word "distance." Then hold the **Shift** key while you use the right arrow to select the word. It will now be blacked out. Simply click the italic icon on the toolbar. Next use the arrow keys to locate the word "speed" and repeat. Of course, in this example it would have been faster to use the mouse to select each word by wiping over each of them.

Entering Equations

We'll see that *entering* equations in Mathcad is very easy, but *editing* previously typed equations is somewhat tricky, until you get used to Mathcad's editing logic (and version 7 has a different editing logic from previous versions). For this reason, we'll treat these as two different topics. While learning how to enter equations in the following sections, if you make an error, you may find it easier to delete an equation completely (by repeatedly using the **Backspace** and/or the **Delete** keys) and retyping, rather than trying to edit it.

Mathcad is very much like, and very much unlike, a word processor when you're entering equations. It's like a word processor in that you pretty much type an expression using the keys you might expect. For example, multiplication, division, and powers are invoked with the asterisk (*), slash (*/*), and accent (^) keys.

It's unlike a word processor in several ways. For example, you'll see a little later that the **Backspace** and **Delete** keys don't always delete quite what you'd expect, based on how a word processor works. It also doesn't follow a rigid line structure: you can place an equation anyplace you like, and not necessarily below the previous one. In this way, it's just like writing math longhand on a blank sheet of paper. You can write equations anywhere you like on a sheet of paper. The only constraint on where you place equations (by longhand or in Mathcad) is that you should (in fact in Mathcad you *must*) write them in a sequence that makes sense. Mathcad always—with one exception, which we'll see shortly—reads a worksheet from the top left to bottom right, so you must write your equations in the appropriate order. If you try to ask Mathcad to evaluate something before you have defined it, you'll get an error, unless it's something Mathcad already knows, such as π and e. A common error for beginners is to type two equations side by side and assume the one on the left will be encountered by Mathcad first. Mathcad *will* do so, unless the equation on the right is even *slightly* above the level of the one on the left. This can be very tricky because it's not always apparent that an error occurred, because the right-hand equation might still be computable (albeit incorrectly). To avoid this error it's always a good idea to use the Align Across icon on equations that you've typed in a row.

When you're typing an equation, bear in mind that Mathcad uses the standard hierarchy you're probably familiar with. For example, in a complicated expression it will evaluate multiplications and divisions before additions and subtractions, unless you impose an order by using parentheses.

The concept that Mathcad has some quantities built in is important. Not only does Mathcad have built in to it common constants, such as π and e, but as we'll soon see, it also has practically all the units you'll be likely to need. This means that, for example, Mathcad will understand m to be meters (actually, one meter). You are allowed to redefine m as anything you wish, such as the mass of an object, but if you do so the underlying unit system will be seriously in error for that worksheet. Hence, it's *always* a good idea to try and avoid using symbols that you might expect Mathcad to have already used for a unit. For example, use *M* or *mass* for the mass of an object, and avoid defining anything using symbols like ft, J, and so on.

Mathcad's Four Equals Signs

Mathcad has four different equals signs, each with its own purpose. Let's list them:

1. The *assignment* equals sign, which is generated using the colon (:) key or by clicking the Assign Value icon on the Arithmetic palette. This is used to *define* entities such as variables and functions. Even though it is created using the colon key, it appears on the worksheet as ":=" (without the quotes). This is the equals sign you'll use most frequently, so you should memorize the fact that it's created using the colon key. Once you've typed an equation, to end press the **Enter** key, use the arrow keys, or click on any empty region with the mouse.

You should note that math regions, unlike text regions, do not allow you to type in spaces (Mathcad will automatically space out math expressions as appropriate). This leads to an important point about the **Space bar:** *to move out of a particular location in a math expression* [e.g., an exponent or a denominator (as in the last equation shown below)], simply press the **Space bar** (or, less predictably, use the right-arrow key). We'll see when we do editing, and when we do more complicated math, that the **Space bar** is also very useful for selecting expressions on which to operate.

Let's practice using the assignment equals by continuing Example 2.1. Try doing the following in Mathcad (remember that if something unexpected happens, you can always delete the entire expression and start over by repeatedly pressing the **Delete** and/or **Backspace** keys; also, don't worry at this stage about the meaning of the vertical and horizontal *editing lines* that appear):

$a := 3$

$Vo := 10$

$t := 5$

$V := Vo + a \cdot t$

$x := Vo \cdot t + \dfrac{1}{2} \cdot a \cdot t^2$

2. The *evaluation* equals sign, which is generated using the regular equals (=) key, by clicking on the Calculate icon in the toolbar, or by clicking the Assign Value icon on the Arithmetic palette. This is used to *evaluate* (give the value of) whatever is on the left of the equation. As we just stated above, you can only evaluate something that Mathcad knows, and Mathcad only knows those things that are built in (e.g., the value of π or e) or that you have previously defined with the assignment equals (or priority equals sign, as we'll see below). As soon as you type an evaluation equals key, Mathcad will give you on the right side of the equation the value of the entity. As we'll see, you'll be able to change the format and units of the answer.

Let's continue with our example by asking Mathcad to evaluate what you just defined. In a space anywhere *below* the five previous equations, type the variables t, x, V, M, and g, following each with the evaluation equals sign for all five equations (the fourth expression is exited by pressing **Enter** or by clicking on an empty region with the mouse). Your screen will display the following:

$$t = 5 \qquad x = 87.5 \qquad V = 25 \qquad M := \blacksquare \qquad g = 9.807 \cdot m \cdot s^{-2}$$

What happened here? The first three equations came out okay, as you might expect. The last one produced a result, because although *you* never defined a quantity g, Mathcad knows of one (the acceleration of gravity), and even gave it units! So far we've intentionally not used units, for simplicity, but we'll see shortly how easy it is to do. The fourth expression is a bit of a surprise. Mathcad cannot give us a value for M (the object mass) because no such quantity exists. In previous versions of Mathcad, this condition would have generated an error signal. Version 7 has a new feature, the Smart Assignment operator. What this does is assume you *meant* to type the *assignment* equals if you type the evaluation equals with an undefined entity. In this example, then, Mathcad assumed we wanted to define a new quantity M using the assignment equals instead of the evaluation equals that you actually typed.

3. The *priority* equals sign, which is generated using the tilde (~) key or by clicking the Global Assignment icon on the Evaluation and Boolean palette. This works in the same way as the assignment equals sign, except for one major feature: when Mathcad computes a worksheet, as we have mentioned, it computes from the top left to the bottom right, *except* it first looks for all expressions with the priority equals sign and evaluates these first, in the top-left to bottom-right order. In this sense, these expressions will be global: Mathcad is aware of them before doing anything else. Why would you want such an equals sign? As we'll see, you often end up with a worksheet with a large number of calculations, leading, for example, to a graph. The graph might be on the last of several pages but be affected by an input on the first page. It's inconvenient to go back and forth between these pages to see how changing the input affects the graph. To be able to put an input adjacent to the graph, you would use the priority equals, so that Mathcad would find it first, then scan through all the pages performing all the other math.

Let's use the priority equals, and while we're at it see that Mathcad is indeed *live*.

Define M anywhere below all the previous expressions, using the priority equals. Next, click on the first M expression and use the backspace and/or delete keys until you delete the assignment equals and type the evaluation equals. You should get something like the following (showing all our equations so far):

$a := 3$

$Vo := 10$

$t := 5$

$V := Vo + a \cdot t$

$x := Vo \cdot t + \frac{1}{2} \cdot a \cdot t^2$

$t = 5$ $x = 87.5$ $V = 25$ $M = 25$ $g = 9.807 \cdot m \cdot s^{-2}$

$M \equiv 25$

Everything now works! Why did we have to delete the assignment equals in the equation for M? Because once Mathcad's Smart Assignment operator has converted the intended evaluation equals to an assignment equals, no matter what you do later it will leave it as an assignment equals (albeit incomplete). To see that the worksheet is live, try clicking on the first equation for t and replacing the value 5 with 10 (if this proves difficult, just delete and/or backspace until the equation is erased and type it again). After doing this, you'll immediately see the new values of x and V appear (250 and 40).

4. The *Boolean* equals sign, which is generated using the **Ctrl + =** keys or by clicking the Boolean Equals icon on the Evaluation and Boolean palette. This will be useful when we ask Mathcad true-false logical questions and also when we ask it to solve one or more equations (see Chapter 5 for more details on this).

As a practice exercise, you should tidy up the worksheet by inserting explanatory text at appropriate locations, deleting unneeded regions, and so forth save it (as "Example 2.1") in a location of your choice, and print it.

Try to make it look something like the following:

<u>Uniform Acceleration</u>

By (Your Name)

This worksheet computes the *distance* x traveled and the *speed* V of an accelerating object.

First, let's enter the given data:

Acceleration (ft/s^2): $a := 3$ Initial speed (ft/s): $Vo := 10$

The time duration is (s): $t := 5$

The equations of motion are: $x := Vo \cdot t + \frac{1}{2} \cdot a \cdot t^2$ $V := Vo + a \cdot t$

Finally, the results are:

At time (s): $t = 5$ Distance traveled (ft): $x = 87.5$ Speed (ft/s): $V = 25$

Exercises

In the following, *you* should take care of units and not attempt doing them in Mathcad. Hint: to get π, type **Ctrl + P.**

2.1 A shaft has a diameter of $D = 0.125$ ft and a length of $l = 10$ ft. The density of the shaft material is $\rho = 150$ lb/ft^3. Find the shaft mass M (lb).

2.2 Find the surface area A (m^2) and volume V (m^3) of a sphere of diameter $D = 0.25$ m.

2.3 You have the choice of depositing \$1,000,000 for 5 years in either Bank A or Bank B. Bank A provides interest of 3 percent, compounded monthly. Bank B provides interest of 3.25 percent, compounded annually. Which bank will pay you more? *Compounding* means, for example, that *each month* Bank A computes the amount of interest by multiplying what you currently have in the bank by 0.03/12 (the interest rate, on a decimal basis, for the month), and adds this amount to your deposit. After the first month, then, your deposit will be \$1,000,000 + \$1,000,000 × 0.03/12 = \$1,002,500. For the next month, the computation will be \$1,002,500 + \$1,002,500 × 0.03/12 = \$1,005,006.25. Compounding essentially adds interest to *previous* interest payments. The more frequent the compounding, the more rapidly the growth in the amount accumulated. To solve this problem, use the following: it can be shown that the formula for the total amount F accumulated by the principal (initial) amount P after n compounding periods, with an annual interest i (expressed as a decimal), with k compounding periods per year, is

$$F = P\left(1 + \frac{i}{k}\right)^n \tag{2.3}$$

We're almost ready to practice editing equations. We'll do this by changing the above worksheet so that it uses *functions*. Before getting into editing techniques, let's discuss how functions are created and used in Mathcad.

Mathcad has all of the common mathematics operators and functions built in. First of all, if you ever want to find out about an operator, one thing you can do is invoke Mathcad's *Help* and type in the Index window the word *operators*. You'll eventually be able to find help on the arithmetic operators (as well as Boolean, calculus, etc., operators), as shown in Figure 2.8.

Mathcad also recognizes all the common functions, and then some! You can find information on them in the same way as you can for operators (just type *functions* in the Index window). Mathcad has hundreds of functions built in, from Bessel functions to the If function to vector functions. To be able to use them you just need to type them in the form Mathcad recognizes. Let's

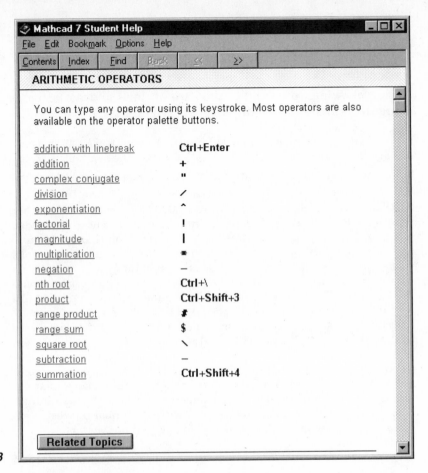

Figure 2.8

demonstrate this by creating a new worksheet (you don't need to close your current Example 2.1 worksheet because Mathcad can have any number of worksheets open at the same time). The quickest way to open a new worksheet is to click on the New Worksheet icon on the toolbar.

Let's ask Mathcad to evaluate $\sin(\pi/4)$ (note that Mathcad assumes angles are measured in radians). To do this, click anywhere on the new worksheet and simply type the expression as you'd expect, except the following: to create Greek symbols, you click on the Greek Symbol palette or alternatively type the corresponding Latin letter (here, p) and immediately press **Ctrl + G.** Actually, π is so commonly used it can also be invoked directly in Mathcad by typing **Ctrl + P.** (This last method violates one of Windows' standard mnemonics: in most applications, **Ctrl + P** invokes printing.) Also, recall that to exit from the denominator after typing 4, you can press the **Space bar.** In this particular case, however, this is not necessary, because Mathcad will automatically match up the opening and closing parentheses and not

leave the closing parenthesis in the denominator. If you do all of
this, after pressing = to get the evaluation equals you should end
up with:

$$\sin\left(\frac{\pi}{4}\right) = 0.707$$

Note that Mathcad is case-sensitive: it does not recognize
$\text{Sin}(\pi/4)$ (try typing it!).

How do you type a less common function? For example, let's
find the value of the fifth-order Bessel function of the second kind
at $x = 0.5$ (don't worry if you don't know what this is). Let's click
in an empty area to do this. You could try guessing how this is
typed in Mathcad, or you could look in *Help,* or, best of all, you
could click on the Insert Function icon on the toolbar (as shown
in Figure 2.4). This last option will bring up the Insert Function
window. To find the desired function, scroll through the list, or
start typing what you think are the first few letters of the function. You should eventually find Yn(m,x), as shown in Figure 2.9.

Note that some explanatory text is also displayed. Inserting
this will produce:

Yn (■ , ■)

where the black nodes are placeholders. The explanatory text
indicates that the first placeholder holds the Bessel function
order and the second the argument x. Click on the first placeholder and enter its value. To get to the second placeholder you
can either click on it with the mouse or **Tab** to it [this works with
all expressions (and graphs) that have multiple placeholders].
Note that if you *knew* the syntax for this Bessel function, you'd
just directly type it and the placeholders would not appear.

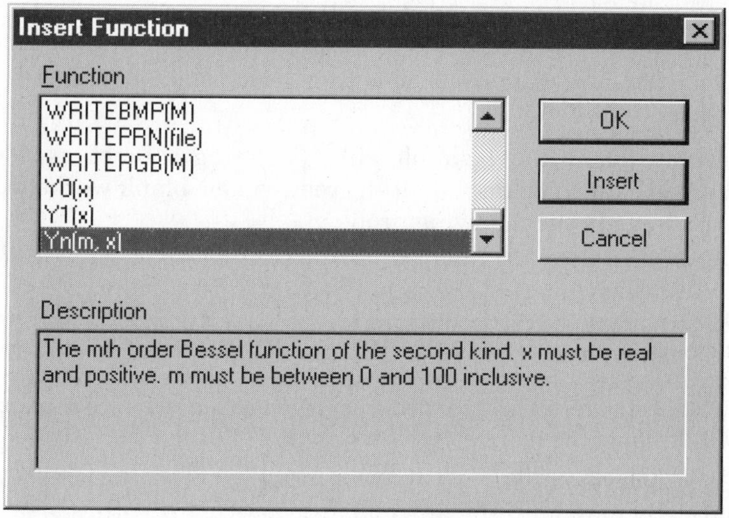

Figure 2.9

Entering the correct values and pressing the evaluation equals key (=) will produce the final results for this practice worksheet:

$$\sin\left(\frac{\pi}{4}\right) = 0.707 \qquad \text{Sin}\left(\frac{\pi}{4}\right) = \qquad \text{Yn}(5, 0.5) = -7.946 \cdot 10^3$$

Of course, if you're not sure how to type even a common function, you can use this Insert Function method.

In the above examples, we looked at built-in functions by evaluating them. More typically, they would be on the right of an equation. For example, try doing the following in your worksheet:

$$x := 0.5 \qquad y := \cosh(x) \qquad y = 1.128$$

We've now finished with this practice worksheet, so close it without saving. Let's now see how you define your own functions.

2.5

Defining Functions

Defining your own functions is simply a matter of typing them in as you would with a word processor, except that there are a few rules. First of all, of course, the assignment (or priority) equals must be used. We can summarize the additional specific rules for defining functions using as an illustration the ideal gas equation, given by

$$pV = MR_{\text{gas}}T \qquad\qquad (2.4)$$

where p, V, M, and T are the pressure, volume, mass, and temperature of an ideal gas and R_{gas} is its gas constant.

The rules are:

1. Functions can have any number of arguments; for example, $p(T, V) = MR_{\text{gas}} \frac{T}{V}$ is a function of two variables.

2. The function arguments (e.g., T and V) do not have to be defined before a function is defined.

3. Any other variables (e.g., M and R_{gas}) on the right-hand side must have been previously defined.

4. Functions and their arguments can include units, as long as these units are consistent.

If you follow these simple rules, creating a function is very easy. Let's do an example. First, create a new blank worksheet in which we'll do the following problem.

Example 2.2 The pressure of an ideal gas In an industrial process 1 lb of nitrogen (treated as an ideal gas with $R_{\text{N2}} = 0.3830$ psia-ft^3/lb-R) is expanded from a volume of 500 ft^3 to a volume of 1200 ft^3 while the temperature drops from 900 R to 600 R. By defining the pressure as a function of T and V, find the change in pressure (psi). Note that the volume expansion and temperature drop both lead to a reduction in pressure.

We'll do something new here. We'll create what are called *literal sub-scripts*. These are subscripts used in variable names. To create these, Mathcad has a unique procedure: you *must* use the period (.) where you wish the subscript to begin in the variable name. For instance, typing R.N2 produces R_{N2}. To exit from the subscript you press the **Space bar.** (For more on literal subscripts, as well as what are called *vector* or *array* subscripts, see Chapter 6.)

To begin solving Example 2.2, start by typing something like the following:

Pressure Change of Nitrogen

By (Your Name)

This worksheet computes the change in pressure of nitrogen during an industrial process.

Let's first define the gas constant: $R_{N2} := 0.3830$

Next, let's define the function for computing pressure as a function of T and V (note that the value of M must be given first!):

$M := 1 \qquad p(T,V) := M \cdot R_{N2} \cdot \dfrac{T}{V}$

We've been careful to use M and R.N2 and not m and R because, it turns out, Mathcad uses these latter terms for the units meter and degrees Rankine. We've set up the function $p(T,V)$, so now we can compute the change in pressure (using the literal subscript so that, for example, V.1 appears as V_1):

Next, let's enter the given data:

$V_1 := 500 \qquad T_1 := 900 \qquad V_2 := 1200 \quad T_2 := 600$

Finally, we can compute the change of pressure in one step:

$\Delta p := p(T_2, V_2) - p(T_1, V_1) \qquad \Delta p = -0.498$

The Δ symbol was created by typing D (no quotes) and then **Ctrl + G**.

Once you've defined a function, it can be used just like any built-in function, such as sin( ).

This example is still not very elegant because we've completely ignored units (in this particular example, the numerical values are not affected by the units). We'll soon learn how to include units. On the other hand, it includes use of literal subscripts and functions. Save this as "Example 2.2." Try the following exercises.

Exercises

In the following *you* should take care of the units and not attempt to use Mathcad for them.

2.4 In an industrial process air (an ideal gas with R_{air} = 0.3704 psia-ft^3/lb-R) is compressed from a pressure of 14.7 psi to 100 psi while the temperature changes from 500 R to 700 R. By defining the volume (ft³) as a function of p and T, find the change in volume (ft³) of 10 lb of air.

2.5 A person who falls into an icy river will quickly experience a temperature drop on their skin. A scientist comes up with a theory that the skin temperature T (°F) is given by

$$T = T_w + (T_{in} - T_w)e^{-\alpha t} \tag{2.5}$$

where t is the time in minutes and T_w and T_{in} = 98.6°F are the water temperature and initial body temperature, respectively. The coefficient α = 0.005 min⁻¹.

By expressing the temperature T as a function of T_w and t, find the skin temperature of someone after 10 minutes and after 60 minutes of immersion in water that is at (a) 35°F and (b) 60°F. Note: Mathcad uses the symbol T for Teslas (a unit for magnetic flux density), but as we're not using any units here, this should not be a problem, unless you attempt to use the Smart Assignment Operator.

Hint: After defining T_{in} and α, create a function $T(T_w,t)$. Then all you need to do to find the temperature after, for example, 10 minutes in 35°F water is to evaluate $T(35,10)$.

2.6

Editing Equations

As we've mentioned earlier, creating equations is fairly easy, but editing equations is a little tricky, until you get used to how Mathcad's editing syntax works. For a fairly complete explanation of this, click on the Help icon on the Toolbar, and in the Index window, begin typing *editing equations* until this topic appears as a choice. Choose it, and under Topics Found you'll find an option *editing an expression (generally)*. This is shown in Figure 2.10.

Let's now return to Example 2.1, in which you solved a motion problem using very rudimentary Mathcad techniques. Let's redo this problem in a more general way, by creating functions. As we do this, you'll practice using Mathcad's equation editing techniques.

First, if it's not already open, open your Example 2.1 worksheet. Let's immediately save the worksheet as a new file, so that if you get stuck at some point you still have your original Example 2.1 file. To save it as a new file, click menu item *File . . . Save As . . .* and save it as "Example 2.1 with Functions." (If you no longer have the Example 2.1 worksheet, simply start a new one and enter regions so that it looks something like the worksheet shown in Example 2.1 above).

Now let's edit this new file. Our goal is to edit the worksheet equations for the distance and speed, so they end up being *functions* rather than just *formulas*. Here we'll just mention a few things to get you started on learning editing.

1. The *editing lines*. These appear when you click on an expression. For example, click on the formula for x. You should see something like:

$$x := \underline{V_0} \cdot t + \frac{1}{2} \cdot a \cdot t^2$$

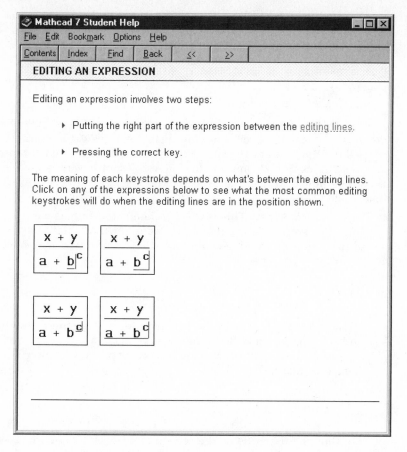

The window shows:

Mathcad 7 Student Help

File Edit Bookmark Options Help

Contents | Index | Find | Back | << | >>

EDITING AN EXPRESSION

Editing an expression involves two steps:

▸ Putting the right part of the expression between the editing lines.

▸ Pressing the correct key.

The meaning of each keystroke depends on what's between the editing lines. Click on any of the expressions below to see what the most common editing keystrokes will do when the editing lines are in the position shown.

$$\frac{x + y}{a + b^c} \qquad \frac{x + y}{a + b^c}$$

$$\frac{x + y}{a + b^c} \qquad \frac{x + y}{a + b^c}$$

Figure 2.10

Don't worry if your lines do not appear in exactly the same location as shown above. The colored lines that appear are the *insertion line* (vertical) and the *underline* (horizontal). They tell you where you are in the expression, and what part of it is currently selected. The size and extent of the lines always tell you what part of the equation you're about to edit.

2. The *arrow keys*. These are used for navigating around the equation. Try using the left and right arrow keys to see how these work. The only slightly surprising thing is that if you use either one of these keys (for example, the left key) enough times you'll move out of the expression. To get back to the expression, just use the opposite key (for example, the right key) or the mouse. Next, try using the up and down arrow keys. Either of these keys will exit you from the equation, unless it makes sense not to do so. For example, if the edit lines are in the denominator of the x equation, using the up arrow will move you to the numerator.

3. The **Space bar.** Using this expands the edit lines to include more of the equation. Once the entire equation is selected, pressing the **Space bar** again cycles back down to the original minimum selection. Try this on the equation for x. This is one of the most useful keys. For example, suppose you wanted to make the entire right-hand side of the x equation be the power to which e is raised (admittedly a nonsensical thing to do, but let's do it anyway!). To do this you first need to select the entire right of the equation. Use the arrow keys until the editing lines are in the 2 of the power of t. Then press the **Space bar** until all of the right-hand side is selected. You'll have:

$$x := \underline{Vo \cdot t + \frac{1}{2} \cdot a \cdot t^2}$$

You can now do anything you wish with the right-hand side of the equation. For example, you could (but here don't) press the multiply (*) key and multiply the entire expression by something else, and parentheses would *automatically* appear. In this little exercise we wish to insert something [namely e and the exponentiation (^)]. For this we need the **Insert** key.

4. The **Insert (Ins)** key. This is used to change the arrangement of the edit lines temporarily to the insertion mode, in which what you type is placed in *front* of an existing expression. Do this now (you may have to do it twice) and you'll get

$$x := \left| Vo \cdot t + \frac{1}{2} \cdot a \cdot t^2 \right.$$

Let's now proceed to type in the exponentiation. To do this press the ^ key and the expression will be immediately made an exponent with a placeholder (the small black rectangle) waiting for you to enter an expression. Type in e and you'll get:

$$x := e^{\left(Vo \cdot t + \frac{1}{2} \cdot a \cdot t^2 \right)}$$

Note that the parentheses did indeed appear. Now that we've seen how to use the **Ins** key, let's change the formula back to its original form by removing this exponentiation.

5. The **Backspace** and **Delete** keys. These work pretty much as you'd expect. The location of the insertion line tells you what is erased with these keys. For example, pressing the **Backspace** key in the expression above will delete the e:

$$x := \blacksquare^{\left(Vo \cdot t + \frac{1}{2} \cdot a \cdot t^2 \right)}$$

Pressing the **Delete** key will delete the placeholder and remove the exponentiation:

$$x := \left(Vo \cdot t + \frac{1}{2} \cdot a \cdot t^2 \right)$$

How do we delete the parentheses? In this example, just press the **Delete** key, which deletes whatever is immediately to the right of the insertion line (in this case a parenthesis). Note that both parentheses disappear, giving you back your original x equation:

$$x := Vo \cdot t + \frac{1}{2} \cdot a \cdot t^2$$

Working with these basic rules, you should eventually pick up the details of editing equations. Some unexpected things will still happen. For example, suppose you wanted to delete the right-hand side of the equation for x. If you use the arrow keys and **Space bar** as necessary so that the entire right side is selected and then press the **Backspace** key to try and delete it (try it!), you will not see the right side disappear; instead you will see

$$x := \boxed{Vo \cdot t + \frac{1}{2} \cdot a \cdot t^2}$$

You would then, it turns out, have to press the **Backspace** key again (don't do it!) to finish the deletion. This happens because Mathcad assumes you intend to delete a single symbol (letter, number, or operator) when you use the **Backspace** or **Delete** key. To delete an *expression* you've selected, you have to press the **Backspace** key twice. Click somewhere else on the worksheet to cancel this selection of the right side of the equation (we don't really want to delete it).

In this example, then, to delete the right side of the equation you would have used the **Backspace** key twice. Alternatively, you could have used the techniques we've described to first select the right side of the equation, and then either clicked the Cut icon on the toolbar or right-clicked with the mouse to bring up a small menu with various editing options, including *Cut*.

Even with these rules in mind, you'll find that sometimes you'll get frustrated editing an equation, especially if it's large. If unexpected things happen during editing (for example, a numerator disappears), you could click the Undo icon on the toolbar. If you get *really* frustrated, you can delete the entire equation and type it over again.

Finally, if you wish to delete, align, or move *several* equations at once, you can use the techniques described in Section 2.2 on editing text regions.

Let's now practice all of this by editing the Example 2.1 with Functions worksheet in the following way.

Example 2.1 (Continued)   Uniform acceleration (using functions)   Modify the worksheet Example 2.1 with Functions, using functions, so that you can conveniently compute the distance traveled and speed at any time t. Compute the distance and speed after 5 s and 10 s.

We'll edit the worksheet so that the equations for x and V become functions, but first let's use the period (.) to create a literal subscript, making Vo become V_o. To do this use the arrow keys as necessary to get the insertion line between V and o, and simply press the period key. Note that after you change Vo to V_o the subsequent equations will no longer compute, because Vo no longer exists! When you edit the equations, they'll again compute correctly. Edit the equations so that they are *function* definitions and so that they use V_o. After these changes, and deleting an unwanted region (the one creating the time duration), your worksheet should look something like:

Uniform Acceleration Using Functions

By (Your Name)

This worksheet computes the *distance* x traveled and the *speed* V of an accelerating object.

First, let's enter the given data:

Acceleration (ft/s^2): $a := 3$ Initial speed (ft/s): $V_0 := 10$

The equations of motion are: $x(t) := V_0 \cdot t + \frac{1}{2} \cdot a \cdot t^2$ $V(t) := V_0 + a \cdot t$

Another way you could have accomplished these modifications would have been to select and delete all regions below the given data regions. You could then have typed the new equations. However, we wished to practice editing, so instead we edited individual equations.

Note that we used a variable t on the right side of two equations without previously defining it. You recall that the reason no error arises is because you have made functions $x(t)$ and $V(t)$. The argument t in both formulas is simply a cipher and does not have to have a value when the functions are created.

Once these functions are defined, you can evaluate them at any value of the argument. For example, simply click somewhere below the above material and type the following [with the evaluation equals (=)] to find the distance and speed at $t = 5$ and $t = 10$:

Hence, after 5 seconds: $x(5) = 87.5$ $V(5) = 25$

After 10 seconds: $x(10) = 250$ $V(10) = 40$

We've just created our first function in Mathcad, and while doing so practiced our editing techniques. We'll get lots more practice in editing as we proceed through the rest of this text.

Exercises

2.6 Create the following worksheet:

$x := 2$ $y := x^2 - 4$ $y = 0$

Edit the second equation so it computes the expression $y = e^{\sqrt{x^2 - 4}}$. Hint: Use the backslash (\) for the root sign.

2.7 Create the following worksheet:

$x := 2$ $y := 0$ $z := 3$ $x^2 + y \cdot z - 4 = 0$

Use the editing techniques you've learned to change the last equation so you get:

$x := 2$ $y := 0$ $z := 3$ $(x^2 + y) \cdot (z - 4) = -4$

Hint: There are several ways to do this, but try using the arrow keys and **Space bar** as necessary so that the terms $x^2 + y$ are selected. Then type the right parenthesis, which will enclose the terms in matched parentheses. Use a similar method for $z - 4$.

Finally, edit the new expression to return it to its original form. Hint: Select just the y (with the insertion line to its right), press **Delete,** and observe what happens.

2.8 Create the following worksheet:

$$x := 1 \qquad y := 2 \qquad z := 3 \qquad \frac{x-4}{y+2} \cdot z - 2 \ = \ -4.25$$

Hint: Don't forget to use the **Space bar** after typing 4 in the last equation so that $x - 4$ is selected before you use the divide (/) key, and again after typing the denominator to escape from it.

Use the editing techniques you've learned to change the last equation so you get:

$$x := 1 \qquad y := 2 \qquad z := 3 \qquad (x-4) \cdot (y+2) \cdot (z-2) = -12$$

Hint: There are several ways to do this but try selecting the 4 and then pressing **Delete** to remove the division. You can then insert a multiply. Then you can work on combining z and 2.

As we mentioned earlier, the worksheet you've been working on would look much more professional if you used units, and if you computed the distance and speed for a *range* of time values. We'll look at units later, but first let's consider ranges.

To evaluate a function at many points you first define those points using a *range variable*. Range variables can be used not only for this purpose, but they can also be used for setting up the range of values for which a graph is plotted (see Chapter 3) and for working with vectors and matrices (see Chapter 6). A *range* in Mathcad is defined by a beginning value and an ending value. Mathcad assumes that you wish to have unit step sizes between these two values. If you want some other step size, you must specify *not* the step size, but the *second term* of the series when you define the range. In this case Mathcad uses the first and second values to figure out what the step size is and then generates values at this step size, until it reaches the last value.

We'll formally summarize the procedure later, but for now let's create, on a blank worksheet, a range x with values $(2,-2,-6,-10)$. Notice that here the series *decreases* in value [the step size computes to $-2 - (+2) = -4$]. To create this range you type *x:2,–2;–10.* Do this, with some explanatory text, and you'll get:

The range is: $x := 2, -2 .. -10$

Notice that the two periods were created by typing the semicolon. It's important to note that if you were to try typing two periods, Mathcad would not understand! What we've created is a range whose first value is 2, whose second is –2 (overriding the default, which Mathcad assumes is 3), and whose last is –10. If you now evaluate x, you'll get:

The range is: $x := 2, -2 .. -10$

x

2
–2
–6
–10

Instead of the usual equals sign (=), the sign disappeared and a column of the range values appeared.

It's a very common error in creating ranges to assume that the middle term is the step size rather than the second value of the series. Using the correct logic, we got the result shown above. If you had used the incorrect logic, of assuming that the middle term is the step size (–4), you would have ended up with:

The range is: $x := 2, -4 .. -10$

x

2
–4
–10

Here Mathcad interpreted this as a sequence whose first term is 2 and whose second term is –4, so that the step size is –6. Hence the next (and last) term is –10! If the last term had been a value that would not have been encountered in the computation of the series (e.g., in this example if it was, say, –9), the series would stop at the immediate previous step (e.g., –6).

Now that we've been introduced to the idea of range creation, let's close this practice worksheet without saving (we don't need it), open the Example 2.1 with Functions worksheet (if it's not already open), and create a time range for it. Continuing in your worksheet somewhere below the previous material, define a variable t by typing t:0,2;10 and pressing **Enter.** You should see (after including some explanatory text) the following:

The time range (s) is: $t := 0, 2 .. 10$

Now that you've defined a range of values for t, if you evaluate the time, distance, and speed (using the evaluation equals sign), you'll get these evaluated at all of the values of time t:

The times, distances, and speeds are:

t	$x(t)$	$V(t)$
0	0	10
2	26	16
4	64	22
6	114	28
8	176	34
10	250	40

This worksheet can now be printed if you wish, saved, and closed. We can point out three important features of ranges:

1. On the right side of a range definition, you can use constants (e.g., 2, π, etc.) or predefined variables (e.g., $v_{initial}$, v_{final}, etc.)

2. The second (middle) value is *optional*. If it's not specified, Mathcad assumes a unit step size.

3. Ranges can have units (although care should be taken if the middle value is not specified because Mathcad will assume a unit step size in the default units, whatever they happen to be).

With these ideas in mind, the general procedure for creating ranges in Mathcad can now be summarized:

1. Decide on the beginning and ending values. For example:

$v_{initial} := 10 \qquad v_{final} := 5$

2. If the step size is unity, just use these limits to create the range, using the semicolon (;) to separate the limits. For example:

$V := v_{initial} .. v_{final}$

V

10
9
8
7
6
5

3. If the step size is *not* unity, define the second term and create the range by using the beginning term, a comma (,), the second term, a semicolon (;), and the ending term. For example:

$v_{next} := 8.5$

$v := v_{initial}, v_{next}.. v_{final}$

v

10
8.5
7
5.5

Let's do another example illustrating the things we've learned so far.

Example 2.3 Radioactive decay The radioactive decay of a substance is given by

$$N(t) = N_o e^{-0.693\frac{t}{\tau}} \qquad (2.6)$$

where N is the level of radioactivity after time t, normalized to $N_0 = 100$, which is the initial level of radioactivity, and $\tau = 50$ is the half-life of the radioactivity. Set up a worksheet so that, given the values of τ and N_0, the radioactivity at $t = \tau$ is computed (it should be equal to half of N_0). Also, set up the worksheet so that it computes the radioactivity from $t = 0$ to 2τ with time steps of size τ/n, where n is a user input. Set $n = 4$. See if you can generate the following:

Radioactive Decay

By (Your Name)

First, enter the initial radioactivity and the half life:

$N_0 := 100 \quad \tau := 50$

The radioactivity decay formula is: $\quad N(t) = N_0 e^{-0.693 \cdot \frac{t}{\tau}}$

Let's compute the radioactivity at the half-life time:

$N(\tau) = 50.007$ . . . which is about half of N_0.

Or, perhaps more elegantly: $\quad \dfrac{N(\tau)}{N_0} = 0.5$

Finally, let's set up the time range: $\quad t := 0, \dfrac{\tau}{n}.. 2 \cdot \tau$

$N(t)$

100
84.093
70.716
59.467
50.007
42.053
35.363
29.738
25.007

Note that we've used a trick to enable us to specify the number of steps for the range. By defining a variable n and using it in the definition of the second term, the number of steps is directly controlled by the user, rather than being computed internally by Mathcad. There will be ($2n$ + 1) terms, as you can easily verify. Not only will the number of terms in the range change if the value of n is changed, but so will the step size.

Exercises

2.9 Define a range x that goes from 0 to 10π, in steps of 2π.

2.10 Define a range x that starts at x_{start} and ends at x_{end}, where $x_{start} =$ 0 and $x_{end} = 20$, with unit step size.

2.11 Define a range x as follows: 20, 17, 14, and so on, down to −1.

2.12 Define a range x that starts at x_{start} and ends at x_{end}, where $x_{start} =$ 0 and $x_{end} = 20$, with $k = 8$ terms. To do this, define x_{start}, x_{end}, and k, and

then define the *second* term to be $x_{sec} = \dfrac{(x_{end} - x_{start})}{k - 1} + x_{start}$.

2.8

Symbolic Math

So far we've seen how Mathcad can do quite a bit of number crunching. However, sometimes what we want Mathcad to do is perform mathematical manipulations in *symbolic form*. This capability is a major feature of Mathcad. In this chapter we'll merely introduce the topic and do a few quick examples to illustrate the feature. In subsequent chapters we'll see, for example, how to perform symbolic calculus (Chapter 4), symbolically solve an equation for an unknown (Chapter 5), and perform matrix manipulations symbolically (Chapter 6).

Let's do some practice examples just to hint at the possibilities. Start a blank worksheet by clicking on the New Worksheet icon on the toolbar. Let's see if we can symbolically factor the following equation:

$$f(x) = x^3 - x^2 - 4x + 4 \tag{2.7}$$

If we're lucky it will have factors. We'll see shortly whether or not Mathcad can do this for us.

As a second quick example, let's try to find the Taylor series expansion about $x = 0$ of

$$g(x) = e^{x^2} \tag{2.8}$$

You may be wondering what the Taylor series of a function is. A Taylor series is a power series representation of a function. In other words, if it exists for a given function (and it sometimes doesn't), it represents a function as an infinite series of increasing powers of the function argument. In the case of Equation (2.8), it means the function $g(x)$ would be represented by

$$g(x) \approx \sum_{i=0}^{\infty} a_i x^i = a_0 + a_1 x + a_2 x^2 + \ldots \tag{2.9}$$

The trick is to find the values of the coefficients a_i. It turns out that these can be obtained by performing repeated differentiations of the function. Let's avoid this by getting Mathcad to do it for us (it happens to be built in to Mathcad!).

Why would you want such an infinite series? There are several reasons, but the main one is that sometimes it's easier to manipulate a Taylor series than the original function. For example, integrating Equation (2.8) is trickier than integrating Equation (2.9). The disadvantages are first that in reality we always need to *truncate* the infinite series, introducing errors, and second that a Taylor series will always have a finite *radius of convergence*, outside of which the representation becomes invalid.

Let's type Equations (2.7) and (2.8) into Mathcad (using, of course, the assignment equals):

The equations are: $f(x) := x^3 - x^2 - 4 \cdot x + 4$

$$g(x) := e^{x^2}$$

How do we do all this symbolic math in Mathcad? There are several ways to gain access to Mathcad's symbolic mode:

1. Use the menu item *Symbolics*.

2. Click on the Symbolic Keyword palette on the Math palette.

3. Use the accelerator keys **Ctrl + Shift + .** (one more original Mathcad combination!). If all you wanted to do with an expression is *simplify* it, you could just use the **Ctrl + .** .

The first method gives you access to several symbolic commands. The other two methods allow you to perform the same symbolic commands but, unlike the first method, as we'll soon see, they will be live. Let's explore the use of each of these methods in detail by working on Equations (2.7) and (2.8).

Symbolic Math Using the Menu Bar

Before invoking the symbolic menu, you must select the expression or term with which you wish to work. In the case of Equation (2.7) we wish to factor the entire right-hand side, so it should be selected, using the arrow keys and **Space bar** as necessary. Then select menu item *Symbolics . . . Factor.* You'll see that the right-hand side is immediately factored for you [and the equation for $g(x)$ will be automatically moved down as necessary!]:

$f(x) := x^3 - x^2 - 4 \cdot x + 4$

$f(x) := (x - 1) \cdot (x - 2) \cdot (x + 2)$

If you got some other answer you probably selected either less than or more than just the right-hand side, in which case you should delete your result and try again. It turns out that the expression for $f(x)$ *could* be factored. If it had been an expression without factors, Mathcad would have just given you back the original expression.

In this example, we're not quite finished, because the last two factors would look neater if they were combined. To do this, you can select just them, again using the arrow keys and **Space bar,** and use the menu item *Symbolics . . . Expand.* You should end up with:

$f(x) := x^3 - x^2 - 4 \cdot x + 4$

$f(x) := (x - 1) \cdot (x - 2) \cdot (x + 2)$

$f(x) := (x - 1) \cdot (x^2 - 4)$

(You may have to manually insert the last parentheses.) Hence, we can see that you can symbolically manipulate an entire expression, or a part of it.

Let's now find the Taylor series for Equation (2.8). Here, we need to select just the x in the expression, because this is the variable for which we wish to create the power series. Having done this, you'll find that under the menu item *Symbolic . . . Variable* the item *Expand to Series . . .* is now available (it was previously grayed-out). Select this, and an Expand to Series window will appear, waiting for you to tell Mathcad how many terms in the series to compute. Select 10 for this example. Almost immediately you'll get

$$g(x) := e^{x^2}$$

$$g(x) := 1 + x^2 + \frac{1}{2} \cdot x^4 + \frac{1}{6} \cdot x^6 + \frac{1}{24} \cdot x^8 + O\left(x^{10}\right)$$

Mathcad symbolically computed the series for us! The last term (which you would delete if you wished to use the equation) indicates the order of the series. Mathcad did all the work necessary to find the coefficients of the series.

These two examples illustrate how simple the use of Mathcad's symbolic manipulator is. The only rule for using the menu bar is that, before using the menu, you must have selected the expression or variable with which you wish to work.

We've seen how to use the *Factor*, *Expand,* and *Expand to Series* features, but there are quite a few more. For guidance on these a good place to look is under *Help*. In the Index window you should be able to find the *Symbolics* menu commands. This, as shown in Figure 2.11, provides explanations on all of the various symbolic features.

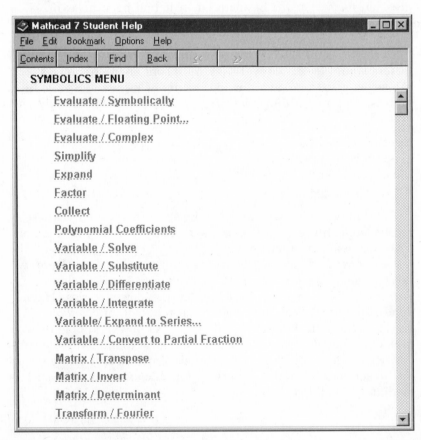

Figure 2.11

Symbolic manipulations made with the menu bar are *not* live. This means that if you change an equation, the subsequent symbolic manipulations of it will *not* be updated. This is obviously a disadvantage of using the menu bar for symbolic math.

Try editing the expression for $g(x)$ to confirm this:

The modified function is: $g(x) := e^x$

The series is still: $g(x) := 1 + x^2 + \dfrac{1}{2} \cdot x^4 + \dfrac{1}{6} \cdot x^6 + \dfrac{1}{24} \cdot x^8 + O(x^{10})$

The series was *not* updated.

Finally, an advantage of the menu bar method is that you have *some* control over the output format. You can have Mathcad place the results of the symbolic math below (the default) or to the right of the original expression, or even replace it. Mathcad can also be made to automatically create explanatory text for you, if desired. To see these options (which we won't explore here), try clicking on menu item *Symbolics . . . Evaluation Style. . . .*

Symbolic Math Using the Symbolic Keyword Palette

In this approach you need to have open the Symbolic Keyword palette (accessed from the Math palette). The palette is shown in Figure 2.12. If you move your mouse over an icon, an explanatory bubble of text will appear, although the icon names themselves are pretty much self-explanatory.

Let's clean up the worksheet by deleting everything except the two original equations. Then, for the equation for $f(x)$, simply click anywhere on the right-hand side and then click the Factor icon. The word factor, a placeholder, and a right arrow ($\rightarrow$) will appear. The placeholder is there in case you wish to factor with respect to a particular expression. In our case, we don't, so you should click on it and press **Backspace** to delete it. To finish just

$\blacksquare \rightarrow$	$\blacksquare\blacksquare \rightarrow$	Modifiers
float	complex	assume
solve	simplify	substitute
factor	expand	coeffs
collect	series	parfrac
fourier	laplace	ztrans
invfourier	invlaplace	invztrans
$M^T \rightarrow$	$M^{-1} \rightarrow$	$\|M\| \rightarrow$

Figure 2.12

press **Enter** (or use arrow keys to exit the expression). You should get:

The equations are: $f(x) := x^3 - x^2 - 4 \cdot x + 4$ factor $\rightarrow (x-1) \cdot (x-2) \cdot (x+2)$

$$g(x) := e^{x^2}$$

It's done! We can make three points here:

1. When using the Symbolic Keyword palette, sometimes placeholders will appear with no obvious purpose (as in this example). If this happens, you should refer to Mathcad's *Help*, and in the Index search for *keywords for symbolic evaluation*. This will lead you to information, including QuickSheet Examples, on using all of the various icons.

2. In this method, the symbolic math is always performed on the *entire* expression (although judicious use of the optional placeholders can help you get around this).

3. The symbolic manipulation is *live*, so if you change the original equation, the resulting equation is updated automatically.

Let's illustrate this last point by computing the Taylor series of $g(x)$. To do this, click anywhere on the right-hand side of the equation and click on the Series icon. This time *two* placeholders appear. For guidance on these you can again refer to *Help*, where you'll find that the first placeholder is for the variable with respect to which you want to create the series (in this case x), and the second *optional* one is for specifying the value of x around which the expansion should be created. We can delete this placeholder to use the default point of expansion ($x = 0$). Finally, to specify the number of terms to compute, you add a comma, then that number (in this example, 10).

If you do all this, you'll get:

The series is:

$$g(x) := e^{x^2} \text{ series, } x, 10 \rightarrow 1 + x^2 + \frac{1}{2} \cdot x^4 + \frac{1}{6} \cdot x^6 + \frac{1}{24} \cdot x^8$$

To demonstrate the live nature of this method, edit the function so it's just e^x, and so that it computes the series through 4 terms. After exiting the equation the series will be immediately updated:

The series is: $\quad g(x) := e^x \text{ series, } x, 4 \quad 1 + x + \frac{1}{2} \cdot x^2 + \frac{1}{6} \cdot x^3$

Symbolic Math Using Symbolic Accelerator Keys

In this final method you essentially end up with the same results as with using the Symbolic Keywords palette, except to do so you simply type in the operator you wish to use. The advantage of this method is that it's quick to do, but on the other hand you need to know the symbolic operator and its exact syntax.

To use the method, click anywhere on the equation and then press **Ctrl + Shift + .** (which means hold down the **Ctrl** and **Shift** keys while you press the period (.) key). A single placeholder accompanied by the right arrow will appear. You can then simply type into the placeholder the operation you want, including any required conditions.

For example, for factoring $f(x)$, you'd type *factor* in the placeholder, and you'd get the same result as with the Symbolic Keyword palette method. For expanding $g(x)$ into a series, at the placeholder you'd type, for example, *series,x,10* to get the same result as before.

Finally, if all you want to do with an expression is simplify it, you can just use the **Ctrl** key while you press the period (.) key. The only caveat here is that the word "simplify" is somewhat ambiguous. For example, is the function $f(x)$ "simplest" when it's factored, or when it's not? Try cutting and pasting both expressions and using this method:

$$x^3 - x^2 - 4 \cdot x + 4 \rightarrow x^3 - x^2 - 4 \cdot x + 4$$

$$(x - 1) \cdot (x - 2) \cdot (x + 2) \rightarrow (x - 1) \cdot (x - 2) \cdot (x + 2)$$

Neither "simplify," implying that both forms are the "simplest"!

We've now finished with this practice worksheet, so you can close it without saving.

In this mini-review we've just barely introduced the use of symbolic math. There is obviously a lot more to this feature of Mathcad and, as we mentioned earlier, we'll get to use some of them in subsequent chapters.

Exercises

In the following use all three methods (the menu item *Symbolics*, the Symbolic Keyword palette, and an accelerator key combination). Before using the menu item, modify the Evaluation style so that the results are presented horizontally, with comments.

2.13 Simplify the expression $\dfrac{x^2 + 2x - 8}{x + 4}$.

2.14 Expand the expression $\sin(3\theta)$ around $\theta = 0$, using 10 terms. Also, expand the expression around $\theta = \pi/6$, using 10 terms.

2.15 Collect the expression $x^2 + (y + x^2)\,y - x + y^2x$ in terms of powers of x.

2.16 Collect the expression $x^2 + (y + x^2)\,y - x + y^2x$ in terms of powers of y.

2.9

Working with Units

We've looked at Example 2.1 several times but still don't have it in a form that's acceptable to an engineer: it has not been presented with units. To introduce units let's rework this example one more time.

Example 2.1 (Continued)   Uniform acceleration (using units)

Modify Example 2.1 with Functions so that the acceleration $a = 3$ m/s^2 and the initial speed $V_0 = 10$ mph. By defining x and V as functions of time, compute the distance in feet and speed in mph after 5 and 10 seconds. Also, generate the distances in meters and speeds in ft/s for the first 10 seconds, in time steps of 2 seconds.

Note that this example intentionally has mixed units (feet, meters, meters per second squared, miles per hour, and feet per second).

You'll notice that we're continuing this example from where we left off in Section 2.7. In Section 2.6 we saved this file as Example 2.1 with Functions. Open this file now, and let's immediately save it as a new file called "Example 2.1 with Units." If for some reason you don't have the Example 2.1 with Functions file, simply create a new file and make it look like that shown in Section 2.7 and save it as Example 2.1 with Units.

Let's now get to work inserting units into this worksheet. Click with the mouse on the equation for a (or use the arrow keys to move the cursor into the equation). Then use the arrow keys as necessary to get the insertion line to the end of the equation:

$$a := 3|$$

Then simply multiply the right-hand side by m and divide by s^2, then press **Enter** (or use the arrow keys) to exit. You should get, after also doing some text editing, something like the following (showing the first few lines):

Uniform Acceleration (with Units)

By (Your Name)

This worksheet computes the *distance* x traveled and the *speed* V of an accelerating object.

First, let's enter the given data:

Acceleration: $a := 3 \cdot \dfrac{m}{s^2}$ Initial speed (ft/s): $V_o := 10$

The equations of motion are: $x(t) := V_o \cdot t + \dfrac{1}{2} \cdot a \cdot t^2$ $V(t) := V_o + a \cdot t$

Hence, after 5 seconds: $x(5) =$ $V(5) =$

There are two things worth pointing out here:

1. Mathcad understood what m and s were without us having to define them. This is because they are built-in units. As we have previously mentioned, all of the common units, in various unit systems (including SI and US) are built-in.

2. The evaluations of x and V no longer work. This is because the formulas for them are no longer dimensionally consistent. For example, the first term $V_0 t$ on the right of the equation for x has no dimensions (actually it has the dimensions of t, but t is not defined yet), and the second term, $\frac{1}{2}at^2$, now has the dimensions of m/s^2. It is, of course, not possible to add terms that have different dimensions or units. If you click on the equation for evaluating x, for example, you'll see some advice from Mathcad:

$x(5|) = \blacksquare\blacksquare$

The units in this expression
do not match.

Both of these points reveal very important rules in using Mathcad:

1. Mathcad uses lots of common symbols and phrases for built-in units. If you plan to use units anywhere in a worksheet, in order to not seriously damage the units for that worksheet, do not define a variable using symbols that Mathcad already uses for units.

For example, don't use m for the mass of something (it's used for meters), but instead use M or *mass* or some other expression. Sometimes it's not obvious that a symbol is used by Mathcad. For example H and *henry* are both used by Mathcad for electrical inductance. If you ever encounter an error, or if you get unexpected results in a worksheet, it's a good idea to examine the names of your variables to see if you've accidentally redefined a unit. This is probably one of the most common errors in using Mathcad! You can see if you've inadvertently used a built-in function by moving to a location on your worksheet above where you've *first* used the variable. If you now type the variable with the *evaluation* equals, you'll quickly see if Mathcad already knows it as a built-in unit.

If a particular worksheet does not use units, then of course none of this applies.

2. Use of units must be dimensionally consistent. This consistency must include function arguments, range definitions, graph axes, and so forth.

With all this in mind, let's fix the worksheet so it works. Let's edit the equation for V_0 so that the right side is multiplied by mph.

After you've done this you'll see that the evaluation of x and V are *still* in error! This is because now that we've started to use units, time t cannot be specified without units. To make the evaluations work, you must edit them so that the arguments are multiplied by s or sec (for seconds).

If you do all this, with a little tidying up of the text, you should have for the math:

Acceleration: $a := 3 \cdot \dfrac{m}{s^2}$ Initial speed: $V_0 := 10 \cdot mph$

The equations of motion are: $x(t) := V_0 + t + \dfrac{1}{2} \cdot a \cdot t^2$ $V(t) := V_0 + a \cdot t$

Hence, after 5 seconds: $x(5 \cdot s) = 59.852 \cdot m$ $V(5 \cdot s) = 19.47 \cdot m \cdot s^{-1}$

After 10 seconds: $x(10 \cdot s) = 194.704 \cdot m$ $V(10 \cdot s) = 34.47 \cdot m \cdot s^{-1}$

Look what happened here. Mathcad used the mixed units of a and V_o and gave us results for x and V in SI units! We didn't have to tell Mathcad that x, for example, has the dimension of length. The reason it gave us x in m and V in m·s⁻¹ is because SI units are the *default* units for each worksheet you create. You can change the default unit system for a worksheet by clicking on menu item *Math . . . Options*, where you'll find a tab for Unit System. You don't have to change the default units if you want all or most of your answers in SI units. On the other hand, if you're looking for answers mostly in US units, you'd want to change the default to those units.

Note that, whatever default units you use, *any* individual expression can be expressed in any units you wish. For example, we want the position x in ft and speed V in miles per hour. Click on the equation for evaluating x. You'll get something like:

$$x(5 \cdot s)| = 59.852 \cdot m \quad \blacksquare$$

The small black rectangle is called the *unit placeholder*, and it's the place where you can type in any units you wish. In this case we want feet, so use the arrow keys or mouse to get to the placeholder and type *ft*. As soon as you press **Enter,** Mathcad recomputes the answer in the desired units:

$$x(5 \cdot s) = 196.365 \cdot ft$$

What happens if you either type in units that Mathcad doesn't know or use units that are not correct for a particular answer? Edit the expression by changing *ft* to *feet*. This is what you'll get:

$$x(5 \cdot s) = \cdot feet$$

Mathcad doesn't know *feet*. If it was important to you that feet show up as *feet,* you would have to type an equation defining the variable *feet* as being equal to ft. Now edit the expression so that instead of *feet*, you have *joule*. You'll then have:

$$x(5 \cdot s) = 59.852 \cdot kg^{-1} \cdot m^{-1} \cdot s^2 \cdot joule$$

Mathcad gave us an answer including joules, and adjusted other units so that the answer has the dimension of length!

Let's edit the equation one last time (as well as the equation evaluating x at 10 seconds) to give the answer in feet. Also, edit the right of the two evaluations of V so that their answers are in mph. You should end up with:

Hence, after 5 seconds: $x(5 \cdot s) = 196.365 \cdot ft$ $V(5 \cdot s) = 43.554 \cdot mph$

After 10 seconds: $x(10 \cdot s) = 638.793 \cdot ft$ $V(10 \cdot s) = 77.108 \cdot mph$

Finally, let's format the right side of these equations. To format a number, simply double-click the number. The menu shown in Figure 2.13 will appear. The contents of this window are pretty much self-

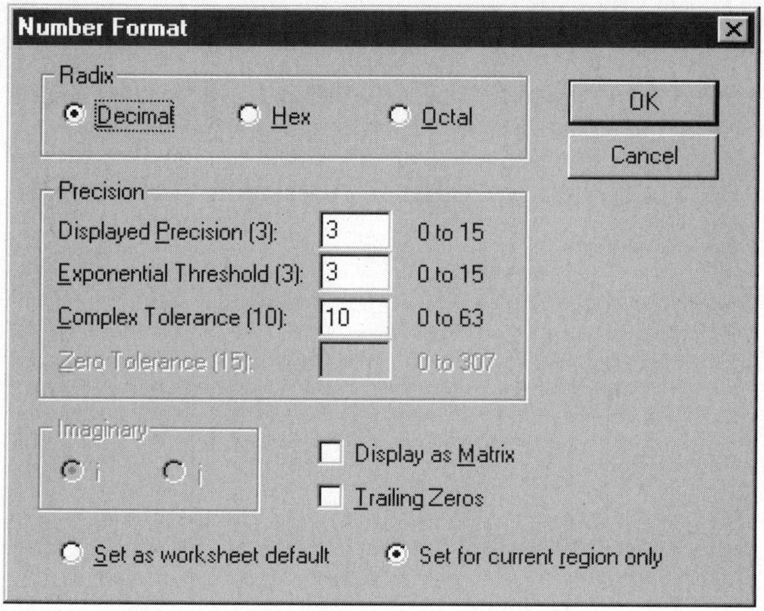

Number Format

Radix
- (•) Decimal   ( ) Hex   ( ) Octal

OK

Cancel

Precision

Displayed Precision (3): `3`   0 to 15

Exponential Threshold (3): `3`   0 to 15

Complex Tolerance (10): `10`   0 to 63

Zero Tolerance (15):   0 to 307

Imaginary
- (•) i   ( ) j

☐ Display as Matrix

☐ Trailing Zeros

( ) Set as worksheet default   (•) Set for current region only

Figure 2.13

explanatory. Let's change the *displayed precision* to 0 and set this as the *worksheet default*. After doing this you'll have:

Hence, after 5 seconds: $x(5 \cdot s) = 196 \cdot ft$ $V(5 \cdot s) = 44 \cdot mph$

After 10 seconds: $x(10 \cdot s) = 639 \cdot ft$ $V(10 \cdot s) = 77 \cdot mph$

Note that Mathcad keeps the same computational accuracy, even though fewer significant figures are displayed.

Finally, let's fix the range computation, which up to now has been in error. To do this, simply multiply by s *each* term (a common error is to forget to put units in the middle term) in the definition of the time range.

After doing so you'll have:

The time range (s) is: $t := 0 \cdot s, 2 \cdot s .. 10 \cdot s$

The times, distances, and speeds are:

t	$x(t)$	$V(t)$
$0 \cdot s$	$0 \cdot m$	$4 \cdot m \cdot s^{-1}$
$2 \cdot s$	$15 \cdot m$	$10 \cdot m \cdot s^{-1}$
$4 \cdot s$	$42 \cdot m$	$16 \cdot m \cdot s^{-1}$
$6 \cdot s$	$81 \cdot m$	$22 \cdot m \cdot s^{-1}$
$8 \cdot s$	$132 \cdot m$	$28 \cdot m \cdot s^{-1}$
$10 \cdot s$	$195 \cdot m$	$34 \cdot m \cdot s^{-1}$

The answers don't look quite the way we want them to. We want the distances in meters, which they are, and the speeds in ft/s, which they are not. Unfortunately, in this columnar kind of output, there is no units placeholder. The only way you can impose a particular set of units for the output is to not compute, for example, $V(t)$, but instead $\frac{V(t)}{ft/s}$. In other words, divide the expression you're evaluating by the units you wish it expressed in. Edit the outputs for time t, distance x, and speed V so that they have similar output formats. Your worksheet should then finally look like

Uniform Acceleration (with Units)

By (Your Name)

This worksheet computes the *distance* x traveled and the *speed* V of an accelerating object.

First, let's enter the given data:

Acceleration: $a := 3 \cdot \dfrac{m}{s^2}$ Initial speed: $V_o := 10 \cdot mph$

The equations of motion are: $x(t) := V_o \cdot t + \dfrac{1}{2} \cdot a \cdot t^2$ $V(t) := V_o + a \cdot t$

Hence, after 5 seconds: $x(5 \cdot s) = 196 \cdot ft$ $V(5 \cdot s) = 44 \cdot mph$

After 10 seconds: $x(10 \cdot s) = 639 \cdot ft$ $V(10 \cdot s) = 77 \cdot mph$

The time range (s) is: $t := 0 \cdot s, 2 \cdot s .. 10 \cdot s$

The times, distances, and speeds are:

$\dfrac{t}{s}$	$\dfrac{x(t)}{m}$	$\dfrac{V(t)}{ft/s}$
0	0	15
2	15	34
4	42	54
6	81	74
8	132	93
10	195	113

This was a quick introduction to units, in which we saw one method for inserting units. There are other methods for inserting units. Let's now summarize these, and other important features about using units in Mathcad.

Inserting Units

Units can be inserted anywhere on the *right* of an equation that uses the *assignment* or *priority* equals. They can be inserted on the *left* or *right* of an equation that uses the *evaluation* equals.

To insert units at a point in an expression do any *one* of the following:

1. Directly type in the unit or units you want.
2. Click on menu item *Insert . . . Unit*.
3. Use the accelerator keys **Ctrl + U.**
4. Click on the Insert Unit icon on the toolbar.

The last three give you access to the window shown in Figure 2.14. Try one of them to get this window to appear.

To find the units you want, first use the Dimension window. Either scroll to the dimension you want or press its first letter. In Figure 2.14 we typed the letter *l*. The units window will then list all the units Mathcad knows for that particular dimension. Select the one you want, and click the Insert button. Note that you also have an option of replacing a current unit. If you wish to replace an existing unit in an expression, double-clicking on that unit would bring up the window shown in Figure 2.14, and you would then click on the unit you want and press the Replace button.

Let's do another engineering example to bring all these notions together.

Example 2.4 Air-conditioner performance Most air-conditioning (*AC*) systems consist of a *compressor* (driven by an electric motor), which compresses and pumps the working fluid (e.g., Refrigerant-134a) as a gas; the *condenser* coil, where the pressurized gas condenses to a liquid and throws off heat; the *throttle,* where the fluid is allowed to drop to a low pressure; and the *evaporator* coil, where the now-low-pressure liquid evaporates and draws in heat. The evaporator coil is located in the room that is being cooled, and the condenser coil is located outside. The circuit is illustrated in Figure 2.15.

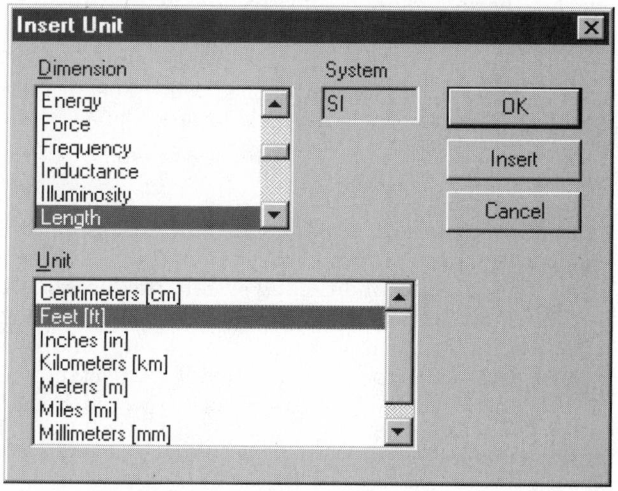

Figure 2.14

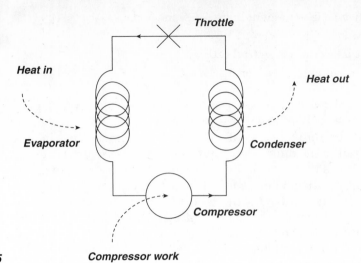

Figure 2.15

The idea is that a fluid will tend to condense when it's at a high pressure and to evaporate when it's at low pressure. This means that the fluid will condense in the condenser coils even though they are outside in the hot summer environment, and will evaporate in the evaporator coils in the (hopefully!) cooler building.

The performance of the AC system depends on two things: the mechanical efficiency of the electric motor/compressor unit and the thermodynamics of the circuit itself. The efficiency of the motor/compressor unit is given by:

$$\eta_{motor} \equiv \frac{W_{comp}}{W_{elec}} \tag{2.10}$$

where W_{comp} is the rate of work (e.g., hp) done by the compressor and W_{elec} is the electrical power (e.g., kW) supplied to the unit.

The thermodynamic effectiveness with which an air conditioner works is called the *coefficient of performance* (COP). It is a measure of the amount of cooling produced by each unit of work provided, so that the higher the COP, the better the device. The formula for the COP is

$$COP \equiv \frac{Q}{W_{comp}} \tag{2.11}$$

where Q is the rate of cooling (e.g., BTU/hr). Equations (2.10) and (2.11) enable the overall performance of an AC system to be analyzed.

A particular air conditioning system produces 19,000 BTU/hr of cooling. The motor/compressor unit efficiency is 70 percent, and it uses 3 kW of electricity. What is the work rate (in hp) of the motor/compressor? What is the COP of the AC? Finally, if the system is improved by using better evaporator and condenser coils (but with the same motor/compressor unit), so that it now has a COP of 3, what will the new cooling rate (BTU/hr) be?

Let's create a new worksheet to solve this problem. First, give it the following title and enter the given data:

<u>Air Conditioner Performance</u>

By (Your Name)

First, enter the cooling rate and electricity usage:

$$Q := 19000 \cdot \frac{BTU}{hr} \qquad\qquad W_{elec} := 3 \cdot kW$$

The motor/compressor efficiency is: $\eta_{motor} := 70 \cdot \%$

Note that percentage (%) is a built-in "unit." Its effect is to divide by 100. To get the other units (BTU, hr, and kW) you could have just typed them, or used the other unit insertion methods we've learned. Now we have everything we need to compute the compressor work and system COP:

We can then compute the work of the compressor: $W_{comp} := \eta_{motor} \cdot W_{elec}$

$$W_{comp} = 2.816 \cdot hp \qquad \ldots \text{compared to} \ldots \qquad W_{elec} = 4.023 \cdot hp$$

Now the COP can be computed: $COP := \dfrac{Q}{W_{comp}} \qquad COP = 2.652$

The COP, because it is a ratio of two *power* terms, is dimensionless. Mathcad took care of the fact that Q and W_{comp} have different units. We needed to fix the right-hand side of the equations evaluating W_{comp} and W_{elec} so that they compute hp. Remember, to do this, click on each equation, and at the units placeholder type in *hp*.

Finally, the new AC system performance can be analyzed:

The new AC system COP is: $COP_{new} := 3$

Then: $Q_{new} := COP_{new} \cdot W_{comp} \qquad Q_{new} = 2.15 \cdot 10^4 \cdot \dfrac{BTU}{hr}$

To change the answer in the last equation to a more attractive numeric format, double-click on the number, and in the Number Format window that appears, select 0 for the Displayed Precision and 5 for the Exponential Threshold. You should obtain:

Then: $Q_{new} := COP_{new} \cdot W_{comp} \qquad Q_{new} = 21496 \cdot \dfrac{BTU}{hr}$

You can now save this worksheet as "Example 2.4."

This example illustrates Mathcad's power and convenience for working with problems involving units. Without Mathcad even this straightforward problem would have been tedious, because you would have had to look up and use conversions from BTU/hr to hp to kW.

Exercises

2.17 Suppose you weigh 150 lbf. What is your mass in lb and in kg? What is your weight in newtons? What will your weight be in lbf and newtons on the moon (assuming g_{moon} is approximately a sixth of that on earth)? Hint: Don't use m for the mass!

2.18 Consider the cantilever beam shown in Figure 2.16. The deflection δ of the end of the beam is given by

$$\delta = \frac{Fl^3}{3EI} \tag{2.12}$$

where $F = 100$ newton is the end load, $l = 3$ ft is the beam length, $E = 30$ x 10^6 psi is the beam material Young's modulus, and I is the beam cross-section moment of inertia. For the rectangular cross-section shown:

$$I = \frac{bd^3}{12} \tag{2.13}$$

with $b = 1$ in. and $d = 2$ in. Find the deflection δ in inches and in mm.

2.10

Comments and Summary

This chapter has introduced you to:

1. Mathcad's interface: You should now be getting comfortable with using the various icons, palettes, and accelerator keys. As you progress through the other chapters, this will be reinforced.

2. Working with text regions: You've now had some practice in entering and editing text. We haven't spent a lot of time on text formatting and using templates, but these techniques are very similar to those in word processors, such as Microsoft Word.

3. Working with math regions: You've now been exposed to the very simplest concepts in creating and editing equations. This is still probably somewhat frustrating to you, but the more you use Mathcad, the more the equation editing logic will become second nature to you. We've also just scratched the surface of Mathcad's collection of built-in functions and operators. Again, the more you use Mathcad, the more you'll realize how comprehensive this collection is. Finally, we've introduced the notions of ranges and had a little practice in using them to create columns of data (actually, vectors).

4. Using Mathcad's symbolic math: We saw that Mathcad can symbolically simplify and factor expressions and expand a function into a series. As we'll see in subsequent chapters, Mathcad can also symbolically integrate, differentiate, and solve equations for one or more unknowns. This is obviously an extremely powerful feature of Mathcad.

Figure 2.16

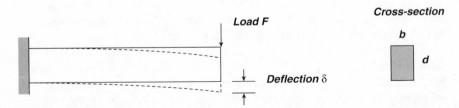

5. Working with units: As is probably apparent to you at this point, Mathcad's handling of units is one of its most useful features. As an engineer, you already know how tedious performing computations involving units can be, but now you can have Mathcad perform this task for you. We've also seen this can be a double-edged sword, in that choosing variable names unwisely (e.g., using m for the mass of something) can lead to problems. An additional benefit of using units in Mathcad is that Mathcad will flag you if you're trying to do something that doesn't make sense (e.g., adding two quantities with different dimensions).

Some Useful Keystrokes

We list here some accelerator keys and other keystrokes that are probably worth committing to memory (although, as we've mentioned, there are other ways to accomplish each task, so you don't *have* to). Some we've already seen, and others will be useful to us as we move on to other chapters:

:	Produces the *assignment equals*
Ctrl + =	Produces the *Boolean equals*
~	Produces the *global assignment equals*
Ctrl + .	Produces *symbolic evaluation* of an expression
Spacebar	Useful for selecting/deselecting within a math region
Ctrl + G	Used after a Roman letter to convert it to Greek
Ctrl + P	An alternative way to generate π
Ctrl + M	Opens a window for creating a *vector* or *matrix*
[	Used to generate a *vector or array subscript*
.	Used in a math expression to create a *literal subscript*
;	Used to generate the two dots (..) in defining a *range*
@	Inserts a blank *X-Y plot*
****	Generates the *square root sign*
Ctrl + I	Generates an *integral sign* with limits
Shift + /	Generates a *differential*
Ctrl + R	Refreshes the screen
Ctrl + End	Moves to the top of the worksheet
Ctrl + Home	Moves to the end of the worksheet
Esc	Cancels or halts a current calculation

Where to Find More

We've covered quite a bit of basic material in this chapter, and hinted at much more. The next chapter will discuss one more basic topic, namely graphing. Subsequent chapters will discuss some of this material in a more comprehensive way. For example, several times we've referred to both *literal* and *vector* or *matrix subscripts*. In Chapters 3 and 6 we'll discuss these in more detail.

The remaining chapters are aimed at exposing you to features of Mathcad that go beyond the basics. For example, Chapter 5 will introduce Mathcad's methods for solving an equation or a set of equations in one or more unknowns.

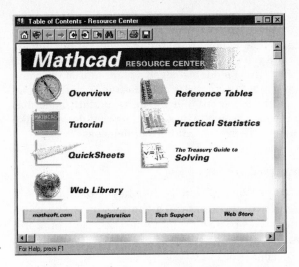

Figure 2.17

Mathcad version 7 is extremely feature rich (not surprising after seven iterations!), and in this introductory text we cannot cover *all* of these features. For more details on anything we've covered in this, or any other, chapters, you should consult the Mathcad *User's Guide* included in the Mathcad 7 package.

Mathcad 7 also has an excellent Help facility called the *Resource Center* (found either under the *Help* menu or by clicking on its icon), shown in Figure 2.17.

You should certainly feel free to explore the various topics listed. It would be a good idea at this point to look at the material in the Overview, Tutorial, and Quicksheets topics, as these have details on the basic material we've covered in this chapter. For example, the Tutorial window is shown in Figure 2.18. Finally, don't overlook Mathcad's web site at http:/www.mathsoft.com, which we'll discuss in Chapter 9.

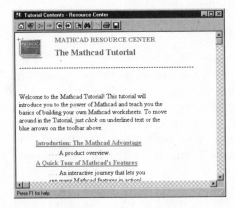

Figure 2.18

2.19 Expand the following:

$$(x - 3)(x + 5)(x - 4)(x + 1) \tag{2.14}$$

2.20 Factor the following:

$$x^6 + 7x^5 - 5x^4 - 41x^3 - 42x^2 + 30x + 210 \tag{2.15}$$

2.21 Expand the following into partial fractions:

$$\frac{x^2 - 7}{x^2 - x - 2} \tag{2.16}$$

2.22 Expand the following:

$$\sum_{n=0}^{4} (x - y)^n \tag{2.17}$$

Then collect in powers of x.

Hint: One way to get the summation sign is to use the icon in the *Calculus Palette* of the *Math Palette*.

2.23 Expand $\sin^2(\theta)$ into a Taylor series of order 10 about $\theta = 0$. Expand $\cos^2(\theta)$ into a Taylor series of order 10 about $\theta = 0$. If you were to add these two series what would you get, and why?

Hint: To type in $\sin^2(\theta)$, first type $\sin(\theta)$, and *then* square it.

2.24 Expand $\tan(\theta)$ into a Taylor series of order 6 about $\theta = 0$. Copy and paste the result and delete the last term $(O(\theta^6))$. Then square this entire expression and simplify. You will have found the square of the Taylor series of $\tan(\theta)$. Now find the Taylor series of order 12 of $\tan^2(\theta)$. Compare the two results. Should you expect the Taylor series of the square of a function to be equal to the square of the Taylor series of a function?

2.25 Define the following function:

$$f(x) = e^{-x} \tag{2.18}$$

Expand this into a Taylor series of order 6 about $x = 0$. Edit the result (delete the last term $O(x^6)$, and call this series $g(x)$. Then define a function $E(x)$ which computes the error between the original function and the Taylor series approximation:

$$E(x) = \left| \frac{f(x) - g(x)}{f(x)} \right| \tag{2.19}$$

Evaluate the error over the range $x = -4, -3.5 .. 2$. If we want the Taylor series to be accurate to better than 0.5 percent, what approximate range of x should we limit the series to?

Hint: The absolute value signs can be obtained from the **SHIFT + ** accelerator keys. You should evaluate $E(x)$ divided by percent.

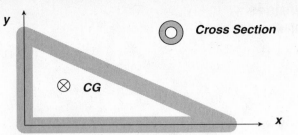

Figure 2.19

2.26 Part of a bicycle frame with the geometry shown in Figure 2.19 is made of an aluminum alloy tubing of density 2500 kg/m³. The inside and outside diameters of the tubing are 2.5 cm and 3.5 cm, and the sides are 40 cm, 96 cm, and 104 cm.

Find the mass M (lb) of the frame, and its center of gravity (CG) with respect to the x-y coordinates shown.

Hint: The CG can be found by taking moments about each axis:

$$M X = m_1 x_1 + m_2 x_2 + m_3 x_3$$
$$M Y = m_1 y_1 + m_2 y_2 + m_3 y_3$$

(2.20)

where M is the total mass of the frame and the m_1, m_2 and m_3 are the masses of each piece, X and Y are the locations of the CG, and x_1, x_2 and x_3 and y_1, y_2 and y_3 are the locations of the center of mass of each piece (the values of x_3 and y_3 are straightforward, if you think about it). Once the various masses have been computed, the total mass can easily be obtained, and Equations (2.20) can be solved for X and Y.

2.27 What is the RMS current I_{RMS} (amps) in the RLC circuit shown in Figure 2.20 when it is connected to a voltage source of $V_{RMS} = 120$ volts with a frequency f of 60 Hz? The resistor is $R = 100$ ohm, the inductor is $L = 377$ mH, and the capacitor is $C = 35$ μF. What are values of the RMS voltage drops $V_R = R\ I_{RMS}$, $V_L = \omega\ L\ I_{RMS}$, and $V_C = \frac{I_{RMS}}{\omega C}$ across each component? Do you know why they do not add up to the value of V_{RMS}?

Hint: It can be shown that the equation for this is:

$$I_{RMS} = \frac{V_{RMS}}{\sqrt{R^2 + \left(\omega L - \dfrac{1}{\omega C}\right)^2}}$$

(2.21)

where $\omega = 2\pi f$ is the frequency expressed in radians per second.

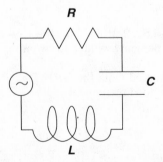

Figure 2.20

Note: If you solve other exercises on the same worksheet be sure to redefine R as $\frac{5}{9} \cdot K$ so that problems involving degrees Rankine (R) will compute correctly!

2.28 A house hot water heater heats Q = 80 gal/day of water from 50°F to 170°F (a ΔT of 120°F). Find the power usage P in kW and in hp.

Hint: The power required is $P = Q \, \rho \, c_p \, \Delta T$ where ΔT is in Rankine (R). Although R = °F + 460, a *difference* in temperatures in each units has the same value: ΔT (°F) = ΔT (R), and Mathcad recognizes R but not °F. Hence, all you need to do is define a variable ΔT with units R. The density of water is ρ = 62.4 lb/ft³, and the specific heat of water is c_p =1 BTU/lb-R.

2.29 Your blood pressure is 120/80. This means that the high pressure (*systolic*) is 120 mm Hg, and the low pressure (*diastolic*) is 80 mm Hg. Find these two pressures in psi. Express them as percentages of atmospheric pressure (101 kPa). Express atmospheric pressure in mm of Hg.

Hint: Pressure can be indicated as the pressure a column of fluid (in this case mercury) would create. The relationship between the two is $p = \rho g h$, where p is the pressure and h is the height of a column of the fluid of density ρ. Take the density of mercury to be ρ = 13,300 kg/m³.

2.30 A pressure cooker works by cooking at a high pressure, which allows water to boil at a higher temperature than 212°F, so that food cooks more quickly. It creates this high pressure by having a weight sit on top of a hole in the top of the cooker, as shown in Figure 2.21.

As the food is heated, pressure builds up because the weight seals the hole. Eventually, the pressure reaches a point where it can lift the weight off the hole, causing some steam to escape, and the pressure to drop a little. The weight will then fall and reseal the hole, causing the pressure to increase again. Hence the weight is essentially floating above the hole, creating a constant pressure in the cooker. If the mass of the weight is 35 gm, and the diameter of the hole is 3 mm, what is the *operating* pressure (psi) in the cooker? Atmospheric pressure is 101 kPa. If the hole gets a little clogged up so that the diameter is effectively reduced to 2.5 mm, what will the *actual* pressure be? Finally, you clean the hole so that it returns to a diameter of 0.3 cm, but you move to Denver, where the atmospheric pressure is only 13.64 psi. What new mass (gm) would you need to use to create the original operating pressure in the cooker?

Hint: Remember that pressure is force (in this case weight) over area, and that the pressure in the cooker is due to this plus atmospheric pressure.

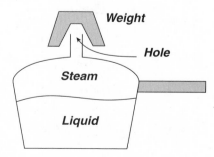

Figure 2.21

2.31 The buoy shown in Figure 2.22 has a diameter $D = 2$ m and height $H = 7$ m and has a density of $\rho_{Buoy} = 850$ kg/m³. Find its weight W in lbf. It is tethered to the bottom of the river by a cable of length $l = 80$ ft. The water density is $\rho = 1000$ kg/m³.

As a safety feature, the cable is designed to snap if the water depth d exceeds 100 ft. What happens is that as the depth of the river increases so does the upwards buoyancy force of the water, making the cable tension increase (you recall that *Archimedes Principle* states that the upward force of a fluid on a body is equal to the weight of fluid displaced). By doing a force balance, find the tension (in lbf) that the cable should be designed to snap at. Suppose the cable snaps. The buoy will now float (its weight will equal the weight of fluid displaced). How much of it (in feet) will project above the surface of the water?

2.32 At the exit to a highway there is a crash barrier that is designed to absorb the energy of a car of mass $M = 2500$ lb hitting it at a speed $V = 60$ mph. It does this by converting all the car's kinetic energy into energy stored in a large spring. The car will be stopped by the barrier in a distance of $x = 10$ ft. Find the *spring constant k* (newton/m) of the barrier, and the maximum "g" force (call it g_{force}) experienced by the car passengers. The barrier is built, and after a few days a motorcycle of total mass of 600 lb hits the barrier at 85 mph. How much (in ft) will the barrier be compressed (in other words, what will x be now), and what is the maximum "g" force experienced by the cyclist?

Hint: The total energy absorbed by a spring when it is compressed a distance x is $\frac{1}{2}kx^2$. The "g" force is not really a force at all, but a measure of the maximum deceleration in terms of multiples of the acceleration of gravity. For example, an astronaut might experience 10 g's for a few seconds during launch. In this problem it is given by $\frac{kx}{Mg}$.

2.33 You are making a model plane of mass $M = 1.5$ kg fly around you in circles by holding a wire, of length 35 ft, attached to it. If the wire will break if the tension in it exceeds 25 lbf, find the maximum speed (mph) the plane can have without breaking the wire. At this speed how many times will the plane go around in 1 minute?

Hint: Recall the formula for the centrifugal force on a body. For the second part, remember that angular rotation is usually expressed in formulas as *radians*, but here we want *revolutions*, so in your formulas you will need to use a factor of 2π as necessary.

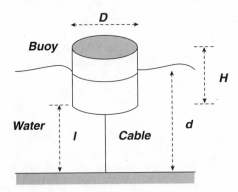

Figure 2.22

2.34 A father and child are playing on a see-saw. One of the games they play is that when the father's side hits the ground, he suddenly holds it down so that the child's end, up in the air, will vibrate, or oscillate. If the child weighs 45 kg, what will be the frequency (cycles per second) the child oscillates at? How long (sec) will one vibration take? If they now continue to ride the see-saw, and this time the child holds his end to the ground, making the father's end oscillate, what frequency will dad vibrate at (he weighs 80 kg), and how long will he take to oscillate once?

Hint: This is essentially a cantilever beam with a large mass on its free end. Assuming the beam mass is small, it can be shown that the frequency f of vibration (in cycles per second, or Hz) is:

$$f = \frac{1}{2\pi}\sqrt{\frac{3EI}{Ml^3}} \tag{2.22}$$

where $E = 10^6$ psi is Young's modulus of the plastic see-saw, $I = 12$ in^4 is the second moment of area of the beam cross-section, $l = 8$ ft is the half-length of the see-saw, and M is the mass of the person on the vibrating end.

2.35 You want to buy a new car, and you decide to take out a loan of $19,000, repayable over three years, at an annual interest rate of 8.25%. What will your monthly payment be? Suppose this monthly payment is too large (the most you can afford is $500/month). You look at other banks and find one that will give you a loan for four years at an interest rate of 7.25%. Can you afford this loan?

Hint: The formula for this is:

$$A = P\left[\frac{\frac{i}{12}\left(1 + \frac{i}{12}\right)^n}{\left(1 + \frac{i}{12}\right)^n - 1}\right] \tag{2.23}$$

where A is the monthly payment, P is the loan amount, and i is the interest rate (and note that % can be treated as a "unit" in Mathcad). Mathcad does not have a "unit" for dollars, so just treat dollar amounts as numbers.

2.36 Find the height h (miles) above sea level and the velocity v (mph) of a satellite in orbit at a fixed point above the earth.

Hint: This involves several steps. First you must define the angular velocity ω. This is one revolution per day. Mathcad doesn't know "revolutions," so you'll have to put in the 2π factor in the definition of ω. Then you can find the radius r, measured from the earth's center, at which the satellite is located. This will be the radius at which the centrifugal force just balances the gravitational force:

$$mr\omega^2 = G\frac{mM}{r^2} \Rightarrow r = \left(\frac{GM}{\omega^2}\right)^{\frac{1}{3}} \tag{2.24}$$

where G is the gravitational constant (and can be obtained from the Mathcad *Resource Center* under the *Reference Tables* section), m is the satellite mass, and M is the earth's mass. How do you find the earth's mass? You could look it up, but let's find it from the earth's radius, which is approximately $r_e = 3950$ miles. You can use the idea that, at sea level, an object that has a mass of m_{sea} weighs $W = m_{sea}g$. Hence you can use the following to find the earth's mass:

$$W = m_{sea}g = G\frac{m_{sea}M}{r_e^2} \Rightarrow M = \frac{gr_e^2}{G} \tag{2.25}$$

Equations (2.24) and (2.25) enable the radius of the satellite's motion to be computed. Finally, this radius can be used to find its height h above the ground and, by also using the angular velocity ω, its velocity v.

2.37 A fresh-water reservoir which holds $V = 100,000$ ft^3 of water is being polluted by salt at the rate of $s = 0.3$ lb/min. This contamination is diluted by run-off of fresh water from streams into the reservoir at the rate of $Q = 1000$ gal/min, which is also the flow rate of water out of the reservoir (keeping the volume in the reservoir constant). Evaluate the salt concentration c (gm/m^3) in the water leaving the reservoir at the following times: 1 hr, 12 hr, 1 day, 2 days, 7 days, 14 days, and 1 year. What can you conclude about approximately how long it takes the concentration level to stabilize, and what level does it stabilize at?

Hint: The formula for the concentration is:

$$c(t) = \frac{s}{Q}\left(1 - e^{-\frac{Q}{V}t}\right) \tag{2.26}$$

It might appear that you could define a *range* for the times, but this is not the case, because each time step is different. Instead, define the function $c(t)$, and then just evaluate it at the seven different times.

2.38 A skydiver whose total mass including equipment is $M = 70$ kg jumps out of an airplane. It can be shown that the velocity of descent $V(t)$ is given by:

$$V(t) = \sqrt{\frac{Mg}{k}}\tanh\left(\sqrt{\frac{gk}{M}}t\right) \tag{2.27}$$

where k is an effective drag coefficient which among other things depends on how the skydiver holds her body. If she bundles up her body so that $k = 0.005$ lbf/mph^2 , evaluate the speed V (in mph) over the time range $t = 0$ s, 5 sec .. 60 sec. From this data, approximately how long does she take to reach terminal velocity (or in other words the steady velocity)? What is the value of the terminal velocity (in mph)? Repeat the calculation if she spread-eagles herself so that $k = 0.0155$ lbf/mph^2. What would the speed be after 60 sec if there was no air drag at all (you can't use Equation (2.27) for this)?

How to Graph Functions

Engineers always work with numerical data obtained, for example, from conducting an experiment or as the results of a theoretical analysis. They must decide how best to present this data. If there is a large amount of it, there are two ways it can be presented: in tabular form or in graphical form. Engineers often present results in graphical form, as this affords the reader an immediate sense of the data trend (and, depending on the need, the data is often tabulated too).

For example, consider the sea-level temperature at a location as a function of time in hours, for a period of one year. If you presented this in *tabular* form, it would have the advantage of enabling the reader to obtain a temperature at any given hour during the year, but it would have the disadvantage that the reader would not be able to see trends or patterns in the data. If you instead presented the data in *graphical* form, the reader would not easily be able to obtain an accurate reading of the temperature at any given hour (a disadvantage of graphical presentations), but on the other hand several trends in the data would be apparent (the major advantage of graphical presentations). These trends would be that the data appears to have an approximate sinusoidal behavior over a 24-hour period (colder at night, warmer during the day); the data would have another approximate sinusoidal behavior superimposed on the first, this time over the entire year (colder in winter, warmer in summer); the data would have *scatter* (random variations of data points around the two sinusoidal trends). In addition, with the graphical presentation, the hottest and coldest hours (or at least days) would be immediately apparent.

Hence, it's clear that being able to produce data in graphical form is a fundamental need of any engineer or scientist.

In this chapter we'll review the basics of how to graph things in Mathcad. This topic is, like many others we're reviewing in this text, quite large. For instance, we'll see that Mathcad has two very useful features called *Zoom* and *Trace* that, as their names imply, allow you to zoom in on a region of a graph and trace (or, in other words, read out) the values of data points on the graph. If you think about it, these features obviate the disadvantage of graphical versus tabular presentations: you can now get detailed information from a graph!

In this introductory text, we can merely scratch the surface of the subject of graphing using Mathcad. We'll see later that Mathcad has lots of built-in resources for giving you help on its graphing capabilities.

3.1

The Graph Palette

Figure 3.1

For this chapter, which focuses on graphing, let's open the Graph palette by clicking on its icon on the Math palette. You should then have visible the palette shown in Figure 3.1. Let's review the icons in this palette. Starting at the top left and proceeding in rows, we have

1. The *X-Y Plot*. We'll study this kind of graph in some detail.

2. The *Zoom* icon. This is currently grayed-out because it's only used when you already have a graph. We'll discuss this.

3. The *Trace* icon. This is also currently grayed-out, for the same reason. We'll discuss this.

4. The *Polar Plot,* which we'll discuss.

5. The *Surface Plot,* which we'll discuss.

6. The *Contour Plot,* which we'll discuss.

7. The *3D Bar Chart,* which we'll discuss.

8. The *3D Scatter Plot,* which we will not discuss. For help on this, see the comments at the end of this chapter.

9. The *Vector Field Plot,* which we will not discuss. For help on this, see the comments at the end of this chapter.

Note that you don't *have* to use one of these icons to create a graph. For example, an *X-Y* graph can be invoked not only by clicking on the *X-Y Plot* icon, but also by pressing **Shift + 2** or the @ key on the keyboard.

3.2

X-Y Plots

Let's begin to examine how to do *X-Y* plots by doing an example, and then we'll summarize what we learned.

Example 3.1   The damped pendulum

A pendulum consisting of a mass M and a string of length $l = 2$ ft, shown in Figure 3.2, is set swinging with an initial amplitude of $\theta_{in} = 4°$.

Because of aerodynamic drag and friction in the mounting, the pendulum will eventually stop swinging. The equation for the motion of the mass can be shown to be:

$$\theta(t) = e^{-at}\theta_{in}\ \cos\left(\sqrt{\frac{g}{l}}t\right) \tag{3.1}$$

Here $a = 0.25$ s^{-1} is a damping coefficient (due to the air drag and friction in the mounting). Plot the motion for the first 10 seconds.

First, in Mathcad, start a new worksheet and save it as "Example 3.1." Give it the following title, formatting it as you wish (the format of the title below happens to be Helvetica 16 point):

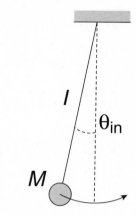

Figure 3.2

The Damped Pendulum

By (Your Name)

Next, let's input the given data:

The pendulum length is: $l := 2 \cdot \text{ft}$

The initial amplitude is: $\theta_{in} := 4 \cdot \text{deg}$

The damping is: $a := 0.25 \cdot \dfrac{1}{s}$

Note that the *literal* subscript was used for creating the subscript in θ_{in}. Also, although Mathcad computes trigonometric functions using *radians*, you can specify the value of a variable in *degrees*, as we've done for θ_{in} in the equation above.

Now we can define the function $\theta(t)$:

The motion is given by: $\theta(t) := e^{-a \cdot t} \cdot \theta_{in} \cdot \cos\left(\sqrt{\dfrac{g}{l}} \cdot t \right)$

In creating the above expression, don't forget: Greek letters can be obtained from the Latin by typing **Ctrl + G** immediately after typing the letter (in this case q); press the **Space Bar** to escape from the exponent *and* the root; and use the period (.) for the literal subscript. To create the root, you type the backslash (\) (another unique Mathcad accelerator key worth memorizing!). For the root, you could also use the Arithmetic palette by opening it from the Math palette.

To plot any graph you always need to decide what range of values to plot. Generally, you will want to control this range (but, as we'll see shortly, Mathcad version 7 has a feature called QuickPlot which will make a guess of what range you wish to plot). In the example we're working on, we're interested in the first 10 s. Here let's define a range of times by typing the following:

The time range is: $t := 0 \cdot s \, .. \, 10 \cdot s$

As you learned in Chapter 2, don't forget that the double period (..) *must* be created by using the semicolon key! Also, note that if you use units in a range, each term in the definition *must* have the same units (except, it turns out, 0 is counted as zero of *anything,* e.g., dimensionless, seconds, meters, etc.).

Once this range is defined, to obtain the graph, click somewhere below the equation definition and range definition, approximately where you want the *top left* corner of the graph to appear, and use any of the following three techniques:

1. Press the @ key (yet another Mathcad accelerator key, again worth memorizing!).

2. Click the X-Y Plot icon on the Graph palette.

3. Use the menu item *Insert . . . Graph . . . X-Y Plot.*

You'll have an empty graph. You need to fill in at least some of the small colored rectangles called *placeholders*. In this example, the one along the horizontal axis will be time *t,* and the vertical axis placeholder will be θ*(t)*. Click on each placeholder (or use **Tab** enough times to cycle around the placeholders) and do this. (We'll discuss the other placeholders that may have appeared later.) When you then press **Enter** or click anywhere outside the graph, you'll get the curve we're looking for.

You should end up with something like

The time range is: $t := 0 \cdot s \, .. \, 10 \cdot s$

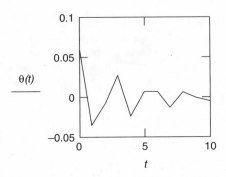

It turns out that if you had *not* defined the time range, the QuickPlot feature would have kicked in, and given you a graph plotted from –10 to 10.

You've just created your first Mathcad graph. However, so far the graph is a bit of a disaster! First of all, the graph is horribly jagged, when we should be expecting a smooth decaying sinusoidal curve. Second, it's a bit small. Third, where do the strange limits on the vertical axis of –0.05 to +0.1 come from? They appear to have nothing to do with our initial 4° angle.

First let's address why the graph is so jagged. It's because the range was not carefully defined, leading to only 11 data points. You recall that in defining ranges, if you *only* specify the beginning and ending ranges, Mathcad assumes you want a *unit* step size. Hence, here Mathcad generated points starting at 0 s and ending at 10 s, *but* the data points were at 0 s, 1 s, 2 s, and so on, so we only ended up with 11 data points. This illustrates a *very* common error in creating graphs: an incorrect or imprecise range specification. Because Mathcad is live, if the range you've created doesn't do the job, simple editing of the range to generate lots of data points will immediately fix the problem.

Edit the time range to make your worksheet look like

The time range is: $t := 0 \cdot s,\ 0.05 \cdot s\ ..\ 10 \cdot s$

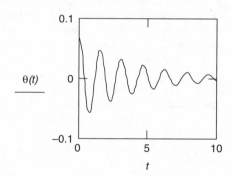

The time step size is now given by the difference between the first and second numbers in the range definition. Here this is $0.05 - 0 = 0.05$ s. With the range defined as above, we have 201 data points, resulting in a smooth-appearing graph. How many data points should you have Mathcad generate? It's basically a matter of personal choice, but you should certainly use enough to guarantee a smooth-looking graph. Mathcad has no problems in generating thousands of data points (depending on overall computer system memory).

Let's now address the second thing that jumps out about this graph: its size. To resize the graph you do what you do with any region: you click on it and use the placeholders on the border. Also, once you've selected the graph region, by moving the mouse over a border you get the small hand appearing, enabling movement of the graph. Try to do this to get something like

The time range is: $t := 0 \cdot s,\ 0.05 \cdot s\ ..\ 10 \cdot s$

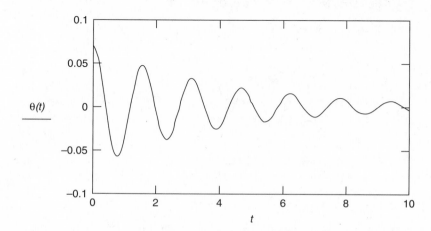

Our graph is now smooth, but it is still a little crude looking, and we still have the third unpleasant feature: the numbers on the vertical axis seem a bit odd. Where do these graph limits of –0.1 and 0.1 come from (your numbers, depending on how you resized your graph, may be different) and how do they fit in with our initial angle of 4°? Also, why do the numbers on the horizontal axis make sense while the vertical ones don't?

The numbers showing up on the vertical axis may be a bit puzzling at first, but they are correct, because Mathcad always computes in its *default* units. To determine the limits on the vertical axis, it computes the maximum and minimum values of the function and then rounds out the numbers to the nearest integer or decimal. In this worksheet, the maximum value of θ is $\theta_{in} = 4°$, or, in other words, about 0.07 radian, so Mathcad sets an upper limit on the axis of 0.1. The other number on the vertical axis is due to rounding down the lowest value θ reaches.

This discussion introduces a small problem in graphing functions with units in Mathcad: If the function has units other than default units (in this case, degrees rather than radians), you'll never get the numbers to appear right, because they'll *always* appear in the default units. This was not a problem for the horizontal axis because the units we chose for time, seconds, happen to be the default time units. This, of course, will also not be a problem if you're working with a worksheet in which you don't have units.

Sometimes this problem can be fixed by changing the default units for the worksheet (click on menu item *Math . . . Options* and in the window that appears switch to the tab called Unit System). In many cases this won't help, but fortunately, there are other ways to get around the problem. For example, we'll see that you can ask Mathcad to not show axis numbers. You could also try restructuring the engineering problem so it is written in standard units (e.g., SI or US). The simplest and best solution, however, is to plot not the function, but the function divided by the units in which you wish it measured. The axis will then be plotting a dimensionless quantity.

To see how this works, click on the $\theta(t)$ on the vertical axis and edit it so it's divided by *deg*. You should see, after pressing **Enter,** the following:

The time range is: $t := 0 \cdot s, 0.05 \cdot s \,.. \, 10 \cdot s$

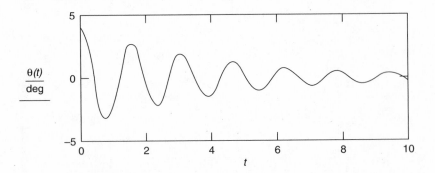

We're finally getting somewhere! All of the numbers now make sense.

Before continuing with this worksheet, let's take a digression to look at the QuickPlot feature.

X-Y Plots

71

Quickplot

Let's start a blank worksheet (you can keep open the Example 3.1 worksheet) and click on an empty region of the worksheet so that we can use QuickPlot to quickly plot, say, $x^3 - 5x$. To do this, one way is to define a variable $f(x)$ to be equal to $x^3 - 5x$ (try it). Then, somewhere below this equation, type $f(x)$ (without an equals sign) and, *while still in this expression,* use any of the graph-generating techniques we already learned:

1. Press the @ key.
2. Click the X-Y Plot icon on the Graph palette.
3. Use the menu item *Insert . . . Graph . . . X-Y Plot.*

A graph will appear. The graph will look incomplete, but when you press **Enter,** the graph just created will be finished:

$f(x) := x^3 - 5 \cdot x$

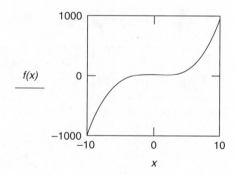

Even though you didn't specify a range to be plotted, the graph worked, because in this QuickPlot method, Mathcad assumed a *default* range of −10 to +10 for the horizontal axis.

Because QuickPlot always *assumes* a range (−10 to 10 or, depending on the function, 0 to 10), no matter what you're plotting, it's only useful as a very quick tool for examining a function: normally, *you* want to control the axes on a graph, so you'll find that you only have an occasional use for it.

You can now close this practice worksheet without saving and return to the Example 3.1 worksheet. There is a lot more formatting of the Example 3.1 graph we can do, but first let's introduce a couple of very nice graph features of Mathcad.

The Zoom Feature

Suppose you want to focus in on part of a graph. For example, let's try focusing in on the peak in θ around $t = 3$ s so we can find at what time the third oscillation is about to begin.

To focus in on a region of an *X-Y* graph:

1. Click on the graph to select it. You *must* do this to get access to the menu item and icon described in the second step.

2. Invoke the zoom mode by either selecting the menu item *Format . . . Graph . . . Zoom* or by clicking on the Zoom icon on the Graph palette (which you opened by clicking on its icon on the Math palette). This will open the window shown in Figure 3.3. Drag with the mouse over the region on which you wish to focus. As you do this, the Min and Max windows will display the corresponding horizontal and vertical coordinates.

3. When you're satisfied with the view you've selected, press the Zoom button and your graph will then focus on the region you've selected.

4. If you're satisfied with your selection, close the Zoom window by pressing the Close button or by clicking on the cross in the top right corner. If you're not satisfied, click Unzoom or Full View to return to the original view.

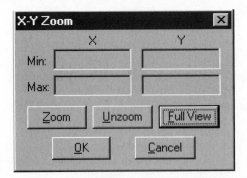

Figure 3.3

If you do all of this, you should have something like

The time range is: $t := 0 \cdot s, 0.05 \cdot s .. 10 \cdot s$

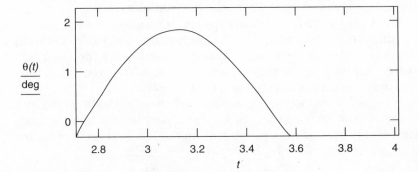

Notice that the original range, although no longer setting the lower and upper limits of the graph, is still needed. If you were to delete it, the graph would no longer plot. Also, if you ever wish to return to the original graph, simply click on it and use the Zoom window again.

This is obviously an excellent tool when you wish to examine the details of a graph. It gets even better, because in addition to or instead of zooming in on a region, you can use Mathcad's Trace feature.

The Trace Feature

To invoke the Trace feature:

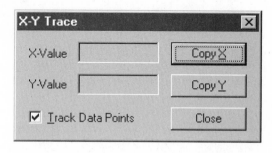

Figure 3.4

1. Click on the graph to select it. You *must* do this to get access to the menu item and icon in the second step.

2. Invoke the trace mode by either selecting the menu item *Format . . . Graph . . . Trace* or by clicking on the Trace icon on the Graph palette (which you opened by clicking on its icon on the Math palette). This will open the window shown in Figure 3.4. Make sure the Track Data Points window is checked (otherwise you won't follow the trace).

3. Click on the graph again. Then, as you either click at different points in the graph window or move the mouse around, you'll see the X-Value and Y-Value windows display the *closest* horizontal and vertical data points of the curve. Instead of the mouse, it's often more convenient to use the left and right arrow keys to move along the trace. In this trace mode, the up and down arrow do not move along a trace, but will, if you have more than one trace, jump from one to another.

4. If you wish to use a data point to which you've moved, simply press the Copy X or Copy Y button. This will copy the number selected to the Windows Clipboard, where it can be pasted somewhere into the worksheet, or into a word processor or other program.

Try using this trace feature to find the time at which the first peak occurs and paste it into the worksheet with some explanatory text. You should have something like

The time (s) for the third oscillation to start is approximately: 3.1

Why do we use the qualifier "approximately" here? Because the time step of data points in both the original *and* zoomed graphs is determined by the original graph range.

In this example, the time step is 0.05 s. If you wish more accuracy in finding the peak, you need to define a finer range. Let's do this by making the second term in the range 0.0025 s (producing 4001 data points!); using zoom again to focus in on a much smaller region; and repeating the trace procedure (delete the previous value found). You should get something like

The time range is: $\qquad t := 0 \cdot s,\ 0.0025 \cdot s\ ..\ 10 \cdot s$

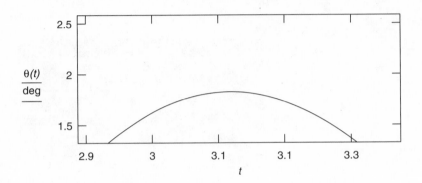

The time (s) for the third oscillation to start is approximately: 3.1175

We'll see in Chapter 5 that there are much more precise and elegant techniques for finding the peak of a function. Now that we've done quite a bit of work on it, it's a good time to save your Example 3.1 worksheet.

Formatting

There are lots of formatting options that can be used on an X-Y Plot graph. Before exploring formatting of our graph, click on it and use the Zoom feature to restore the graph to its Full View.

To access the graph formatting features, either click once on the graph and select the menu item *Format . . . Graph . . . X-Y Plot* or simply double-click on the graph. Using either method brings up the window shown in Figure 3.5, which shows Mathcad's default graph settings.

Most of these check windows are fairly obvious. For example, as we'll see in Chapter 8, sometimes it's important to be able to plot a semilog or log-log graph. All we need to do is check the Log Scale box to make the corresponding axis logarithmic. We'll do some of these types of graphs as exercises at the end of this chapter.

Other options in Figure 3.5 are perhaps less obvious. For example, the Autoscale check box switches on and off the automatic axis scaling. When this is on (checked), Mathcad will scale up the

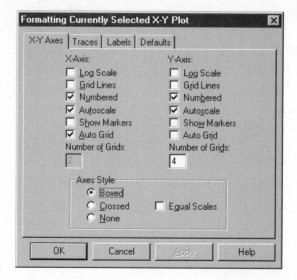

Figure 3.5

axis limits to the closest integer or decimal, as we saw in doing Example 3.1. If it's off (unchecked), the axis limits are the minimum and maximum values of the function (this difference will not be apparent very much in zoom mode).

For specific guidance on any of these features, click on the Help button.

Notice that you have many more options (including changing the graph from line to, among others, point, bar, step, stem, etc.) available by clicking on the tabs for Traces, Labels and Defaults. Again, most of these options are self-explanatory, and those that are not can be understood by clicking on the Help button.

See if you can format your graph by changing the Weight trace option to 3; changing to the Crossed Axes style; adding a Title; and adding X-Axis and Y-Axis labels. You should end up with something like

The time range is: $t := 0 \cdot s,\ 0.0025 \cdot s\ ..\ 10 \cdot s$

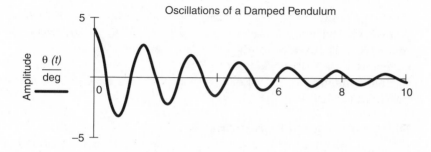

Note that your graph probably looks nicer if you have been using the default fonts for the worksheet (Times New Roman) rather than Helvetica (which all of the worksheets in this text use to distinguish Mathcad's output from the font of the text).

One final interesting point about formatting an *X-Y* plot: you can impose your own graph limits. To illustrate this, suppose for some reason we didn't want to see the amplitudes above 1°, and we only wanted to look at the time from 1 s to 9 s. We can impose these limits on the vertical and horizontal axes. To do this, click once on the graph and you'll see numbers you've been wondering about all along (in this example −3.295037 and 4 on the vertical axis and 0 and 10 on the horizontal axis). These are the extremum values Mathcad found for the functions on the two axes [θ(*t*) and *t*] and are used by Mathcad when it's deciding how to scale the graph. You can click on any or all of these and type other values (*including* units when appropriate). Note that you do not delete the default numbers, but just type over them.

In this example, replace the current values with −1 and 1 on the vertical axis and 1 s and 9 s on the horizontal. After pressing **Enter** you'll have

The time range is: $t := 0 \cdot s, \, 0.0025 \cdot s \, .. \, 10 \cdot s$

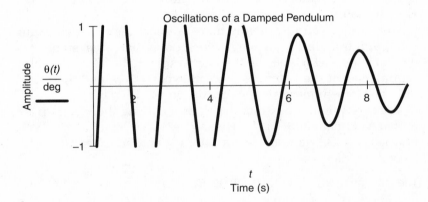

The curve was "clipped" to the limits you imposed. Of course, you could next use all the formatting features to which we've alluded. Now that we've made this graph particularly ugly, you can save and close this worksheet.

Before moving on to other graph types, let's look at two more important aspects of *X-Y* plots.

Plotting Several Functions

Occasionally several functions need to be plotted on the same graph. To illustrate how this is done in Mathcad, let's do another engineering example.

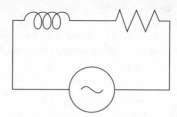

Voltage Source V(t)   **Figure 3.6**

Example 3.2   The RL circuit   Suppose the circuit shown in Figure 3.6 consists of an inductor $L = 0.005$ henry and a resistor $R = 0.5$ ohm connected in series. It is connected to a power source of amplitude $V_0 = 100$ volt and frequency $f = 60$ Hz. The voltage is given by

$$V(t) = V_0 \sin(\omega t) \tag{3.2}$$

where $\omega = 2\pi f$ is the frequency expressed in rad/s.

Plot the current for three cycles starting at $t = 0$ s. For comparison, also plot *one* cycle of the voltage.

To do this example, we need the equation for the current. It can be shown that this is

$$I(t) = \frac{V_0}{\sqrt{R^2 + \omega^2 L^2}} \sin(\omega t - \delta) \tag{3.3}$$

where δ is the *phase angle,* which measures the lag between the voltage and current sinusoids. This phase angle is given by

$$\delta = \tan^{-1}\left(\frac{\omega L}{R}\right) \tag{3.4}$$

Notice, for example, that if there is no inductor ($L = 0$ henry), the phase angle δ is zero, so that according to these equations the current and voltage are in phase, which we should expect from our knowledge of how resistors work. Also, if either the resistor R or inductor L values are large, the current given by Equation (3.3) will be of small amplitude, as we should also expect (because the circuit *impedance* will be large).

First let's create a new worksheet, give it a title, enter the given data, and save it as "Example 3.2." It should look something like

The RL Circuit

By (Your Name)

First enter the given data:

$V_0 := 100 \cdot \text{volt} \quad f := 60 \cdot \text{Hz} \quad \omega := 2 \cdot \pi \cdot f \quad R := 0.5 \cdot \text{ohm} \quad L := 0.005 \cdot \text{henry}$

An interesting point here: both R and L are actually units used by Mathcad, namely degrees Rankine and liter. We discussed in Chapter 2 that you should avoid using for your own variables symbols that Mathcad already uses. However, because we don't intend in this worksheet to express anything using degrees Rankine or liters (neither are fundamental units), we won't encounter any units difficulties.

We can now enter the following:

The alternating voltage is then $V(t) := V_0 \cdot \sin(\omega \cdot t)$

The period of this AC system is: $\tau = \dfrac{2 \cdot \pi}{\omega}$ $\tau = 0.017 \cdot s$

Finally, the current (including phase angle) is:

$$\delta := \operatorname{atan}\left(\frac{\omega \cdot L}{R}\right) \qquad I(t) := \frac{V_0}{\sqrt{R^2 + \omega^2 \cdot L^2}} \cdot \sin(\omega \cdot t - \delta)$$

Remember, to exit from a denominator or a root, use the **Space Bar**, and to invoke the root function (*before* its argument is typed), use the backslash key (\ ).

We're now ready to plot the current for three cycles. Set up the range as shown below to cover three cycles, and then create the graph (which we've resized) with t for the horizontal axis and $I(t)$ for the vertical axis:

We can plot these results: $t := 0 \cdot s, \dfrac{\tau}{100} .. 3 \cdot \tau$

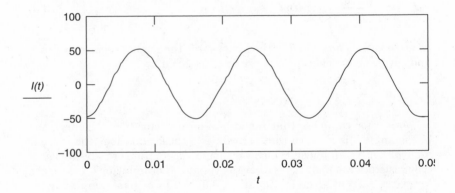

Note that we get a break here, because the functions happen to be expressed in the default units (amps for the current and seconds for the time), so the numbers on the axes immediately make sense. It looks like the current amplitude is around 50 amps. We can easily check this by computing the amplitude (do it by selecting the appropriate expression from the equation for the current and copying and pasting):

The amplitude of the current is: $\dfrac{V_0}{\sqrt{R^2 + \omega^2 \cdot L^2}} = 51.278 \cdot A$

Now we can explore how a second function (the voltage) can be plotted on the same graph. To put a second (and third, fourth, etc.) function on a graph, simply use a comma (,) to separate the functions.

Let's do this. First, there's a little detail we need to take care of: you can't plot current and voltage on the same axis because they have different units! Any graph you create with multiple functions on an axis (horizontal or vertical) must be set up so the functions are dimensionless. Of course, if you're not using units in a particular worksheet, this is not something you need to worry about.

To edit our graph, divide the current function by *amp,* then use the **Space Bar** to exit this denominator, type a comma (,), and then type the voltage $V(t)$ divided by *volt.* The comma separates the two variables on the vertical axis.

When you exit the graph you should have

We can plot these results: $t := 0 \cdot s, \dfrac{\tau}{100}..3 \cdot \tau$

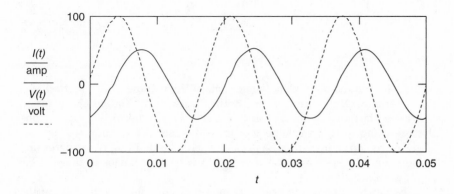

We'll summarize the rules for plotting multiple functions later, but for now let's see how we can further modify the graph so the voltage, as desired, is only plotted for one cycle.

First, note that we have two functions of time plotted against one variable (t). In general, any number of functions can be plotted against one function on the horizontal axis. We can also plot in pairs: that is, each function on the vertical axis can be paired with one on the horizontal axis.

Let's see this by creating a second time range t', which goes from τ to 2τ. To create a prime in a math expression, you *don't* use the prime key (') because this is used by Mathcad to generate parentheses, but instead use the alternate prime key (`)! Define this new range. Then, in the graph, using the comma to separate the two terms, add the second time range t' to the horizontal axis. Before exiting from the graph, edit the voltage function on the vertical axis to be a function of the new time variable t'.

It's *very* important to note that the horizontal and vertical axis functions should be correctly sequenced: the *first* expressions on each axis go together, as do the second pair, and so on. In this example, the first function $I(t)/amp$ goes with t and the second, $V(t')/volt$ with t'. If you don't follow this sequence rule, you're likely to get a mess of a graph, or Mathcad might start computing and not stop for a long while (in which case you should press **Esc** to stop calculation).

If you succeed with this editing, you'll get

We can plot these results: $t := 0 \cdot s, \dfrac{\tau}{100} \, .. \, 3 \cdot \tau$ $t' := \tau, 1.001 \cdot \tau \, .. \, 2 \cdot \tau$

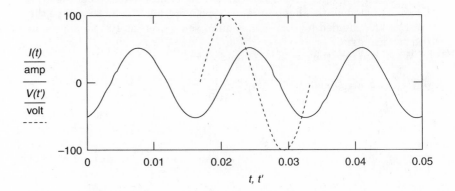

Note that, as desired, only one cycle of the voltage is now plotted.

We've basically finished with this worksheet. You might want to practice formatting the graph (we won't do this here). We can do one more thing to this worksheet to make it more interesting: we can use *global variables* by using the priority equals for defining the resistor and inductor values, so we can conveniently see how changes in these affect the graph.

Somewhere near the graph, create equations for R and L using the priority equals (see Chapter 2 if you've forgotten how to do this). Then edit the previous formulas for these at the top of the worksheet so they are equations using the evaluation equals. If you do all of this, and, for example, change the inductor value to 0 henry, you should have

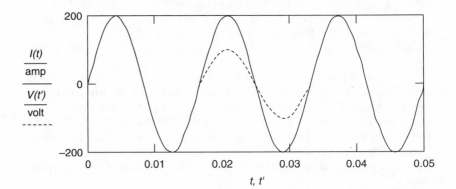

The amplitude of the current is: $\dfrac{V_0}{\sqrt{R^2 + \omega^2 \cdot L^2}} = 200 \cdot A$

$R \equiv 0.5 \cdot \text{ohm}$ $\qquad L \equiv 0 \cdot \text{henry}$

As we should expect, with this data the voltage and current are in phase, and the current ($= V_0 / R$) is 200 amp amplitude.

Let's summarize the rules for creating graphs with several functions on each axis:

1. Each axis can have any number of functions, except the number of functions on the vertical axis should be equal to or exceed the number on the horizontal axis. For example, you can plot one function versus another, or three functions versus one, or two versus two, and so forth, but not two versus three.

2. The functions on each axis are matched together in sequential pairs (the first function on the vertical axis goes with the first on the horizontal, etc.). If the number on the vertical axis exceeds that on the horizontal axis, the functions are paired off and any unmatched functions are matched with the *last* function on the horizontal axis. For example, two functions will both be matched with a single horizontal function, and three functions plotted against two functions will be matched with the first, second, and second horizontal functions.

3. If several functions are assigned to an axis, they must all have the same dimensions (or all be dimensionless).

These rules apply not only to functions but to the following.

Plotting Vectors

Engineers often need to graph not a *function* but instead experimental data. In other words, instead of plotting one function against another, they need to plot one set of data against another set. For example, an engineer might accumulate data on the pressure indicated by a pressure gage as different known pressures are applied. The measurements were perhaps taken for uniform pressure changes, or they might have been taken for smaller pressure changes when the pressure itself was small in order to increase the number of data points at low pressures. This kind of data is usually presented in tabular format. We'll see in Chapter 8 that quite a bit of statistical analysis can be done on such data, and in Chapter 9 how to import and export data from, say, a spreadsheet, but here we'll look into how to graph it.

Mathcad represents columns of data as *vectors*. So far we haven't discussed how Mathcad handles vectors, and we'll postpone exploring this in detail until Chapter 6. Here we'll just introduce them so we can see how to plot them.

Let's start a blank worksheet so we can do another engineering example. Type in the title "Pressure Gage Calibration" and include your name. Format these titles as you wish. Save it as "Example 3.3." We can then tackle the following.

Example 3.3 Pressure gage calibration The accuracy of a pressure gage can be obtained by calibrating it. One way to do this is to read the indicated pressures and compare them to actual pressures. Suppose we have the following data for a particular gage:

Reading	1	2	3	4	5	6	7	8	9	10
p_{act} (*Pa*)	0	5	10	15	20	30	40	50	60	70
p_{ind} (*Pa*)	0	6	11	13	24	32	38	56	61	73

Let's see how we enter this data as two vectors. The first vector will be called p_{act}. First of all, we've already seen literal subscripts. You recall that these are created using the period (.) and are used for conveniently labeling variables. Type this variable name at a location several lines down from the title, and press the colon key to get the assignment equals. We can now create the vector of numbers on the right of the equation.

One way to create a vector (we'll eventually learn others, including using vector or matrix subscripts) is to type **Ctrl + M** (a mnemonic for *m*atrix). Do this and the window shown in Figure 3.7 will appear. This is a window asking what size matrix you'd like to create. In this example, the matrix is a vector, so the number of columns is 1 and the number of rows is 10. Simply type 10, press **Tab** to get to the Columns window, type 1, and either click the Insert button or press **Enter.**

You'll now have a blank column with 10 placeholders ready for your input. If the column spills over onto the worksheet titles, simply drag it down a little. Enter the 10 numbers for p_{act} (to move from placeholder to placeholder, you can use the mouse or press the **Tab** key). When you get to the last number, instead of pressing **Enter,** press the **Space Bar** so that the insertion lines include the entire column. You can then

Figure 3.7

multiply the entire column by the units Pa. After you've done all of this, you can repeat for the p_{ind} vector of data.

After adding some explanatory text, your worksheet should look something like

Pressure Gage Calibration

By (Your Name)

The data for actual and indicated pressures are:

$$
p_{\text{act}} := \begin{bmatrix} 0 \\ 5 \\ 10 \\ 15 \\ 20 \\ 30 \\ 40 \\ 50 \\ 60 \\ 70 \end{bmatrix} \cdot Pa
\qquad
p_{\text{ind}} := \begin{bmatrix} 0 \\ 6 \\ 11 \\ 13 \\ 24 \\ 32 \\ 38 \\ 56 \\ 61 \\ 73 \end{bmatrix} \cdot Pa
$$

We can now plot p_{ind} against p_{act}. Simply use the techniques we've already described to create an *X-Y* plot and place these vectors at the two placeholders. You should get, after resizing the graph and changing the trace to Points with x's, something like

The data looks like:

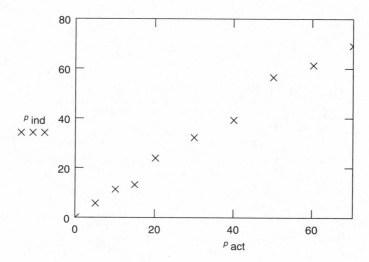

That's it! What Mathcad does when it's asked to plot two vectors against one another is create data points by matching the values in both vectors, one by one, until it runs out of values in one of the vectors (and usually vectors of the same size are plotted against one another, so all data points are used).

This graph is not very interesting. About the only thing we can say is that it appears to be approximately linear, so we can apply linear regression to the data. This means we'd like to get the best straight line to represent the relationship between the indicated and actual pressures. We'll discuss this and other data analysis techniques in Chapter 8, but for now we'll just have Mathcad do it for us so we can see how to plot multiple vectors on an axis, and not worry about how the regression was done. The equation for the regression is

$$p_{\mathrm{reg}}(p_{\mathrm{act}}) = Mp_{\mathrm{act}} + C \tag{3.5}$$

where M is the slope of the best straight-line fit and C is its intercept. How do we get Mathcad to compute M and C? Mathcad has two built-in functions, *slope* and *intercept,* for doing this. As always, Mathcad's *Help* would give you guidance on these (try searching in the Index of the Help window for *regression*), but for now just type the following (where you will need to insert the *Pa* units in the evaluation of C) below your previous work:

The results of the linear regression are:

$M := \mathrm{slope}\,(p_{\mathrm{act}}, p_{\mathrm{ind}})$ $\qquad\qquad M = 1.037$

$C := \mathrm{intercept}\,(p_{\mathrm{act}}, p_{\mathrm{ind}})$ $\qquad\qquad C = 0.286 \cdot \mathrm{Pa}$

Below this, create a new graph by copying the original graph and pasting it. Next, add a second vector to the vertical axis of the new graph (remembering to use a comma to separate the two vectors) to represent the regression line (the best fit).

You should end up with

The regression analysis leads to:

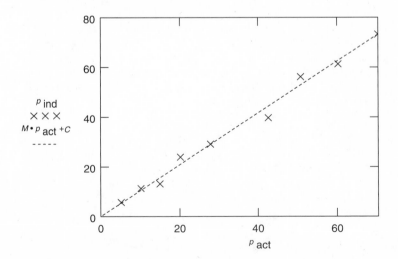

Here Mathcad matched data points from *each* vector on the vertical axis with those of the vector p_{act} on the horizontal axis, following the rules described in the previous section. As we mentioned, you can see Chapter 8 for more on what you can do with this regression analysis.

Finally, sometimes it's convenient to plot vectors using a *parametric* representation, which means the graphing is controlled by another variable. To do this, we need to briefly discuss *Vector or Array subscripts,* not to be confused with literal subscripts! We'll discuss all of these subscripts in detail in Chapter 6, but for now let's note that you can create a vector subscript by using the left angle bracket ([) (one more special Mathcad keystroke).

To see what this is about, let's continue with our example. Move to a region below the previous work. Let's use this new subscript notation to give us the value of the *last* (tenth) data point of p_{ind}. To try to do this, type *p.ind[10=.* Note that this expression uses both the literal (.) and Vector or Array ([) subscripts.

You should get

$p_{ind_{10}} =$

> Value of subscript or superscript is too big (or too small) for this array.

Mathcad could not find the tenth value of p_{ind}! This happened because Mathcad assumes you always want to count vector or matrix elements starting with *zero* rather than *unity*. Hence, to get the tenth, and last, data point, according to Mathcad, you should ask for p_{ind_9}. Furthermore, the data point $p_{ind_{10}}$ does not exist, because it actually refers to a nonexistent *eleventh* element!

Again, we'll discuss the details of this in Chapter 6, but for now let's just state that you can change the starting point for counting vector and matrix elements by changing Mathcad's built-in variable called *ORIGIN.* Let's do this now by clicking on menu item *Math . . . Options,* and in the Math Options window that appears change the Array Origin from 0 to 1. Exiting from this window will immediately lead to the correct result (where, if you like, you can insert *Pa* units):

$p_{ind_{10}} = 73 \cdot kg \cdot m^{-1} \cdot s^{-2}$ ∎

We've now finished with this expression, so you can delete it.

Next, let's create a range i below everything we've done so far that will be used to count vector elements

The counting range is: $i := 1 .. 10$

Finally, use the Vector or Array subscript notation to create yet another graph, this time using the *parametric* representation:

The graph, generated using the parametric notation, is:

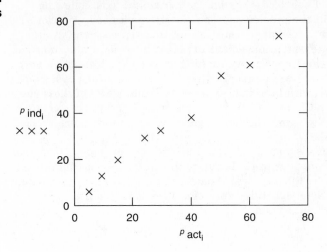

This method of plotting vectors is slightly more versatile than the previous method (which didn't use subscripts). For example, to plot every *other* data point, simply edit the range definition:

The counting range is: $i := 1, 3 .. 10$

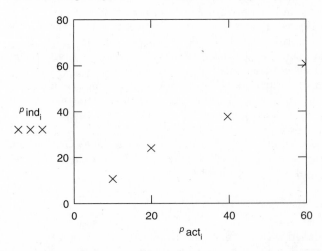

Finally, all of the graphs we've done in this example need further formatting. For example, this last graph should be worked with so that the first and last data points don't sit on the edges of the graph, titles should be added, a linear regression could be plotted, and so on. When you've done this, you can save the worksheet once again.

Exercises

3.1 A block of mass $M = 10$ lb is sitting on an oiled surface that is inclined at an angle $\theta = 10°$ to the horizontal. At time $t = 0$ s the block is released and begins sliding down the incline. Eventually the block will attain a steady speed, when the friction generated by the oil just balances the pull of gravity down the incline. The equation for the block motion is

$$V(t) = \frac{Mg \sin(\theta)}{k}\left(1 - e^{\frac{-k}{M}t}\right) \qquad (3.6)$$

where $k = 0.25$ lbf/mph is a coefficient of viscous friction.

Plot the velocity for the first minute. Then (zooming in on the graph as necessary) use the trace feature to find when the velocity becomes constant (to the accuracy of the trace window) and what this velocity is in mph.

Hint: Plot $V(t)$ divided by mph.

3.2 You have $1000. You want to leave it in the bank for 30 years. The interest rate is 5.25%, compounded annually. *Compounding annually* simply means that at the end of each year, the amount of money accumulated in interest is added to the original deposit, so the next year the interest is accumulated on a slightly larger amount. Plot a bar chart (by selecting Bar as the trace type) showing the *total* amount of interest you have accumulated by the end of each year. Also plot on the same graph the amount you would have accumulated if you had only received simple interest. In contrast to compound interest, *simple interest* means that the amount you accumulate each year is computed *only* on the original deposit. Compute the additional money you will have received after 30 years due to the compounding.

Of course, all banks in fact do compound (some daily, others quarterly or annually). The relevant formulas are

$$S_{comp}(n) = P[(1 + i)^n - 1] \qquad (3.7)$$

$$S_{simp}(n) = Pni \qquad (3.8)$$

where S_{comp} and S_{simp} are the sums accumulated by the two types of interest after n years at the interest rate i (%). P is the amount of the original deposit.

Hint: Express the interest as a percentage by using the "unit" %.

3.3 The following data is available on the cooling of a soot particle after it is ejected from a smoke stack:

t (s)	0	5	10	15	20	25	30	35	40	45	50
ΔT (K)	500	300	150	90	40	30	10	7	4	2	1

The table shows the temperature ΔT (in Kelvin) above atmospheric temperature of the particle as a function of time t (s). Plot the temperature versus time as points without lines. On a second graph, plot temperature versus time again but make the vertical axis a log scale. On this second graph the data will appear approximately linear. In Chapter 8 we'll discuss why sometimes data that is not linear appears linear when plotted on a semi-log graph.

3.3

Polar Plots

Occasionally engineers need to plot information on a *polar plot*. Let's do an example to illustrate how to do this in Mathcad.

Example 3.4   Pressure distribution around a cylinder

One of the basic geometries studied in *inviscid flow theory* (the theory of fluids with no viscosity) is that of the flow over a circular cylinder with rotation, as shown in Figure 3.8.

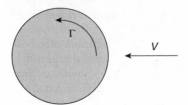

Figure 3.8

Although all real fluids have viscosity, in many aerodynamics problems, the viscous effects of the air are negligible in much of the flow field, so inviscid flow theory is a reasonable model. Furthermore, a cylindrical shape can be mathematically transformed into an airfoil shape, so once the flow around the cylinder is known, flow around an airfoil can be deduced—hence the importance of the study of flow over a cylinder. It turns out that the pressure distribution over the cylinder surface is

$$p(\theta) = p_{\text{atm}} + \frac{1}{2}\,\rho\,[V^2 - (\Gamma + 2V\sin\theta)^2] \tag{3.9}$$

where $p_{\text{atm}} = 14.7$ psi is the atmospheric pressure, $\rho = 1.2$ kg/m^3 is the density of air (notice the mixed units!), $V = 100$ mph is the speed of the air moving toward the cylinder, $\Gamma = 200$ mph is a measure of the cylinder rotation, and θ is the angular position on the cylinder (so that $\theta = 0°$ means the front of the cylinder).

We'd like to plot this distribution. Let's start a new worksheet (which you can save as "Example 3.4"), give it a title, and enter the given data and the equation for the pressure distribution:

<u>Pressure Distribution around a Cylinder</u>

By (Your Name)

The given data are

$$p_{\text{atm}} := 14.7 \text{ psi} \quad \rho := 1.2 \cdot \frac{\text{kg}}{\text{m}^3} \quad \Gamma := 200 \cdot \text{mph} \quad V := 100 \cdot \text{mph}$$

The pressure distribution is

$$p(\theta) := p_{\text{atm}} + \frac{1}{2} \cdot \rho \cdot [V^2 - (\Gamma + 2 \cdot V \cdot \sin(\theta))^2]$$

What we *could* do is plot the pressure against angular position on an *X-Y* plot. However, it will be more meaningful and intuitive if we use the polar plot. Click on an empty space where you'd like the graph to appear. Then, to invoke the polar plot, you use any of three methods similar to those used for the *X-Y* plot:

1. Press the accelerator keys **Ctrl + 7.**

2. Click on the Polar Plot icon on the Graph palette (obtained from the Math palette).

3. Use the menu item *Insert . . . Graph . . . Polar Plot.*

If you do this, you'll get an empty graph waiting for you to enter variables at the placeholders. The first one, at the lower center, is for the angle variable, in this example θ. You can then **Tab** to the second one, which is for the radial variable, in this case $p(\theta)$. After entering these and exiting the graph, you should have (adding some text):

The plot looks like:

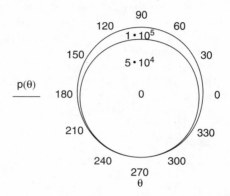

You may have noticed that we didn't specify a range for the independent variable θ. This is because Mathcad assumes that polar plots are for 360°, unless you specifically define a range.

Once you have the graph, you can customize it with basically all the options you have for the *X-Y* plot. See if you can get the graph to look like

The plot looks like:

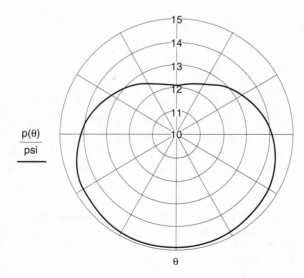

In case you're wondering, to get this graph from the original, do the following: resize it; divide $p(\theta)$ by psi so that the radial axis will count in numbers that make sense; insert the values 10 and 15 in the radial axis limit placeholders; double-click on the graph to open the Formatting Currently Selected Polar Plot window, where the Radial axis Grid Lines box can be checked, the Angular axis Grid Lines box checked, and Numbers box unchecked.

This graph is a famous result in fluid mechanics, because it shows that the cylinder with rotation will have relatively low pressure on the top surface and high on the bottom, leading to *aerodynamic lift*. The same general trend, of lift generation, happens for an airfoil, to which the rotating cylinder can be transformed [for fairly complicated theoretical reasons, the amount of rotation of the cylinder dictates the detailed shape (e.g., the curvature or *camber*) of the airfoil]. Once you have the worksheet laid out, you can see what happens as you change the value of the rotation. For instance, you might want to try changing this value to 0 mph and −200 mph.

This example is as far as we'll go with polar plots. However, all the things you can do with *X-Y* plots can also be done with polar plots. You can use QuickPlot, use the Zoom and Trace features, plot several functions, and plot vectors.

Exercise

3.4 The pressure distribution around a cylinder in a *real* fluid flow is

θ (°)	0	30	60	90	120	150	180	210	240	270	300	330	360
p (psi)	14.1	13.3	12.4	12	12.4	13.3	13.5	13.5	14	14	14.6	14.7	14.1

Plot these two vectors as a polar plot to look similar to the one in Example 3.4, except make the trace Symbols rather than Lines. Then, generate theoretical pressures at these angles according to Equation (3.9), and add these to the radial axis on the same graph, so you can compare experimental and theoretical data.

3.4

Surface Plots

The third major graph type we'll look at is the *surface plot*. This, as the name implies, is a graph designed to show the surface, or shape, of a function in 3-D space [the two horizontal directions are, for example, x and y, and the vertical is $f(x,y)$].

It turns out that the only thing that can be plotted as a surface plot in Mathcad is a *matrix*. We won't spend a lot of time in this chapter on matrices (we'll do this in Chapter 6), but we will discuss them just enough to learn how to do surface plots.

Let's consider an example to see how we create such plots.

Example 3.5 Vibration of a rectangular membrane

Consider an elastic membrane stretched across a square opening whose sides are length $L = 1$ ft. If this is disturbed (e.g., struck with a stick), as shown in Figure 3.9, it will vibrate with a very complicated vibration pattern.

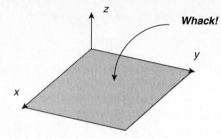

Whack!

Figure 3.9

It turns out that any such vibration can be represented as the addition of an infinite number of simpler vibration patterns, called the *eigenvectors* for the problem. The derivation of the equation for these eigenvectors involves fairly advanced theory, but this theory eventually leads to the following, for what is called the *m-n* mode:

$$z = f(x, y) = \sin\left(\frac{m\pi x}{L}\right)\sin\left(\frac{n\pi y}{L}\right) \tag{3.10}$$

Here z is the height of the membrane above the equilibrium position of the membrane. Note that this gives the *envelope* of the *m-n* mode of vibration, meaning it gives the shape of the amplitude of that mode. This *is* a vibration, so this function of the coordinates (x,y) would have to be multiplied by a function of time to obtain the complete solution for that mode. We won't do this here.

If you're a bit puzzled by this discussion of *m-n* modes, don't worry because we'll quickly see, using Mathcad to plot the surface, what it means.

As usual, create a new worksheet, give it a title (as shown below), and save it as "Example 3.5." We need to tell Mathcad how many points we'd like to plot in the x and y directions, and then generate those points. To accomplish this, do the following [using Vector or Array subscripts, ([), and assuming you kept the default value of the built-in constant ORIGIN as zero]:

Vibration of a Rectangular Membrane

By (Your Name)

The number of points on each axis is determined by:

$N := 50$ and $L := 1 \cdot \text{ft}$

Next, we can set up ranges for counting points on the axes:

$i := 0 .. N$ $j := 0 .. N$

The x and y values will then be:

$$x_i := i \cdot \frac{L}{N} \qquad y_j := j \cdot \frac{L}{N}$$

If you wish to check that the x and y values are correct, you could just evaluate them, but this would generate a large, and pretty uninformative, column. In fact, look what happens if you evaluate x:

The x and y values will then be: $\quad x_i := i \cdot \dfrac{L}{N} \qquad y_j := j \cdot \dfrac{L}{N}$

	0
0	0
1	$6.096 \cdot 10^{-3}$
2	0.012
3	0.018
4	0.024
5	0.03
6	0.037
7	0.043
8	0.049
9	0.055
10	0.061
11	0.067
12	0.073
13	0.079

$x = \qquad \qquad \qquad \cdot m$

The column is so large Mathcad switched its format to that of a spreadsheet! If you really wanted to see this column in Mathcad's normal format, you would double-click on it, and you'd get a Number Format window, where you could click on the option Display as Matrix.

Instead of displaying this unwieldy column (delete it if you created it), you could do a test by evaluating the last terms, x_{50} and y_{50}. Do this as a check and then delete them (we don't really need them):

$$x_{50} = 1 \cdot \text{ft} \qquad y_{50} = 1 \cdot \text{ft}$$

Here we inserted the *ft* units.

Next, we can define the *m-n* mode we're interested in (let's look at the *fundamental* one, $m = 1$ and $n = 1$) and define the function $f(x,y)$:

The mode is defined by *m* and *n:* $\qquad m := 1 \qquad n := 1$

. . . and is given by: $\quad f(x, y) := \sin\left(\dfrac{m \cdot \pi \cdot x}{L}\right) \cdot \sin\left(\dfrac{n \cdot \pi \cdot y}{L}\right)$

We've now set up all the engineering. Now let's see how we create the surface plot.

First of all, as we stated at the beginning of this section, we can only plot a matrix. A matrix, simply put, is a collection of numbers arranged in a row and column format. One way (we'll eventually learn others) to create a matrix vector is to type **Ctrl + M.** If you were to do this (don't), the window shown earlier in Figure 3.7 would appear, where you could specify the matrix size, create it, and then enter values into the matrix placeholders. Another way, which we'll use here, is to use the Vector or Array subscripts we previously mentioned and a predefined function. Type the following:

$$z_{i,j} := f(x_i, y_j)$$

What this expression does is compute the values to be placed in each of the cells. This matrix z has 51 ($i = 0$ through N, and $N = 50$) rows and 51 ($j = 0$ through N) columns. The counter i moves us through the x values, and counter j moves us through the y values, while both i and j control which cell value is being computed. The equation says that the (i, j) cell of matrix z is equal to the function evaluated at point (x_i, y_j).

We've now (finally!) generated a matrix we can plot.

To generate the surface plot, click on the approximate point where you'd like the plot to appear and use any one of the following:

1. Press **Ctrl + 2** (yet another Mathcad accelerator key, this time not really worth memorizing!).

2. Click on the Surface Plot icon on the Graph palette.

3. Use the menu item *Insert . . . Graph . . . Surface Plot.*

You'll find a single placeholder, where you should type z (the matrix you'd like to plot, without subscripts), and then press **Enter.**

You should get (after resizing the graph)

$$z_{i,j} := f(x_i, y_j)$$

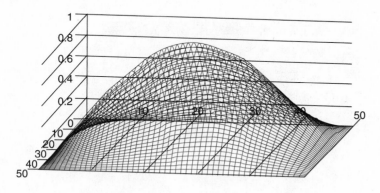

z

This is the shape (or envelope) of the vibration if the membrane was made to vibrate in its simplest, or fundamental, mode, in which the entire membrane moves up and down in phase.

Isn't this graph a bit disappointing? We need to work on its formatting a little, but first let's note the meaning of $m = 1$ and $n = 1$. These determine how many peaks and troughs occur in the x and y directions. To see this, change the value of n to 3 and look at the graph (another demonstration of the *live* nature of Mathcad). You should see

$$z_{i,j} := f(x_i, y_j)$$

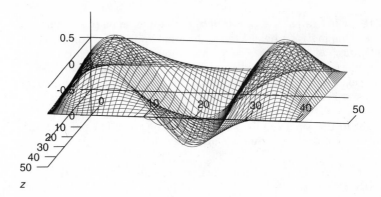

The value of n controls how many peaks and troughs appear in the y direction (the plot conforms to the right-hand rule).

Now let's format this graph. The quickest way to format *any* graph is to *double-click* on it. You'll get the window shown in Figure 3.10.

You can really do no harm by playing around with all these options, and most of them are self-explanatory. If you're not sure about any option, click the Help button on the bottom right for guidance.

Figure 3.10

On the View page, deselect Show Border and under Axes select None; on the Color & Lines page under Shading select Color and under Hide select Mesh; and on the Titles page click on Show Title and type a title (check Show Title). After exiting this window, you should get something like

$z_{i,j} := f(x_i, y_j)$

Vibration of a Rectangular Membrane

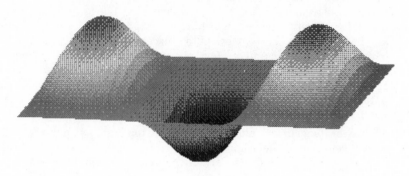

z

Let's finally change the mode to $m = 3$ and $n = 5$, and increase the size of N. The size you're allowed to choose depends on the memory and speed of your computer. If the computation takes too long, press **Esc** and choose a smaller value. You should be able to get something like

$z_{i,j} := f(x_i, y_j)$

Vibration of a Rectangular Membrane

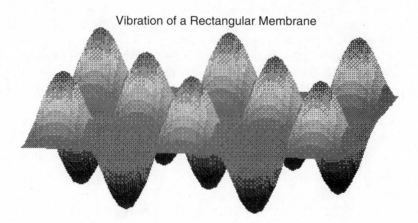

z

These graphs show various modes of vibration of the elastic membrane, meaning shapes the membrane *could* have, with purely sinusoidal motion in time. It turns out that the *fundamental* mode ($m = 1$ and $n = 1$) will vibrate with the lowest frequency, and the higher the mode (e.g., $m = 3$ and $n = 5$), the higher will be the corresponding vibration frequency.

Exercises

3.5 Plot the shape of the rectangular membrane of Example 3.5 when it is vibrating with a *combination* of two modes [mode (2,2) plus 0.5 times mode (3,7)]. To do this, create a function $f(x_i, y_j)$ as in Example 3.5 and another function $g(x_i, y_j)$ identical to it except that m and n are replaced with new constants p and q. Then, above these formulas, define m and n to be 2 and 2 and p and q to be 3 and 7. Finally, the equation for z will be $z_{i,j} = f(x_i, y_j) + 0.5g(x_i, y_j)$. You can then experiment with different combinations of modes by changing the values of $m, n, p,$ and $q,$ and by changing 0.5 to some other number.

3.6 Generate a surface plot that shows the top half of a sphere of radius $r = 1$ ft centered at the origin.

Hint: To do this, define a variable x_i that runs from $-r$ to $+r$ as i runs from 0 to some number N (which you should have previously defined as, for example, being equal to 50), and a variable y_j that runs from $-r$ to $+r$ as j runs from 0 to N. Then you can define and graph the function

$$z_{i,j} = \sqrt{r^2 - x_i^2 - y_j^2}$$. Note that this will actually generate values of z that are complex when $x^2 + y^2 > r^2$. Mathcad will plot just the real parts of these points, which are zero!

3.5

Contour Plots and 3-D Bar Charts

The last two types of plots we'll look at, *contour plots* and *3-D bar charts*, are really variations on the theme of the surface plots.

To immediately see this, let's return to the Example 3.5 worksheet on the vibration of the rectangular membrane. If you don't have this file open, open it and double-click on the graph in that worksheet to get access to the 3D Plot Format window shown in Figure 3.10. You'll see that on the View page you can select Contour Plot or 3D Bar Chart. Select Contour Plot and, while you're at it, on the Color & Lines page, check the Greyscale box and uncheck the Numbering box. After exiting from this window you should have something like

$z_{i,j} := f(x_i, y_j)$

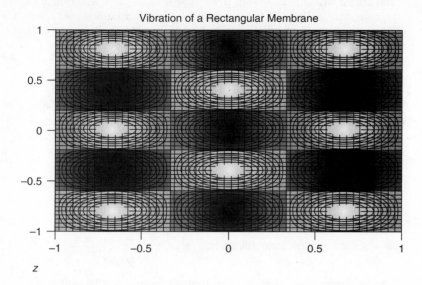

Vibration of a Rectangular Membrane

z

This is the contour plot version of the shape of the $m = 3$ and $n = 5$ mode of vibration of the membrane. You could do a similar thing with the 3-D bar chart option, but using a bar chart for this particular engineering problem wouldn't make much sense: using bars to represent the surface of a membrane would be a little odd.

The basic point, however, is that contour plots and 3-D bar charts, like surface plots, will only plot a matrix of numbers and, again like surface plots, there are quite a few customization options.

Let's do an example of each, just to get some practice in using them.

Example 3.6 Inviscid flow over a cylinder Let's return

to the same kind of inviscid flow physics discussed in Example 3.4 and Figure 3.8, except here we'll assume no cylinder rotation. A classic result is that the equation for the streamlines for uniform flow over a cylinder is

$$\psi(x, y) = y - \frac{y}{x^2 + y^2} \tag{3.11}$$

Here ψ is the *stream function*. This gives the shape of the stream-lines. For example, the *zero* streamline is obtained from setting $\psi = 0$. What curve will this be? Well, if $y = 0$, $\psi = 0$, so the horizontal x axis is the zero streamline. There is another zero streamline: suppose we choose points so that $x^2 + y^2 = 1$. Inspection of Equation (3.11) shows that for these points $\psi = y - y = 0$. Hence the circle of radius 1 is also the zero streamline. You can begin to picture what's happening here, but let's use Mathcad's Contour Plot to do all the work for us.

Start a new worksheet, called "Example 3.6," and, after providing a title and a little explanatory text, define the function $\psi(x,y)$ (one way to create the symbol ψ is to type y then press **Ctrl + G**):

Inviscid Flow over a Cylinder

By (Your Name)

The equation for the streamlines is: $\psi(x, y) := y - \dfrac{y}{x^2 + y^2}$

As for the surface plot, we need to use this function to generate a matrix. First, let's set up the calculation of the x and y values so that we can easily change the number of data points plotted. Try to do the following:

The number of data points in each direction is: $N := 50$

The x values are: $i := 0.. N$ $x_i := -5 + 10 \cdot \dfrac{i}{N}$

The y values are: $j := 0.. N$ $y_j := -5 + 10 \cdot \dfrac{j}{N}$

This will create an x-y region from $x = -5$ to 5 and $y = -5$ to 5 (the radius of the circle is 1). If you're not sure about this, try, for example, evaluating x_0 and x_{50}.

Next, we need to define the matrix of values, just as we did in Section 3.4:

The matrix of values is: $F_{i,j} := \psi(x_i, y_j)$

Finally, we can create the contour plot by doing any one of the following:

1. Press **Ctrl + 5.**
2. Click on the Contour Plot icon on the Graph palette.
3. Use the menu item *Insert . . . Graph . . . Contour Plot.*

After inserting F at the placeholder and exiting, you should have

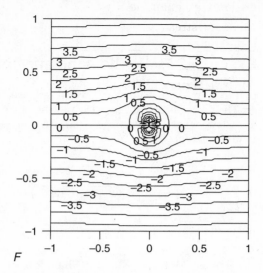

As we predicted, the zero streamlines are the horizontal axis and the circle. Notice also that there are streamline patterns *inside* the cylinder! This is a mathematical artifact, which we can ignore (it's because the flow over a cylinder is actually modeled by placing a *source doublet*, which is a source and a sink, rather than the cylinder, in the flow).

This graph can now be formatted. We don't really want the axes or numbers showing. See if you can modify the graph so it looks like

The flow field looks like

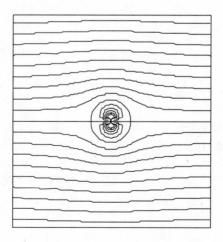

If you wish, you can try different values for N to see what happens.

Finally, we can briefly introduce use of 3-D bar charts, again by doing an example.

Example 3.7   Per item income/cost analysis   Suppose a manufacturer wishes to graphically present the income from, and the cost to manufacture, each of several proposed models of a new dishwasher. The data on the selling price and the labor and material costs are given below, where parentheses indicate a negative amount (a cost to the manufacturer).

	Model 1	Model 2	Model 3	Model 4	Model 5
Price	100	125	140	180	200
Labor	(20)	(25)	(40)	(25)	(50)
Material	(45)	(55)	(60)	(80)	(80)

Let's use Mathcad's 3D Bar Chart feature to do this. As for the other types of 3-D graphs, only data in a matrix format can be plotted.

In a new worksheet (call it "Example 3.7"), we need to set up a matrix (which, you remember, can be created starting with **Ctrl + M**), with the data:

Per Item Income/Cost Analysis

By (Your Name)

$$Amounts := \begin{bmatrix} 100 & 125 & 140 & 180 & 200 \\ -20 & -25 & -40 & -25 & -50 \\ -45 & -55 & -60 & -80 & -80 \end{bmatrix}$$

This Amounts matrix can then be plotted.

To create a 3-D bar chart, do either of the following:

1. Click on the 3D Bar chart icon on the Graph palette.
2. Use the menu item *Insert . . . Graph . . . 3D Bar Chart.*

If you use one of these methods, and add some text, you'll get something like

The data look like:

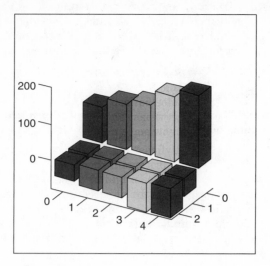

Amounts

Once again we have a graph that, at first blush, isn't very interesting. If you double-click on it, you'll get the 3D Plot Format window, where you can customize the graph to some degree. For instance, try to get something like

The data look like

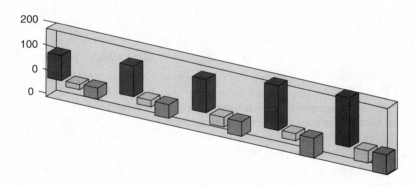

Amounts

Price and Cost Data

As you can see, even if you work at it a bit, a 3-D bar chart still looks a little crude. In fact, in most situations, if you need to present information in such a format, you might prefer to use a spreadsheet (such as Microsoft Excel). All current spreadsheet applications have extensive bar chart formatting features that go well beyond what can be accomplished in Mathcad.

Exercise

3.7 Create a worksheet for plotting a contour plot of the following function ψ:

$$\psi(x, y) = y - \frac{y}{x^2 + y^2} + \frac{k}{20} \ln(x^2 + y^2 + 0.0001) \qquad (3.12)$$

The graph should be plotted from $x = -5$ to 5 and $y = -5$ to 5, and the variable k should be defined to have the value 15. This represents flow around a cylinder with rotation. The 0.0001 factor doesn't really belong in the equation, but it is there just so that we will never accidentally try to compute $\ln(0)$.

3.6

Where to Find More

For complete details on Mathcad's graphing capabilities, consult the *Mathcad User's Guide*. In addition, you can click on the menu item *Help* or the ? icon on the toolbar to get the Help Topics window to look for guidance on creating any of the various kinds of graphs. Finally, Mathcad's *Resource Center* (also accessed via the *Help* menu item or by clicking on the Resource Center icon on the toolbar), shown in Figure 2.17, has lot's of information. Here you can click on Overview or Tutorial for guidance.

In many of the examples in this chapter, we typed in data that was then plotted, but in many (if not most) situations, you'll be importing data from some other application, or from a data file. We didn't do this in this chapter in order not to make the material here too complicated, but you should note that this topic is covered in detail in Chapter 9.

Additional Exercises

Note: In these exercises you should select the plotting range so that the graph looks smooth. This means that you should make sure you plot at least 100 points, and preferably many more (1000 points is not difficult for most computers to be able to compute). Also, you should format each graph so that it looks professional by using, for example, limits on the axes, appropriate line types, titles, and so on. Finally, remember that when you plot a function that has units, it is usually better to plot that function divided by the units in which you want it displayed.

3.8 Define the following functions using literal subscripts (they will appear with errors because a, b and ω have not yet been defined):

$$f_1(t) = a \cos (\omega t)$$

$$f_2(t) = b \sin (\omega t)$$

$$F(t) = f_1(t) + f_2(t)$$

(3.13)

Then, below these, using the priority assignment equals [you recall that one way to do this is to use the tilde (~) key], define a, b and ω to be 1, 2 and 1, respectively. This should remove the error flags on the three functions. The three constants a, b and ω are defined globally so that they will be in a location which will be convenient when you want to change their values. Then plot $f_1(t)$ $f_2(t)$ and $F(t)$ on separate graphs from $t = 0$ to $t = 4\pi$. What do you get for $F(t)$? Is it always true that when you add a sine of any amplitude to a cosine of any amplitude (but with the same frequency) it will result in a sinusoid (a shifted sine)? Test this hypothesis by trying different values of a, b and ω.

Hint: It's a good idea to set limits of 5 and –5 on the vertical axes of these graphs.

3.9 In computer technology we often refer to "Moore's Law" (named after a co-founder of Intel Corporation), which states that the computational power of the average PC sold doubles about once every eighteen months. This means that the power P increases exponentially:

$$P(t) = e^{\lambda t}$$

(3.14)

where it is assumed, as a benchmark, that the power of an average PC now ($t = 0$ yr) is one. The constant λ is obtained from Equation (3.14) by setting $P = 2$ when $t = 1.5$ yr (in other words, the power doubled in 1.5 years):

$$\lambda = \frac{\ln(2)}{1.5 \cdot \mathrm{yr}}$$

(3.15)

Plot a graph of $P(t)$ against time t for $t = 0$ yr to 20 yr. Then copy and paste the graph and edit this copy so that it is a semi-log graph. Should you expect this curve? Why? How much more powerful will a PC be 20 years from now, based on Moore's Law?

Hint: Make sure you define the time range so that you control the step size! If you don't, Mathcad will try to generate data points every *second* over a 20 year span.

3.10 Find the approximate values of all the positive roots of

$$\sqrt{x^4 + 3} = 5x \sin(2x)$$

(3.15)

To do this, define a range of x from 0 to 10. Then, plot on the same graph both $\sqrt{x^4 + 3}$ and $5x \sin(2x)$ against x. The roots of Equation (3.15) will be where the two curves intersect. You can use *Zoom* and *Trace* to estimate what the roots are (and remember that the finer the range is defined, the more accurate the answers will be). We'll see in Chapter 5 that there are much better ways to solve this problem.

3.11 In a brewery, a settling tank is used to let solid microparticles of dead yeast settle out so that the beer clears. The equation for the speed $V(t)$ of descent of the particles is

$$V(t) = kg\left(1 - e^{-\frac{t}{k}}\right) \tag{3.16}$$

where k is a constant given by

$$k = \frac{2\Delta\rho r^2}{9\mu} \tag{3.17}$$

where $r = 1$ mm is the average particle diameter, $\Delta\rho = 500$ kg/m^3 is the difference in density between the particle and beer densities, and $\mu = 0.001$ N-s/m^2 is the viscosity of the beer. Plot the speed (ft/s) for the first five seconds. Use Zoom and Trace as necessary to find approximately how long a particle takes to reach a steady speed. What is the value of this steady speed? If the beer is warmed up so that the viscosity falls to $\mu = 0.0002$ N- s/m^2, how long will a particle now take to reach its steady speed, and what will it be?

Hint: Depending on how you set up the graph and your worksheet's default units, you will have to be careful in reading speed values using Trace.

3.12 When two musical notes are close in frequency we get what are called beats (a phenomenon that musicians take advantage of when they tune an instrument). To see what this is like, add together two sound waves:

$$S(t) = S_1 \sin(2\pi f_1 t) + S_2 \sin(2\pi f_2 t) \tag{3.18}$$

where $S_1 = 1$ Pa and $S_2 = 2$ Pa are the amplitudes of each sound wave, and $f_1 = 500$ Hz and $f_2 = 550$ Hz are the frequencies. Plot this combined sound wave over a period of 0.05 s. You should see a wave that has a high frequency and whose amplitude *also* appears to vary in a sinusoidal manner. This low frequency amplitude variation is the beat phenomenon. Use Zoom and Trace as necessary to estimate the *period* of the high frequency signal, and the period of the amplitude variation (you can obtain these by measuring the time from one peak to another). Can you explain these results in terms of f_1 and f_2? Try changing the values of S_1 and S_2 to see if this has any major effect.

3.13 In advanced mathematics we sometimes encounter Bessel functions. For example, when oscillations of a physical phenomenon occur in a radial direction (in other words, in a cylindrical coordinate system), the amplitude of the oscillation can often be described using Bessel functions. An example of this is the vibration of a drumskin. There are many kinds of Bessel functions, but the most commonly used one is called the Bessel function of the first kind—of order zero—given the symbol $J_0(x)$. It, as well as the other Bessel functions, are built into Mathcad. This Bessel function can also be approximated by

$$J_0 x \approx \sum_{n=0}^{N} \frac{(-1)^n x^{2n}}{2^{2n}(n!)^2} \tag{3.19}$$

where the larger the value of N, the more accurately $J_0(x)$ will be computed. Let's compare values of the Bessel function using Equation (3.19) with Mathcad's built-in values. To do this, first define N to have the value 25. Then plot on the same graph Mathcad's built-in Bessel function $J0(x)$, and the function given by Equation (3.19) (call it $J_0(x)$ to distinguish it from $J0(x)$). Set the range of x to be from zero to ten. The resulting curves should be similar. Are they? What happens if N is changed to 30? These curves give, for example, one possible shape for the vibration of a drumskin, where $x = 0$ is the center of the drumskin, and $x = 10$ is the edge of the drumskin.

3.14 Plot the function given in Equation (3.20) below, with N defined as 1, and t varying from 0 to 3π.

$$f(t) = \frac{4}{\pi} \sum_{n=1}^{N} \frac{1}{2n-1} \sin((2n-1)t) \qquad (3.20)$$

What does the curve look like? Now copy and paste to a location lower down on the worksheet the equation for N, the equation for $f(t)$, and the graph. This is so you can keep your original result for $N = 1$ and change N in the copied version to a new value to see what happens. Change the value of the new N to 10. What do you now get? Do you know what Equation (3.20) represents?

3.15 As an improvement on the procedure described in Exercise 3.14, define a function to be a function of t *and* N:

$$f(t, N) = \frac{4}{\pi} \sum_{n=1}^{N} \frac{1}{2n-1} \sin((2n-1)t) \qquad (3.21)$$

Then you can plot on the *same* graph the function evaluated for 1 term ($N = 1$), 2 terms, 4 terms, and 10 terms. To do this, plot on one graph $f(t,1)$, $f(t,2)$, $f(t,4)$ and $f(t,10)$ against t for the range 0 to 3π. Format the graph so that the upper and lower limits on the vertical axis are 2 and –2, and change the line types to produce a tidy looking graph, and use a legend. Depending on the speed of your computer, add one final curve $f(t,X)$, where X is as large a number as you can conveniently compute (and note that when you do this you will probably have to redefine your t range to be much finer so that your curve is not jagged).

3.16 In control theory we are often interested in the response of the system to an input of a given frequency. A physical example of this might be the vibration of a door panel on a car due to engine vibration. Depending on the speed of the engine, the door panel might not vibrate at all, or it might vibrate with a relatively large amplitude, generating an annoying noise for the driver. It can be shown that an equation that can sometimes be used to describe the amplitude A of the response of a system to an input of frequency ω is

$$A(\omega) = \frac{1}{\sqrt{\left(1-\left(\frac{\omega}{\Omega}\right)^2\right)^2 + c^2\left(\frac{\omega}{\Omega}\right)^2}} \qquad (3.22)$$

Here Ω is the *natural frequency* of the system and c is a coefficient that determines the amount of *damping* (or friction) in the system. Note that if $\omega = 0$ Hz (in other words, if the input was constant rather than being a vibration), Equation (3.22) gives $A = 1$, so that the equation is a *normalized* equation: the value of A at any given frequency is indicative of the *relative* amplitude of vibration of the system. Suppose you have an automobile whose engine will run through a range of speeds (ω values) from 0 to 3000 rpm, and the natural frequency of vibration of a door panel is 20 Hz, with a damping coefficient $c = 0.15$. Plot the amplitude response curve $A(\omega)$ versus ω. Use *Zoom* and *Trace* as necessary to find the maximum amplitude of the response.

3.17 Find the 10th order Taylor series about $x = 0$ of $y(x) = e^{x^2}$ and copy and paste the result. Edit this copy (you will need to delete the $O(x^{10})$ term) and call it $y_{\text{Taylor}}(x)$. Then plot $y(x)$ and $y_{\text{Taylor}}(x)$ on the same graph against x for $x = 0$ to 2. Is the Taylor series a good fit? To get a better sense of this, also define an error function:

$$E(x) = \left| \frac{y_{\text{Taylor}}(x) - y(x)}{y(x)} \right| \qquad (3.23)$$

and plot this (actually, plot $E(x)$ divided by %) on a new graph over the same x range. Use *Zoom* and *Trace* as necessary to find the value of x at which the error exceeds 2.5% [and a good way to display this is to plot on the vertical axis (with $E(x)/\%$) the "function" 2.5]. Finally, repeat this exercise for a Taylor series of order 16. Is this series accurate for a wider range of x values? Why?

3.18 Consider the following table for the predicted U.S. population:

Year	1998	1999	2000	2001	2002	2003	2004	2005	2006	2007
Pop. (x 10^6)	251	253	253	254	257	258	259	261	261	263

Plot this data as a bar chart.

3.19 Mechanical systems sometimes consist of gears rolling inside other gears. For example, in an automobile automatic transmission there is usually a set of gears similar to that shown schematically in Figure 3.11.

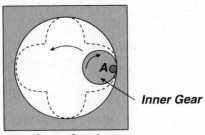

Figure 3.11   **Outer Gearbox**

The small inner gear rolls inside the outer gearbox in a counterclockwise direction, so its own rotation is clockwise. It is sometimes necessary to find the path of a tooth of the inner gear. This is shown in the figure, where the path of the tooth labeled A is shown by the dashed line. This kind of curve is called a *hypocycloid*. It can be shown that the equation for this is

$$r(\theta) = \sqrt{\cos(\theta)^n + \sin(\theta)^n} \qquad (3.24)$$

where r is the radial distance from the gearbox center of gear tooth A when it is at angle θ ($\theta = 0°$ when A is at the position shown in Figure 3.11). Note that in Equation (3.24) it is the cosine and sine that are squared and not their argument θ! The constant n is a factor that depends on the ratio of the two gear radii. Plot, on a polar graph, the path of A for $\theta = 0°$ to $360°$, with $n = 6$. Format the graph as necessary. Try different values of n (equivalent to making the inner gear smaller or larger) to see what you get.

3.20 You wish to evaluate two different audio speakers for use in a large room. The speakers project sound according to the following equations:

$$S_1(\theta) = a_1 + b_1 \cos^2\left(\frac{\theta}{2}\right)$$

$$ \qquad (3.25)$$

$$S_2(\theta) = a_2 + b_2 \cos^4\left(\frac{\theta}{2}\right)$$

In Equation (3.25) $S_1(\theta)$ and $S_2(\theta)$ are the amplitude of the sound (in Pa) emitted in direction θ, where $\theta = 0°$ corresponds to directly forward from the speaker, and $\theta = 180°$ corresponds to directly backwards from the speaker. The constants are $a_1 = 1$ Pa, $b_1 = 3$ Pa, $a_2 = 1.5$ Pa, and $b_2 = 2.5$ Pa. Plot both of these functions on the same polar graph for $\theta = 0°$ to $360°$. By inspection of the graph which, if any of the two speakers is best if you sit directly in front of the speaker? Which is best if you sit to the side of the speaker? Which is best if you sit directly behind the speaker? Finally, if people are sitting around the speaker in all directions, which speaker will be heard best by most people?

3.21 In Exercise 3.13 we saw that Bessel functions can be used to model the instantaneous shape of a drumskin. More generally, we can say that these functions usually arise when many kinds of wave phenomena occur in a radial direction. For example, the surface of water waves created when a stone is thrown into a pond can sometimes be described by the Bessel function of the first kind of order zero. To see this, generate a surface plot of Mathcad's built-in Bessel function *J0*. You recall that surface plots need a matrix of values in order to plot a function, so here several steps will be needed. First, you need to define a function which will generate the radial distance r across the surface of the pond from the point at which the stone entered. Using Cartesian coordinates x and y (which you can imagine to be distances from the stone impact point measured along the surface of the pond), r will be given by

$$r(x, y) = \sqrt{x^2 + y^2} \qquad (3.26)$$

The instantaneous height of the wave created by the stone impact will be given by $h(x,y)$:

$$h(x, y) = J0(r(x,y)) \tag{3.27}$$

The way these equations work is that if you provide a value for x, say one, and for y, say five, Equation (3.26) will compute the radial distance for this point, and then Equation (3.27) will compute the corresponding height of the wave. The next step is to set up computations of x and y values. Define a variable $L = 25$, and a counter $N = 20$, and then generate ranges i and j to run from 0 to N. Use these to set up variables x_i and y_j to run from $-L/2$ to $+L/2$. (If you're thoroughly lost by now you can refer back to Example 3.5 where we followed a similar procedure.) Finally, you can plot the following as a surface plot

$$H_{i,j} = h(x_i, y_j) \tag{3.28}$$

After some formatting of the graph, you should end up with a surface that looks like a surface wave on the pond. Depending on your computer's memory and power, try increasing the values of N and L to see how the wave shape changes.

3.22 Generate a contour plot showing the lines of constant potential due to a pair of oppositely charged source lines of equal strength separated by a distance $a = 1.5$.

Hint: it can be shown that the equation for this is:

$$\phi(x, y) = \ln\left(\left(x - \frac{a}{2}\right)^2 + y^2\right) - \ln\left(\left(x + \frac{a}{2}\right)^2 + y^2\right) \tag{3.29}$$

You need to set up x and y values. To do this, follow the procedure described in Exercise 3.21, except here set variable $L = 5$ and make the counter $N = 30$. Then you can graph the function

$$\Phi_{i,j} = \phi(x_i, y_j) \tag{3.30}$$

The graph—after formatting—should show a symmetric series of circles. Depending on your computer's memory and power, try increasing the values of N and L to see what happens (but be aware that some values of these might cause an accidental computation of $\ln(0)$, leading to an error).

Symbolic and Numeric Calculus

When performing an engineering analysis of a problem, engineers sometimes need to evaluate either an *integral* or a *differential*. An example of the former might be finding the total amount of charge in an electrical capacitor by expressing the current flow as a function of time and integrating. An example of the latter might be, given the instantaneous temperature distribution in a grain of rice that's being dried in a packaged-food factory, finding the temperature gradient (the rate of change of temperature in the rice material) so that the thermal stresses due to temperature variations can be computed.

In this chapter we'll review Mathcad's capabilities in integrating and differentiating. As we do so we'll mention some of the traditional methods for doing this calculus, so that, after completion of this chapter, you'll have a context for understanding how useful and powerful Mathcad's calculus methods are.

4.1

The first step in performing any kind of calculus in Mathcad is creating the integral and differential signs. There are several ways to do this, which we can summarize.

Creating Integrals and Differentials in Mathcad

The Integral Symbol

You can use either of the following methods to generate an integral sign:

1. Press **Shift + 7** (or in other words **&**).

2. On the Calculus palette (accessed from the Math palette and shown in Figure 4.1), click on the Definite Integral icon, in the second row.

When we do *symbolic* integration, it will sometimes be convenient to generate an *indefinite* integral. For this symbol use either of the following:

Figure 4.1

1. Press **Ctrl + I**.
2. On the Calculus palette, click on the Indefinite Integral icon, in the third row.

On a blank practice worksheet, let's try these techniques. Try to generate one integral symbol of each kind, using any of the methods you wish:

$$\int_{\blacksquare}^{\blacksquare} \blacksquare \, d\blacksquare \qquad\qquad \int \blacksquare \, d\blacksquare$$

The placeholders are obviously for you to enter the constants or expressions you're interested in. Once you're in an integral, to jump from placeholder to placeholder either use the mouse or the **Tab** key.

Let's jump the gun a little by using them to evaluate some simple integrals, both numerically and symbolically. See if you can reproduce the following, where the right arrow is the *live* symbolic evaluation symbol and can be created by typing **Ctrl + .**, as you learned in Chapter 2:

$$\int_0^3 x^3 - 2 \cdot x \, dx = 11.25 \qquad \int_a^b x^3 - 2 \cdot x \, dx \rightarrow \frac{1}{4} \cdot b^4 - b^2 - \frac{1}{4} \cdot a^4 + a^2$$

$$f(x) := 3 \cdot \ln(x + 1)$$

$$\int_1^2 f(x) \, dx = 2.729 \qquad \int f(x) \, dx \rightarrow 3 \cdot \ln(x + 1) \cdot (x + 1) - 3 \cdot x - 3$$

The first two integrals evaluate $x^3 - 2x$ numerically and symbolically. Note that these reveal a slight flaw in Mathcad: it doesn't always *automatically* insert parentheses when you want it to (the two integrands were typed in without using parentheses), even though the results are correct. It's a good idea to always type in the parentheses when you think they are needed for appearances' sake. The last two integrals evaluate the previously defined function $f(x)$.

Mathcad had no problem performing these integrals for us, and once again we see that to perform a mathematics operation, all you need to be able to do is type in the expression!

We'll do some engineering examples of both kinds of integrals, but next let's see how you create differentials.

The Differentiation Symbol

To create a differentiation symbol in Mathcad you can use either of the following:

1. Press **Shift + /** (or in other words **?**).
2. On the Calculus palette, click on the Derivative icon.

To create a higher-order derivative, use either of the following:

1. Press **Ctrl + Shift + I**.
2. On the Calculus palette, click on the Nth Derivative icon.

In the same practice worksheet, try using one method for each of these derivatives, and you'll get

$$\frac{d}{d\blacksquare}\blacksquare \qquad\qquad \frac{d^{\blacksquare}}{d^{\blacksquare}}\blacksquare$$

You might be tempted to create a derivative by simply typing, say, the expression dy and dividing by dx. It won't work! Mathcad would assume you're simply dividing a variable called dy by a variable called dx.

Again let's jump the gun a bit by quickly doing a few examples of both numeric and symbolic differentiation. See if you can do the following (using **Ctrl + .** as necessary):

$$y(x) := 5 \cdot \sin(2 \cdot x)$$

$$\frac{d}{dx}y(x) \rightarrow 10 \cdot \cos(2 \cdot x) \qquad\qquad \frac{d^2}{dx^2}y(x) \rightarrow -20 \cdot \sin(2 \cdot x)$$

$$\frac{d}{dx}\ln(x^2 + x) \rightarrow \frac{(2 \cdot x + 1)}{(x^2 + x)} \qquad\qquad \frac{d^2}{dx^2}\ln(x^2 + x) \rightarrow \frac{2}{(x^2 + x)} - \frac{(2 \cdot x + 1)^2}{(x^2 + x)^2}$$

$$x := 5$$

$$\frac{d}{dx}y(x) = -8.391 \qquad\qquad \frac{d^2}{dx^2}y(x) = 10.88$$

$$\frac{d}{dx}\ln(x^2 + x) = 0.367 \qquad\qquad \frac{d^2}{dx^2}\ln(x^2 + x) = -0.068$$

The first four differentials demonstrate differentiating a function $y(x)$ and $ln(x^2 + x)$ symbolically and numerically, and the last four demonstrate the same differentials evaluated numerically. You might want to check these results by hand (which will confirm for you how convenient using Mathcad is). It turns out that symbolic differentiations don't need a value for x to proceed (which makes sense), but numeric ones do (which also makes sense), which is why x was set to 5 before the last four differentiations. It's interesting to note what happens with the symbolic differentiations if this x definition is moved to a location above them:

$$x := 5$$

$$\frac{d}{dx}\ln(x^2 + x) \rightarrow \frac{11}{30} \qquad\qquad \frac{d^2}{dx^2}\ln(x^2 + x) \rightarrow \frac{-61}{900}$$

The symbolic differentials still work, with numerical values inserted (without simplification) for us!

We've finished with this practice worksheet, so you can close it without saving.

Now that we've seen one or two ways to integrate and differentiate in Mathcad, and before learning about other techniques in Mathcad for doing calculus, let's review methods that have traditionally been used for such tasks.

4.2

Symbolic Integration

Symbolic integration simply means performing the integration *analytically*, using all the rules of calculus with which you're familiar. Let's do an engineering example to illustrate this.

Example 4.1 Charging of a capacitor—symbolic integration

Consider the resistor-capacitor (RC) circuit shown in Figure 4.2. Suppose you wish to find the charge accumulated in the capacitor in the RC circuit after the switch has been closed a time t_{meas}.

It can be shown that the current in the circuit at any instant is given by

$$I(t) = I_0 e^{-\frac{t}{\tau}} \tag{4.1}$$

where I_0 is the initial current and $\tau = RC_{cap}$ is the capacitive time constant of the circuit. R and C_{cap} are the circuit resistance and capacitance. We've used C_{cap} rather than C so that we don't mess up the electrical units of the worksheet (Mathcad uses C for coulombs). On the other hand, using R for resistance is okay, because we won't be using temperature units, or be working with anything including temperature as a unit (you recall that R is used by Mathcad for degrees Rankine).

The charge Q accumulated over a time t_{meas} is given by the integral of the current. Obtained symbolically, this is

$$Q = \int_0^{t_{meas}} I(t)dt = I_0\tau\left(1 - e^{\frac{-t_{meas}}{\tau}}\right) \tag{4.2}$$

This is an example of doing a symbolic integration by hand.

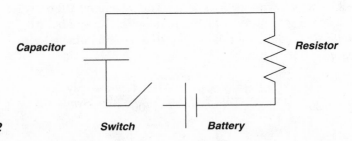

Figure 4.2   *Capacitor*   *Resistor*   *Switch*   *Battery*

Note that it turns out that $I_0 = \dfrac{V_0}{R}$, where V_0 is the battery voltage, so that Equation (4.2) can be simplified by replacing $I_0\tau$ with $C_{cap}V_0$ if desired.

This example is an illustration of the importance of symbolic integration: it gives you a final answer that can give insight to the physics. For example, Equation (4.2) shows that the capacitor has an exponential charging curve, and also, if you let t_{meas} go to infinity, you get the result that the total resulting charge in the capacitor will be $C_{cap}V_0$, so that the final charge in this circuit is determined only by the capacitor and battery and is not affected at all by the resistor value. If we had done a numerical integral, all we would have would be a number (e.g., 0.049 C), which would not allow you to draw any such general conclusions.

Let's have Mathcad do this symbolic integral for us (we'll pretend it was beyond our capabilities).

Symbolic Integration Using Mathcad

First, start a new worksheet in Mathcad and type in text and the equation for the current:

<u>Charging of a Capacitor</u>

By (Your Name)

The equation for the current is: $\quad I(t) := I_0 \cdot e^{\frac{-t}{\tau}}$

Save the worksheet as "Example 4.1" in your desired location.

You'll notice that I_0 and τ are both colored in your worksheet, indicating that they haven't been defined. The reason we haven't defined these constants is because if we had done so, then when we eventually ask Mathcad to symbolically integrate, it would substitute their values, giving us just a number. We want the integral to remain in complete symbolic form.

Let's proceed to ask Mathcad to perform the symbolic integration. Type the following (remembering to use a literal subscript):

The charge is given by: $\quad Q := \displaystyle\int_0^{t_{meas}} I(t)\,dt$

Once again, you'll see that Mathcad doesn't know something, this time t_{meas} and $I(t)$. Let's proceed anyway!

To perform symbolic integration, you can use any of the following methods:

1. Select the entire integral on the right of the equation only, so that it is enclosed in the editing lines, and click on menu item *Symbolics . . . Evaluate . . . Symbolically*.

2. Select the entire integral on the right of the equation only and press **Shift + F9**.

3. Place the cursor *anywhere* in the integral and click on the Symbolic Evaluation icon on the Symbolic Keyword palette (accessible via the Math palette).

4. Place the cursor *anywhere* in the integral and press **Ctrl + ..**

As we learned in Chapter 2, you can have Mathcad perform symbolic math that is either *not live* or *live*. The first two methods listed above are *not* live, and in fact produce identical results; the last two *are* live and have the same effect as one another. Most of the time you'll probably end up using the first method for nonlive and the last for live integrals.

Let's try the first and last methods. Using the first method, you should get something like

The charge is given by: $\quad Q := \int_0^{t_{meas}} I(t)\,dt$

$$Q := -\tau \cdot \exp\left(\frac{-t_{meas}}{\tau}\right) \cdot I_0 + \tau \cdot I_0$$

If you didn't get quite this (for example, if you just have the right side appearing), then you probably selected more or less than just the right side. In that case delete what you got and try again.

We obtained, as we should, the same result as we obtained by hand [Equation (4.2)], except not quite as compactly. All you need to do is edit it as you wish, collect terms, and perhaps replace the *exp* representation with *e* (using ^ for the exponentiation). (It's worthwhile asking Mathcad to try and tidy up an expression it produces symbolically, as discussed in Chapter 2.)

We can make two points here: first, you can change the way Mathcad presents the results of integrals by clicking on menu item *Symbolics . . . Evaluation Style . . .*; second, don't forget that the result is not live, so that if you edit the integral, the result will *not* update. This last point might have you wondering why you would even use this method if a live version is available. The answer is that this method, unlike the live method, gives you output in a format that is immediately understandable, even to a non-Mathcad reader of your worksheet. This will be especially true if you change the evaluation style so that Show Comment is activated.

Let's now try the *live* method (the last one listed above). Delete the result you just obtained and use the method. You should get

The charge is given by: $Q := \int_0^{t_{meas}} I(t)\,dt \rightarrow -\tau \cdot \exp\left(\frac{-t_{meas}}{\tau}\right) \cdot I_0 + \tau \cdot I_0$

The symbolic method produces a symbolic result arrow (a symbol that *might* be puzzling to a non-Mathcad reader) and the correct result. To see that it's live, try changing, for example, the upper limit on the integral to infinity, so we can obtain the final charge in the capacitor. You can invoke this by pressing the Infinity icon on the Calculus palette (an odd place to put it!) or by pressing **Ctrl + Z**.

You'll get, after exiting the equation,

The charge is given by: $Q := \int_0^\infty I(t)\,dt \to \lim_{t \to \infty^-} -\tau \cdot \exp\left(\frac{-t}{\tau}\right) \cdot I_0 + \tau \cdot I_0$

The result *did* update, even if it's a bit disappointing! What happened here was that Mathcad was clever enough to figure out that the value of this integration could be either *finite* or *infinite* (or in other words *singular*) depending on the sign of τ (if τ was negative, you'd end up with a positive infinite power for *e*). Hence, it left the integral in this lim format. Of course, in general, editing an existing integral will not lead to such a problem: the result will simply be updated unambiguously.

Mathcad can even do a better job with this tricky integral! Let's edit out this previous result to start over with our integral.

All we need to do is tell Mathcad that τ is positive; in other words, we need to use a *condition* on the symbolic evaluation. There are several ways to do this. First, click anywhere in the integral. Then do one of the following (and note that moving the mouse over the Symbolic Keyword palette icons reveals explanatory text bubbles):

1. In the Symbolic Keyword palette click on the relevant condition. In this case, you click on the Assume icon and, in the placeholder that appears, type $\tau > 0$.

2. In the Symbolic Keyword palette click on the Symbolic Keyword Evaluation icon. In the placeholder that appears, type *assume*, $\tau > 0$.

3. Press **Ctrl + Shift + .**. In the placeholder that appears, type *assume*, $\tau > 0$.

Try any of these and you should get the result:

The charge is given by: $Q := \int_0^\infty I(t)\,dt$ assume, $\tau > 0 \to \tau \cdot I_0$

Mathcad can do not only symbolic integrals, but it can even handle the special value of infinity!

A final point on symbolic integration: instead of typing in the integral, you can type in just the *integrand*. Try this somewhere below the current work by typing in (without any kind of equals sign) the expression $x^3 \ln(x)$. Then, to integrate it, you click on any place in the integrand where the integration variable appears (in this case, either one of the two appearances of x) and select menu item *Symbolics . . . Variable . . . Integrate.* You should end up with

$x^3 \cdot \ln(x)$

$$\frac{1}{4} \cdot x^4 \cdot \ln(x) - \frac{1}{16} \cdot x^4$$

This method, while convenient for getting quick "scratchpad" type results, doesn't present results in a format that's immediately useful (unless you've carefully customized your evaluation style using the menu item *Symbolics . . . Evaluation Style*). For example, you would have to edit the result to assign some new function to it:

$x^3 \cdot \ln(x)$

$$f(x) := \frac{1}{4} \cdot x^4 \cdot \ln(x) - \frac{1}{16} \cdot x^4$$

One thing you should *not* do is type in a complete integral *and* use this method, because Mathcad will integrate twice!

You can now delete these two lines and close the worksheet (we've finished with it).

By the way, other mathematics computer applications such as Maple (of which, in fact, Mathcad's symbolic math is a subset) and Mathematica can also do symbolic integration, although perhaps not in such a convenient way. Other applications such as spreadsheets (e.g., Microsoft Excel) cannot.

Exercises

4.1 A periodic function can be represented using a Fourier series. For example, the sawtooth wave shown in Figure 4.3 can be represented by an infinite series of sine waves:

$$f(t) = \sum_{n=1}^{\infty} b_n \sin(nt) \tag{4.3}$$

where the constants b_n are obtained from

$$b_n = \frac{2}{\pi} \int_0^{\pi} t \sin(nt) \, dt \tag{4.4}$$

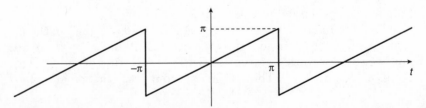

Figure 4.3

Symbolically integrate Equation (4.4) to find a formula for the coefficients. Then define the function given by Equation (4.3), except sum to N instead of infinity, where N is previously defined as having the value 10. Plot this function from $t = -3\pi$ to 3π. Then try different values of N to see what happens.

4.2 The area of a circle of radius r can be obtained from:

$$A = 2\int_{-r}^{r} \sqrt{r^2 - x^2}\,dx \tag{4.5}$$

Evaluate Equation (4.5) symbolically and compare to what you *know* the area of a circle is!

4.3 The velocity of a water jet is given by

$$v(t) = Ve^{-\frac{t}{\tau}} \tag{4.6}$$

where V is the initial velocity and τ is a time constant (assumed positive). If the area of the jet is A, find the total volume of water flow. The volume is given by

$$Q = A\int_{0}^{\infty} v(t)\,dt \tag{4.7}$$

We'll do another engineering example of symbolically integrating later, but let's now move on to *numerically* integrating.

Why don't we *always* do calculus symbolically? The answer is that we usually *try* to but cannot always succeed! When engineers encounter an integration, they attempt to do it analytically (as opposed to obtaining just a number, which is all you get with numeric integration). The reason for this, as we have discussed, is that if a final integrated equation can be obtained, insight into the engineering problem can often be gained. We saw in Example 4.1 that Equation (4.2) yielded the insight that the total resulting charge in the capacitor is $C_{cap}V_0$.

Whether or not you as an engineer succeed with a particular integral obviously depends on how good you are at calculus (e.g., how many tricks, like substitution techniques, you know) or how good a reference you have available [e.g., the *Handbook of Mathematical Functions*, by Abromowitz & Stegun (National Bureau of Standards, 1972) is one of several standard works], or, as we have just seen, whether or not you have Mathcad available to you.

However, there are many cases, especially in engineering science, when your engineering analysis leads you to an integral that is not only difficult but *impossible* to solve analytically (it is not *tractable*).

A second reason symbolic integration cannot always be used is that engineers often have to deal with *data* rather than *functions*. For example, you might have data on the pressure distribution on the surface of a wing. To find the resultant lift force of the wing, you would have to sum, or integrate, the pressure distribution over the wing surface area. In the absence of a theoretical equation for this distribution, a numerical method is needed for this integration.

Actually, we'll see that in many engineering applications, Mathcad's numerical integration is convenient enough and accurate enough that, unless you have a specific reason for *wanting* the symbolic form, you'll end up doing integrals numerically most of the time.

From the engineer's point of view, whether a particular integral is not tractable in *practice*, for him or her, or in *principle* is not really the point: the engineer very often just needs to get the job done. If an analytic integration can be obtained, so much the better, but a numerical result will often suffice.

When a differentiation or integration is not tractable, for whatever reason, a numerical approach is needed.

Before formally presenting Mathcad's method for numerically integrating, let's review some traditional approaches.

Numerical Techniques for Integration

Numeric calculus (whether it's a differentiation or integration) involves evaluating the answer to the problem using some kind of numerical procedure, which will always be approximate (albeit to a high degree of accuracy).

As we've mentioned, if possible, integrals should be done symbolically, or in other words analytically. If this is not possible (because the integral is too difficult or impossible, or you have experimental data), then numerical integration must be used.

How is numerical integration done *without* using Mathcad? The most common methods for integrating are

1. The trapezoid rule.
2. Simpson's rule.
3. Romberg integration.
4. Gauss quadrature.

Each of these methods can be implemented by writing code (e.g., in BASIC, Fortran, or Pascal) or using a spreadsheet (e.g., Microsoft Excel).

The first method is based on the idea that the area under a curve (in other words, the curve's integral) can be approximately represented by cutting it up into a large number of trapezoids. For example, Figure 4.4 shows a function *f(x)* cut up into seven

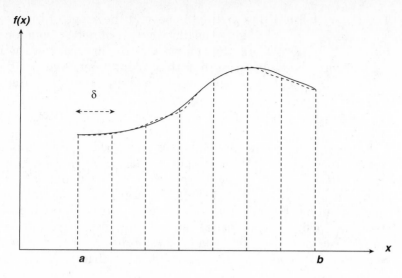

Figure 4.4

trapezoidal segments of width δ. Generally speaking (until round-off errors accumulate), the smaller the δ and, therefore, the more segments created, the more accurately the areas of the segments approximate the area under the curve.

In practice, a formula for this summation is developed:

$$I = \int_a^b f(x)dx \approx \frac{\delta}{2}\left[f(x_a) + 2\sum_{i=1}^{n-1} f(x_i) + f(x_b) \right] \tag{4.8}$$

where n is the number of nodes (and x_a is node 0, so, for example, in Figure 4.4 $n = 7$).

Instead of using straight lines to connect points, parabolas or higher-order polynomials could be used. If this is done, we obtain formulas that are similar in form to, but different in detail from, Equation (4.8). These formulas (which we won't present here) are called *Simpson's rule* methods. Simpson's rule, though a little more complicated, is usually more accurate than the trapezoid method with the same number of nodes. Both the trapezoid and Simpson's methods can be applied to integrating either functions or experimental data points, and to data for which the spacing δ between the points is not constant.

The *Romberg* method is essentially an improvement on the above methods in which trapezoid rule integrations of finer and finer node spacing are performed, and an accurate integral is eventually extrapolated. This method obviously is more complicated to implement but is fast and accurate. (It's interesting to note that Mathcad uses this method internally when you ask it to perform a numerical integration.)

The last method we'll mention in this survey is the *Gauss quadrature* method. This can be applied to integrating functions.

The theory behind this method is beyond the scope of this text, but it amounts to changing the distribution of nodes from a uniform distribution to one that maximizes the accuracy of the integral evaluation. It turns out that using, say, five of these Gauss points will typically provide a more accurate integral than 10 or even 15 points using Simpson's rule. This method is even more accurate than those described earlier but is trickier to implement.

For details on these methods, see any good engineering numerical methods book [for example, *Numerical Methods for Engineers, with Personal Computer Applications,* by Chapra & Canale (New York: McGraw-Hill, 1988]. The trapezoid and Simpson's rule techniques (and even the Gauss quadrature method) can be performed using a spreadsheet such as Microsoft Excel. For detailed descriptions of the spreadsheet approach, see, for example, *Spreadsheet Tools for Engineers,* by Gottfried (New York: McGraw-Hill, 1996).

Numeric Integration Using Mathcad

Let's review how we do numeric integration using Mathcad by doing another example. What we've already seen is that, unlike the rather cumbersome methods just described, in Mathcad pretty much all you need to be able to do to evaluate an integral is to be able to type it in!

Obviously, as we're doing something numerically, we'll be working with numbers, so let's continue with Example 4.1 by adding numerical data.

Example 4.1 (Continued) Charging of a capacitor (numeric integration) Suppose the resistance and capacitance are $R = 1000$ ohm and $C_{cap} = 0.012$ farad. If the initial current is $I_0 = 5$ amp, find the charge after 0.02 s and express this as a percentage of the total charge acquired by the capacitor.

Let's create a new worksheet (call the worksheet "Example 4.1 (Numeric)" and save it in your desired location). First, enter the data provided. It should look something like

<u>Charging of a Capacitor</u>

By (Your Name)

Enter the given data: $I_0 := 5 \cdot amp$ $C_{cap} := 12 \cdot \mu F$ $R := 1000 \cdot ohm$

Then we can compute the capacitive time constant:

$$\tau := R \cdot C_{cap} \qquad \tau = 0.012 \cdot s$$

The time duration is: $t_{meas} := 0.02 \cdot s$

We can make a couple of points here about units. First, as we mentioned earlier, we used C_{cap} rather than C for the capacitor in this entire example because Mathcad wants to use C as the symbol for coulombs (a measure of charge). If we'd used the symbol C, the units of the worksheet would have been seriously compromised. Second, instead of F (farads) for the capacitance unit, it was convenient to use μF (microfarads), which can be found through any of the insert units methods (such as by clicking on the Insert Unit icon on the toolbar).

Next, we can enter the equation for the current $I(t)$ and the integral equation for the charge Q. The integral symbol is created in any of the ways described in Section 4.1. We can then immediately evaluate Q:

The equation for the current is: $I(t) := I_0 \cdot e^{\frac{-t}{\tau}}$

The charge is given by: $Q := \int_{0 \cdot s}^{t_{meas}} I(t) \ dt \qquad Q = 0.049 \cdot C$

(Note that we inserted the unit C for coulombs in the evaluation of Q.) We've just done a numeric integral with Mathcad, and it even included units! As you can see, and as we predicted, doing such an integral amounts to just being able to type it in.

Finally, we can compute the percentage of the final charge acquired after time t_{meas}.

The total charge is: $Q_{max} := \tau \cdot I_0 \qquad Q_{max} = 0.06 \cdot C$

The charge after time t_{meas} as a percentage of the final charge is:

$$\frac{Q}{Q_{max}} = 81 \cdot \%$$

Note that we inserted the "unit" percentage (%) and also double-clicked on the answer to get the Number Format window, where we changed the Displayed Precision to 0.

Of course, your worksheet is *live,* so you can now perform all kinds of tests here, such as changing the resistance value or changing the time at which the charge is computed.

We can even plot the charge as a function of time. To do this, copy the equation for Q in an empty region below your previous work, edit it, and add other material (including redefining the value of t_{meas}) as shown below:

The new final time value is: $t_{meas} := 0.05 \cdot s$

The range of times is: $\quad t := 0 \cdot s, \dfrac{t_{meas}}{20} .. t_{meas}$

The charge, expressed as a function of time, is: $Q(t) := \displaystyle\int_{0 \cdot s}^{t} I(t)dt$

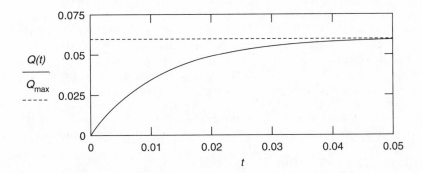

Note that Mathcad does a lot of work in this worksheet: it numerically evaluates 21 integrals (one for each time step).

If you're not sure how to create, or format, a graph, you should refer back to Chapter 3. Here the graph was modified by, for example, imposing a limit of 0.075 on the vertical axis and setting up the axis with 3 grids.

In summary, performing numerical integrations in Mathcad basically amounts to simply being able to type in the integral. In this introduction, we cannot explore all the subtleties of this feature, but you should be aware, for example, that you can request that the integral be evaluated more accurately by changing, via the menu item *Math . . . Options,* the built-in variable TOL to a smaller value.

Exercises

4.4 A ball is attached to a string of length l = 1 ft, as shown in Figure 4.5. At time t = 0 s it is released from rest and starts swinging down due to the effect of gravity. Find the time the ball takes to execute one oscillation. The formula for this is

$$T = \int_{0}^{\pi} \frac{l}{\sqrt{2gl\sin(\theta)}} d\theta \qquad\qquad (4.9)$$

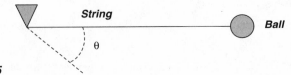

Figure 4.5

Hint: The acceleration of gravity g is built in, so you don't need to define it.

4.5 A jogging track is elliptical in shape. The maximum dimension is $a = 225$ ft and the minimum dimension is $b = 74$ ft. Find the length of the track in feet. The equation for the perimeter of an ellipse is

$$P = \int_0^{2\pi} a\sqrt{1 - \left(\frac{a^2 - b^2}{a^2}\right)\sin^2(\phi)}\, d\phi \qquad (4.10)$$

Hint: When you're typing the equation, type $sin(\phi)$ and *then* square it. You might want to test your answer by setting both a and b equal to one, to generate a unit circle.

Occasionally engineers need to evaluate the differential of a function. For example, if the position of an object is known as a function of time, taking its derivative will produce the object's velocity; if the instantaneous charge on a capacitor is known, its time derivative will give the current. In most instances, in contrast to integration, differentiation is something that can always be accomplished *analytically*, following all the rules of differentiation (such as how to differentiate functions embedded in other functions). However, sometimes we still need to evaluate differentials *numerically* because, for example, the function would produce a very long expression if it was symbolically differentiated or because all we're interested in is numerical answers.

We've already seen in Section 4.1 how to create the differentiation symbols in Mathcad. Let's see now how to do both symbolic and numeric differentiation.

Symbolic and Numeric Differentiation Using Mathcad

To illustrate these methods, let's do another engineering example.

Example 4.2   Thermal stress   In a rice-drying operation in a packaged-food factory, a large percentage of the rice kernels are cracking. This is believed to be due to the fact that thermal stresses are being generated in the kernels. If the outer layers of a kernel are significantly colder than the inner layers, stresses build up as the outer layers contract around the inner. An engineer comes up with a theory that this effect can be summarized by the following equation:

$$\sigma = DE\alpha\frac{dT}{dx} \qquad (4.11)$$

where $D = 1$ mm is the average diameter of the rice kernels, $E = 10^4$ psi is Young's modulus of the rice, and $\alpha = 0.001$ R^{-1} is the coefficient of thermal expansion. Here T is the instantaneous temperature at point x, measured *inward* from the rice kernel surface. The engineer conducts some experiments, which reveal that the instantaneous temperature variation in the rice kernels is approximated by

$$T(x) = 2\Delta T \, \tanh\left(3\frac{x}{D}\right) \tag{4.12}$$

where $\Delta T = 10$ R is the temperature difference between the air and the rice center.

We wish to find the instantaneous stress distribution in the rice kernels. To do this we need to use Equation (4.12) in Equation (4.11). Try to do this by hand. Let's also have Mathcad do it symbolically and numerically. We'll also review other, traditional methods for numerical differentiation.

Start a new worksheet and make it look something like the following (using any of the techniques described in Section 4.1 to create the differential):

Thermal Stresses

By (Your Name)

The temperature distribution is: $T(x) := 2 \cdot \Delta T \cdot \tanh\left(3 \cdot \frac{x}{D}\right)$

The stress distribution is: $\sigma(x) := D \cdot E \cdot \alpha \frac{d}{dx} T(x)$

Once again we've intentionally not given values yet for D, E, α, and ΔT so that we can evaluate the differential symbolically. Note that we've created σ as a function of position, for convenience when we plot the results.

To perform the symbolic integration, you can use any of the following methods:

1. Select *only* the entire differential on the right of the equation, so that it is enclosed in the editing lines, and click on menu item *Symbolics . . . Evaluate . . . Symbolically.*

2. Select *only* the entire differential on the right of the equation and press **Shift + F9.**

3. Place the cursor anywhere in the equation and click on the Symbolic Evaluation icon on the Symbolic Keyword palette (accessible via the Math palette).

4. Place the cursor anywhere in the equation and press **Ctrl + .**.

As we learned in Chapter 2, you can have Mathcad perform symbolic math that is either not live or live. The first two methods listed above are not live, and in fact produce identical results; the last two are live and have the same effect as one another. You'll probably end up using the first method for nonlive and the last for live differentiations most of the time.

For this example let's use the first method. Before doing so, let's change the format of the output by using the menu item *Symbolics . . .*

Evaluation Style and in the window that appears selecting Show Comments. Mathcad will then give you the following:

The stress distribution is: $\quad \sigma(x) := D \cdot E \cdot \alpha \dfrac{d}{dx} T(x)$

yields

$$\sigma(x) := D \cdot E \cdot \alpha \left[6 \cdot \Delta T \cdot \frac{\left(1 - \tanh\left(3 \cdot \dfrac{x}{D}\right)^2\right)}{D} \right]$$

Mathcad inserted some explanatory text for us and then performed a fairly tricky symbolic differentiation! If you examine the result, you'll see that it can be simplified. Select the entire right of the equation and use the menu item *Symbolics . . . Simplify* to get Mathcad to do it for us:

$$\sigma(x) := D \cdot E \cdot \alpha \left[6 \cdot \Delta T \cdot \frac{\left(1 - \tanh\left(3 \cdot \dfrac{x}{D}\right)^2\right)}{D} \right]$$

simplifies to

$$\sigma(x) := 6 \cdot E \cdot \alpha \cdot \frac{\Delta T}{\cosh\left(3 \cdot \dfrac{x}{D}\right)^2}$$

Is it correct? You might want to try and do it by hand as a check.

To be able to use this result we need some data. Move toward the top of the worksheet and press **Enter** a few times to create some space for entering the data:

Thermal Stresses

By (Your Name)

The data are: $\quad D := 1 \cdot mm \quad \Delta T := 10\,R \quad E := 1 \cdot 10^4 \cdot psi \quad \alpha := 0.001 \cdot \dfrac{1}{R}$

The equations below this data will now be computable. We have two formulas, both of which compute σ. Let's have Mathcad plot both the original equation and the final formula. To begin with, copy and paste both equations to a region below the previous work and edit them so the first equation defines a function σ_{num} and the second a function σ_{sym}. The first formula will then be computing a function including a numerically evaluated differentiation (you recall from Section 4.1 that to create a numerical differential, all you need to do is type the differential). The second will compute a function based on having previously performed a symbolic differentiation. As a check, let's ask Mathcad to evaluate each σ at the surface ($x = 0$ mm). If you do all this (including inserting the psi units in the answers), you'll get

$$\sigma_{num}(x) := D \cdot E \cdot \alpha \frac{d}{dx} T(x) \qquad\qquad \sigma_{num}(0 \cdot mm) = 600 \cdot psi$$

$$\sigma_{sym}(x) := 6 \cdot E \cdot \alpha \cdot \frac{\Delta T}{\cosh\left(3 \cdot \frac{x}{D}\right)^2} \qquad \sigma_{sym}(0 \cdot mm) = 600 \cdot psi$$

We can now plot both functions. When you do so, divide each function by psi to impose this as the units for the vertical axis, and also change the trace of σ_{num} to be points. Try to obtain something like

$$x := 0 \cdot mm, \frac{D}{20} .. D$$

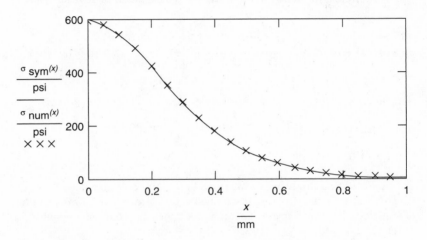

What we've done here is plot σ and evaluated it symbolically (σ_{sym}) and numerically (σ_{num}). This involved Mathcad performing 21 numerical differentiations.

You can see that in this example the numeric (approximate) and symbolic (exact) curves are in very good agreement. You can now save and close this worksheet.

Let's do one more example illustrating the use of symbolic and numeric differentiation.

Example 4.3 Force on a mass
Suppose we know the motion $x(t)$ of a mass M:

$$x(t) = Xe^{-\frac{t}{\tau}}\sin\left(\frac{t}{\tau}\right) \tag{4.13}$$

where τ is a time constant and X is a constant with units of feet. We wish to find the force $F(t)$ required to generate it. This force comes from Newton's Second Law:

$$F(t) = M\frac{d^2 x}{dt^2} \qquad\qquad (4.14)$$

Let's have Mathcad compute this symbolically. First, create in a new worksheet the following (you can create the second derivative in any of the ways we've previously discussed, such as **Ctrl + Shift + /**):

Force on a Mass

By (Your Name)

$$x(t) := X \cdot e^{\frac{-t}{\tau}} \cdot \sin\left(\frac{t}{\tau}\right)$$

$$F(t) := M \cdot \frac{d^2}{dt^2} x(t)$$

You'll notice once again that some terms are colored to flag you that they have not been defined. First let's perform the symbolic differentiation. This time let's use the accelerator keys **Shift + F9**, after first selecting the right-hand side only of the equation:

$$F(t) := M \cdot \frac{d^2}{dt^2} x(t)$$

yields

$$F(t) := -2 \cdot M \cdot \frac{X}{\tau^2} \cdot \exp\left(\frac{-t}{\tau}\right) \cdot \cos\left(\frac{t}{\tau}\right)$$

(If you wish, you can manually edit the exponential term so that it has the same form as the original equation for x.) We can now get some numbers by proceeding to the top of the worksheet and adding some data (note that if we'd used *live* symbolics, when we provided the data, the symbolic evaluation would then have changed because M and τ would have been replaced with values). Let's evaluate both the numeric and symbolic integrals at $t = 0$ s if the mass $M = 10$ lb, $X = 1$ ft, and $\tau = 0.05$ s:

Force on a Mass

By (Your Name)

$$M := 10 \cdot lb \qquad X := 1 \cdot ft \qquad \tau := 0.05 \cdot s$$

$$x(t) := X \cdot e^{\frac{-t}{\tau}} \cdot \sin\left(\frac{t}{\tau}\right)$$

$$F(t) := M \cdot \frac{d^2}{dt^2} x(t) \qquad\qquad F(0 \cdot s) = -248.6 \cdot lbf$$

yields

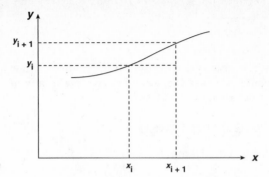

Figure 4.6

$$F(t) := -2 \cdot M \cdot \frac{X}{\tau^2} \cdot \exp\left(\frac{-t}{\tau}\right) \cdot \cos\left(\frac{t}{\tau}\right) \qquad F(0 \cdot s) = -248.6 \cdot \text{lbf}$$

Note that the lbf units were inserted in the answers and that the numbers were formatted. The numerical and symbolic answers agree once again. Of course, if you had a particularly complicated differential, the numerical and symbolic results would slightly disagree.

In summary, we can see that evaluating numerical and symbolic differentiations is extremely easy to do in Mathcad. In contrast, let's just mention the traditional methods for numerical differentiation. The idea behind these is that the differential is replaced with a *difference* equation. For example, the forward difference of order h is

$$\frac{dy}{dx} \approx \frac{\Delta y}{\Delta x} = \frac{y_{i+1} - y_i}{h} \tag{4.15}$$

In this equation y_i and y_{i+1} are the values of the function at the points x_i (where the differential is being evaluated) and $x_{i+1} = x_i + h$, as shown in Figure 4.6. Generally speaking, the smaller term h is, the more accurate will be the approximation. There are lots of other such formulas, many of them designed to produce more accuracy than Equation (4.15).

Just for the fun of it, let's use Mathcad to test how good Equation (4.15) is by doing an example. On a blank worksheet, let's find the slope of

$$y(x) = \sin(\sqrt{2\pi x}) \tag{4.16}$$

at the point $x = 10$.

See if you can do the following:

$$x := 10 \quad y(x) := \sin(\sqrt{2 \cdot \pi \cdot x})$$

$$\frac{d}{dx} y(x)$$

floating point evaluation yields

$-.028777528$

$$h := 0.001 \quad \frac{y(x + h) - y(x)}{h} = -0.028855$$

Note that to create the floating point evaluation, you use the menu item *Symbolics . . . Evaluate . . . Floating Point*, where you can choose (in this example) a 10-point evaluation. As you can see, the difference equation does work, but not very accurately.

Additional Exercises

4.6 Symbolically integrate the following expressions to verify some basic rules of integration:

$$x^n, \; \frac{1}{x}, \; \sin(\omega x) \qquad\qquad\qquad (4.17)$$

4.7 Symbolically differentiate the following expressions to verify some basic rules of differentiation:

$$x^n, \; \ln(x), \; \sin(\omega x) \qquad\qquad\qquad (4.18)$$

4.8 Verify the rule for differentiating a product by symbolically finding the first and second derivatives of the product of two functions $f_1(x)$ and $f_2(x)$. ($f_1(x)$ and $f_2(x)$ do not need to be defined before you do this.)

4.9 Consider the following two functions:

$$f_1(x) = e^{-x}$$

$$\qquad\qquad\qquad\qquad\qquad\qquad (4.19)$$

$$f_2(x) = \frac{x + 1}{x - 1}$$

Evaluate the second derivative of the product and simplify. Then integrate twice and simplify to see if you get back the original product.

4.10 Define constants m and n each to be equal to one (without a decimal point). Then symbolically evaluate the following integrals:

$$\int_{-\pi}^{\pi} \cos(mx)\sin(nx)dx$$

$$\int_{-\pi}^{\pi} \sin(mx)\sin(nx)dx \qquad (4.20)$$

$$\int_{-\pi}^{\pi} \cos(mx)\cos(nx)dx$$

See what pattern emerges as you change the values of m and n to other integers. You should see one pattern when m and n have the same value and another when they have different values. This is because sines and cosines make up what is called an *orthogonal* set. You recall that the dot product of two *vectors* is zero when they are orthogonal (or perpendicular), and not zero when they are not orthogonal. The equations above are one way of verifying that sines and cosines have a similar orthogonality property. This property is an essential part of how the *Fourier* series works.

4.11 Convert $\sin(x^2)$ to a Taylor series about $x = 0$ of order 20 (see Chapter 3 if you've forgotten how to do this). Then symbolically differentiate the series (you may have to edit out the $O(x^{20})$ term). Next, take the symbolic derivative of $\sin(x^2)$, and find the Taylor series about $x = 0$ of order 20 of the result. You will now have two Taylor series: one the derivative of the Taylor series of $\sin(x^2)$; the other the Taylor series of the derivative of $\sin(x^2)$. Do they look the same? Why?

4.12 Find the first and second derivatives of:

$$y(x) = \tan^{-1}(\sin(x)) \qquad (4.21)$$

4.13 Symbolically evaluate the following:

$$\int_{0}^{\infty} e^{-x}dx \qquad (4.22)$$

Note that Mathcad *can* handle *infinity* (and one way to generate this is to use **Ctrl + z**) when it's used in symbolic evaluations. Try numerically evaluating the integral (by typing the integral with an evaluation equals sign). You will not get a result. Can you think why this is?

4.14 The probability density distribution for the *normal* (or *Gauss*) distribution or population is

$$f(x) = \frac{1}{\sigma\sqrt{2\pi}}e^{-\frac{1}{2}\left(\frac{x-\mu}{\sigma}\right)^2} \qquad (4.23)$$

where μ is the *mean* and σ is the *standard deviation*. The mean is the average of the population, and the standard deviation measures how much spread there is in the population: a distribution which is very spread out will have a large value for σ. To find the percentage of a population x that is between the limits a and b, $f(x)$ must be integrated:

$$F(x) = \int_a^b f(x)dx \qquad (4.24)$$

Find the percentage of a normally distributed population between the $\pm\,\sigma$ points. To do this, use Equation (4.24) with a replaced with $\mu - \sigma$, and b replaced with $\mu + \sigma$. Perform the integration symbolically. At the end of the symbolic result enter an evaluation sign and insert the "unit" percent symbol. Repeat this for the $\pm\,2\sigma$ and $\pm\,3\sigma$ points. The results you obtain are well known in statistical analysis and manufacturing (look them up in any book on statistics). As we'll see in Chapter 8, Equations (4.23) and (4.24) are built into Mathcad as *pnorm* and *dnorm*.

4.15 We saw in Chapter 3 that Mathcad can generate the Taylor series of a function $f(x)$ about some point x_0. It turns out that the coefficients a_n in the Taylor series

$$f_{\text{Taylor}}(x) = \sum_{n=0}^{\infty} a_n(x - x_0)^n \qquad (4.25)$$

are given by:

$$a_n = \frac{1}{n!}\frac{d^n}{dx^n}f(x)\bigg|_{x=x_0} \qquad (4.26)$$

In practice a finite number of terms (a *truncated* series) is computed. Using Equations (4.25) and (4.26), find the Taylor series of order 5 about point $x_0 = \pi$ of $f(x) = \sin(x)$. Plot on the same graph $f_{\text{Taylor}}(x)$ and $f(x)$ against x for $x = 0$ to 3π. Set limits on the vertical axis of -2 and 2. Does the Taylor series model the sine wave? Change x_0 to 1.5π and explain what happens. Change x_0 to 0.5π and explain what happens.

Hint: To do this, first set $x_0 = \pi$ and the function $f(x) = \sin(x)$, and define a range $n = 0$ to 5. Then you can compute the a_n from Equation (4.26), *except* that x_0 *must* be used instead of x in *both* places in the equation and the limit symbol is not used. Note that you can find the high-order derivative on the *Calculus Palette*. Finally, in Equation (4.25) replace the infinite upper limit with 5. Be careful to use the right kind of subscripts: *literal* for x_0 and *vector or array* for a_n.

4.16 Find the volume of the cone of height H and radius R shown in Figure 4.7. To do this, find the volume of an infinitesimal disk of thickness dh at arbitrary height h, and sum (in other words integrate) all such disks from $h = 0$ to $h = H$. Derive the following equation and then symbolically evaluate:

$$V = \int_0^H \pi R^2\left(1 - \frac{h}{H}\right)^2 dh \qquad (4.27)$$

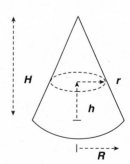

Figure 4.7

You can compare the result you obtain to that given in the *Reference Tables* of the *Resource Center*.

4.17 Derive the formula for the volume of a sphere of radius R by integrating a set of infinitesimal disks in a similar way to Exercise 4.16. You will be integrating using a variable x whose limits will be $-R$ to R, and you will have to deduce the formula for the radius of a disk at arbitrary distance x measured from the sphere center. You can compare the result you obtain to that given in the *Reference Tables* of the *Resource Center*.

4.18 Find the surface area of a sphere of radius R. To do this, use the idea that the surface area of an annular ring, as shown in Figure 4.8, is $2\pi r d\theta$ and that the sphere surface area will be the result of summing (in other words integrating) all these rings from $\theta = -\frac{\pi}{2}$ to $\frac{\pi}{2}$. Derive the following equation and then symbolically evaluate it:

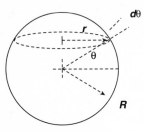

Figure 4.8

$$V = \int_{-\frac{\pi}{2}}^{\frac{\pi}{2}} 2\pi R \cos(\theta) d\theta \tag{4.28}$$

You can compare the result you obtain to that given in the *Reference Tables* of the *Resource Center*.

4.19 The temperature distribution in a rod of length $l = 1$ in is given by

$$T(x) = T_0\left(\sin\left(\frac{2\pi x}{l}\right) + \sin\left(\frac{4\pi x}{l}\right)\right) \tag{4.29}$$

where $T_0 = 500$ R. Find the heat flux distribution $Q(x)$ in the rod. This is given by:

$$Q(x) = -k\frac{dT}{dx} \tag{4.30}$$

where $k = 2$ BTU-ft/R is a conductivity coefficient. Plot the heat flux (divided by BTU) as a function of position x for $x = 0$ in to 1 in.

Hint: This problem should be solved *numerically*. Note that Equation (4.30) must have $T(x)$ rather than T when entered into Mathcad.

4.20 You need to plot the position $x(t)$ and velocity $v(t)$ of the tip of a robot arm as it performs a particular operation. Usually this data is not directly available (it's not convenient to measure distances). Instead, data is generated by an *accelerometer* which, as the name implies, measures the instantaneous acceleration. The instantaneous acceleration data conforms to the following equation:

$$a(t) = \alpha \cos^2(\lambda t) - \beta t \tag{4.31}$$

where $\alpha = 0.75$ m/sec^2, $\beta = 0.25$ m/sec^3, and $\lambda = 1$ sec^{-1}. Plot $a(t)$ (divided by g so the graph will display the number of "g"s for the first 4 seconds of the motion. Then obtain the velocity $v(t)$ and position $x(t)$ by successively numerically integrating

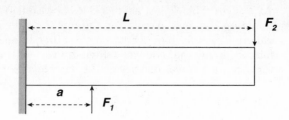

Figure 4.9

$$v(t) = \int_{0 \text{ sec}}^{t} a(t)dt$$

$$x(t) = \int_{0 \text{ sec}}^{t} v(t)dt$$

(4.32)

Plot a second graph showing velocity $v(t)$ (divided by ft/sec) versus time t and a third graph showing position $x(t)$ (divided by ft) versus time t. Use the *Trace* function to estimate the maximum positive velocity (ft/sec) and the maximum distance moved (ft) by the robot's arm.

Hint: Remember to type in the entire cosine and *then* square it. Also, because Mathcad will in essence be computing a double integral for each data point, you should first try computing the time range every second (which will produce very crude graphs), and then, depending on your computer's power, gradually refine the time range to get a set of smooth graphs.

4.21 A cantilever beam of length $L = 5$ ft is built-in at the left end and has two loads $F_1 = -400$ lbf (negative because it is upwards) and $F_2 = 100$ lbf acting on it, as shown in Figure 4.9. The distance $a = 2$ ft, and the beam moment of inertia is $I = 0.125$ in^4, and Young's modulus is $E = 30 \times 10^6$ psi. It can be shown that the *bending moment* $M(x)$ at any point x along the beam is given by

$$M(x) = -F_1a - F_2L + (F_1 + F_2)x - F_1(x-a)\Phi(x-a)$$ (4.33)

In Equation (4.33) $\Phi(x-a)$ is the *Heaviside step function* (built into Mathcad), which is zero for $x < a$ and equal to one otherwise. It turns out that if the moment is integrated twice, the deflection $y(x)$ is obtained:

$$y(x) = \frac{1}{EI} \int_{0 \text{ ft}}^{x} \int_{0 \text{ ft}}^{x} M(x)dx \, dx$$ (4.34)

Plot $y(x)$ (divided by in) against x by numerically evaluating Equation (4.34). What is the end deflection $y(L)$ in inches and in mm? Try different values for F_1 and F_2 (even 0 lbf) and a to see what happens.

4.22 A cubic block of wood has sides $L = 1.5$ ft. You and your friend need to obtain its mass. Your friend assumes its density is constant, with a value of $\rho_0 = 50$ lb/ft^3. You, on the other hand (being much better informed) know that the wood's density varies from this value at the center to a much lower density on the outside, according to:

$$\rho(x, y, z) = \rho_0\left(1 - \frac{r(x, y, z)^2}{L^2}\right) \tag{4.35}$$

where r is the radial distance from the center and x, y and z are Cartesian coordinates measured from the center of the block (you will need to derive the formula for $r(x,y,z)$). The mass of the block is therefore obtained by numerically integrating this density over the block volume:

$$M = \int\limits_{-\frac{L}{2}}^{\frac{L}{2}} \int\limits_{-\frac{L}{2}}^{\frac{L}{2}} \int\limits_{-\frac{L}{2}}^{\frac{L}{2}} \rho(x, y, z)dx\ dy\ dz \tag{4.36}$$

Find the mass of the block in kg and lb as computed by your friend and by you.

4.23 In the kinetic theory of gases, one of the interesting concepts is the *Maxwell Boltzmann* distribution given by:

$$f(v) = 4\pi v^2\left(\frac{mass}{2\pi k_b T}\right)^{\frac{3}{2}} e^{-\left(\frac{mass\ v^2}{2k_b T}\right)} \tag{4.37}$$

This function gives the probability that an individual molecule of a gas at temperature T (K) will have a velocity v. The *mass* is the molecule mass and k_b is Boltzmann's constant. Use Equation (4.37) to find the percentage of molecules of Helium at 25°C (298 K) that will have velocities larger than 1000 m/sec and the percentage with speeds greater than 1000 mph. Plot $f(v)$ for $v = 0$ m/sec to 2000 m/sec. If you increase the temperature by 200 degrees, what is the effect on the curve?

Hint: The percentage of molecules with speeds less than or equal to any speed V is given by

$$P(V) = \int\limits_{0}^{V} f(v)dv \tag{4.38}$$

so that the percentage *above* speed V will be $1 - P(V)$. Also, the mass of a molecule is given by

$$mass = \frac{nM}{N_A} \tag{4.39}$$

where n is the number of atoms in a molecule of the gas (for Helium this will be two), M is the atomic mass of Helium, and N_A is Avogadro's number. These last two terms, as well as Boltzmann's constant, can be obtained from Mathcad's *Resource Center Reference Tables* (except that you should insert the units gm/mole to the definition of M).

How to Solve Equations

Most problems in engineering involve mathematically describing the phenomenon being studied, using one or more fundamental principles of engineering science. In many cases this description leads to one equation to solve for one unknown. The equation can be *linear* or *nonlinear, algebraic, trigonometric,* and so on. It can include *differentials* or *integrals,* and it can be *implicit* or *explicit* in the unknown.

In addition, because the equation represents something in the physical world, the units of all the quantities involved must be carefully allowed for. In a real-world situation, the engineer might gather data from several sources, so some quantities may be given in SI units and others in US units. This mixture of units only adds to the difficulty of solving a problem.

The goal in such analyses is to find an *explicit* expression for the unknown in terms of the given data (in other words, to get the equation in the form $x = \ldots$, where x is the unknown, so that x is isolated), and many times this can be done. Even if such an explicit form *can* be found, Mathcad is still useful because, as we saw in Chapter 2, it's very helpful in handling all the units for you. This chapter, however, will address those situations where the unknown can only be expressed in *implicit* form.

The engineering analysis sometimes results in not *one* equation for *one* unknown, but in *several* equations for *several* unknowns, and they are often *coupled*. This means that all or most of the unknowns appear in all of the equations, so that it's impossible to rearrange the equations to obtain one equation solely for each unknown. The set of equations could be linear or nonlinear. These equations must be simultaneously solved for all the unknowns.

In this chapter we will use Mathcad to solve implicit equations and sets of equations. Let's first look at a detailed example to illustrate these ideas.

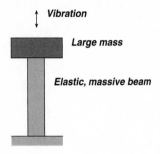

Vibration

Large mass

Elastic, massive beam

Figure 5.1

Example 5.1   Free vibration—continuous medium

Figure 5.1 shows a large mass attached to an elastic beam. The system will vibrate if it is disturbed. Actually, vibration theory shows that because mass is evenly distributed in the beam (a "continuous medium"), even this simple system has an infinite number of what are called *modes of vibration,* and hence an infinite number of natural frequencies. Each mode involves different parts of the beam moving in phase or out of phase with other parts. The *fundamental mode* occurs when all parts of the beam and the mass are moving up and down in phase.

Finding a formula for the natural frequencies involves advanced vibrations theory, leading to what is called an *eigenvalue* problem for the frequencies. This analysis eventually leads to an equation for the possible natural frequencies ω:

$$\omega l \sqrt{\frac{\rho}{E}} \, \tan\!\left(\omega l \sqrt{\frac{\rho}{E}}\right) = \frac{m_b}{M} \tag{5.1}$$

where m_b and M are the masses of the beam and the mass, E and ρ are the Young's Modulus and density of the beam, and l is the beam length. This is an *implicit, nonlinear* equation for the unknown natural frequency ω, because it is impossible to rearrange it in the explicit form ω = . . . , and because the unknown is not represented in a *linear* form. It would be nice if this equation could be written in *explicit* form, because then the problem would be solved.

It is sometimes difficult to tell if a given equation *can* be written explicitly (and we will see shortly that Mathcad's symbolic features are a great help in trying to do this), but it's always a good idea to try so that an exact solution can be obtained. In this example, it turns out, it is impossible to explicitly solve for ω. In other cases it may be possible but too difficult or time consuming to find an explicit solution.

Suppose everything in Equation (5.1) is known except ω. For example, we might have the following data:

Beam density: ρ = 1,500 kg/m^3
Beam area: A = 15 ft^2
Beam length: l = 20 ft
Young's Modulus: E = 5 × 10^5 psi
Large mass: M = 10,000 lb

Even this simple problem is a bit of a mess to solve. First, the mass of the beam $m_b = \rho A l$ must be computed from this data. This in itself is a tedious process because the density is given in SI units and the beam dimensions in US units.

We will postpone solving this example using Mathcad until later. As an exercise (in how tedious such calculations can be!), try using a calculator to insert the above data in Equation (5.1), to obtain

$$\omega A \tan (\omega A) = B \tag{5.2}$$

where A and B are constants (A will have units of seconds and B will be dimensionless).

How do we solve Equation (5.1) or (5.2) for ω? One crude approach would be to try a guess for ω. You could put this value in the left-hand side and see if the result equals the right-hand side. If it does, the guess was correct. In all likelihood it will not be, so a second guess could be made to see if the two sides are any closer in value. By looking at what happens as you repeatedly guess an ω value, you could hopefully eventually focus in on the value that balances the equation. Try this with an initial guess of ω = 300 rad/sec.

This *iterative* process is obviously time consuming to do by hand but, with enough thought, could be programmed. For example, we could rearrange the equation to isolate one of the ω's. Extracting ω out of the tangent

$$\omega = \frac{B}{A}\, \sec(\omega A) \tag{5.3}$$

You could then guess a value of ω on the right and thus obtain a new value on the left. This value would then be substituted into the right, and the procedure repeated until the value of ω no longer changed. This iterative process is cumbersome to execute and doesn't always work (in this example, in fact, it doesn't work because ω diverges wildly).

This is an example of trying to *solve a single equation*. We will find that Mathcad is an excellent tool for such problems, without needing to use an iteration method or any other circuitous process.

Solving a Single Equation

In many engineering problems, we often end up with a single equation for a single unknown in implicit form. First of all, it's a good idea to try and obtain an explicit equation for the unknown, because then the problem is solved except for plugging in numerical values and units. Whether or not you succeed depends on your skill at mathematical manipulations, and, of course, whether or not the equation *can* be made explicit. Mathcad can help you with this.

Symbolically Solving an Equation

As you become more experienced in math, you will develop the ability to tell by inspection whether or not an equation can be made explicit for the unknown. For example, you might already have enough experience to know that Equation (5.2) cannot be solved explicitly for ω

Let's ask Mathcad to try to do this for us anyway! As we'll see, there are several ways to get Mathcad to *symbolically* solve an equation, but here let's just try one method, using the *solve* symbolic keyword.

Before using this method, you first type in the equation to be solved using the Boolean equals (obtained using the **Ctrl + =** combination or by using the appropriate icon on the Evaluation or Boolean palette icon set). After doing this, there are four ways to implement the method:

1. Use the menu item *Symbolics . . . Variable . . . Solve*. Before using this method you must have selected only the variable you wish to solve for (if it appears several times, just choose any appearance).

2. Use the Solve icon on the Symbolic Keyword palette (accessed from the Math palette). First, click *anywhere* in the equation. Then, after clicking on the icon, a placeholder will appear, where you type in the variable you wish to solve for.

3. Use the Symbolic Keyword Evaluation icon on the Symbolic Keyword palette. This is used in the same way as the Solve icon, except you type in at the placeholder *solve,x* (where *x* is the unknown you're solving for).

4. Use the accelerator keys **Ctrl + Shift + .**. This is used in the same way as the previous method.

The last three alternatives, unlike the first, are *live,* so if you change the equation, the symbolic result updates.

In a blank practice worksheet, set up Equation (5.2) :

The equation to be solved is: $\omega \cdot l \cdot \sqrt{\dfrac{\rho}{E}} \cdot \tan\left(\omega \cdot l \cdot \sqrt{\dfrac{\rho}{E}}\right) = \dfrac{m_b}{M}$

Using the Solve icon (the second method), with ω as the unknown, see if you can get

The equation to be solved is: $\omega \cdot l \cdot \sqrt{\dfrac{\rho}{E}} \cdot \tan\left(\omega \cdot l \cdot \sqrt{\dfrac{\rho}{E}}\right) = \dfrac{m_b}{M}$ solve, $\omega \rightarrow$

As we should have expected, Mathcad couldn't find an explicit solution to this equation!

Nevertheless, this method is always one you can try for symbolically solving an equation. Just so you don't get the idea that this solving method doesn't work at all, let's try solving another equation.

Find θ in $a\,\sin(\theta) - b\,\cos(\theta) = 1$. Repeat the above procedure with this expression. You should obtain

Symbolic solution yields:

$$a \cdot \sin(\theta) - b \cdot \cos(\theta) = 1 \text{ solve, } \theta \rightarrow \begin{bmatrix} 2 \cdot \operatorname{atan}\left[\dfrac{1}{(2 \cdot (b-1))} \cdot \left(-2 \cdot a + 2 \cdot \sqrt{a^2 + b^2 - 1}\right)\right] \\ 2 \cdot \operatorname{atan}\left[\dfrac{1}{(2 \cdot (b-1))} \cdot \left(-2 \cdot a - 2 \cdot \sqrt{a^2 + b^2 - 1}\right)\right] \end{bmatrix}$$

Mathcad generated two symbolic solutions to this equation!

What you could do next is copy each solution to a new location and simplify it using the *Symbolics* menu item. For example, try to get something like

$$\theta_{solution} := 2 \cdot \text{atan}\left[\frac{1}{(2 \cdot (b-1))} \cdot \left(-2 \cdot a + 2 \cdot \sqrt{a^2 + b^2 - 1}\right)\right]$$

simplifies to

$$\theta_{solution} := -2 \cdot \text{atan}\left[\frac{\left(a - \sqrt{a^2 + b^2 - 1}\right)}{(b-1)}\right]$$

The symbolic solve method described above can also be used to find the *roots* of an expression (that is, the values that make the value of the expression zero). To do this, you simply type the expression *without* an equal sign and use any one of the three techniques for generating the *solve* expression. Try finding the standard expression for the roots of a quadratic using Mathcad. You should get

The roots of the quadratic are:

$$a \cdot x^2 + b \cdot x + c \text{ solve}, x \rightarrow \begin{bmatrix} \frac{1}{(2 \cdot a)} \cdot \left(-b + \sqrt{b^2 - 4 \cdot a \cdot c}\right) \\ \frac{1}{(2 \cdot a)} \cdot \left(-b - \sqrt{b^2 - 4 \cdot a \cdot c}\right) \end{bmatrix}$$

As you can see, Mathcad can be quite useful in performing symbolic math manipulations for you. In many cases, however, there *is* no symbolic solution possible, so the nonsymbolic (numerical) techniques, which are the main thrust of this chapter, must be used. You can close this practice worksheet without saving, because we've finished with it.

We'll see later that there is another method for symbolically solving an equation (the *Given . . . Find* method), but let's see now how to solve an equation *without* using Mathcad.

Traditional Methods for Solving a Single Equation

There are a number of traditional methods for solving single equations. These methods usually involve writing code (in, for example, BASIC, Fortran, or Pascal). The most well-known methods are

1. The Newton-Raphson method.
2. The Secant method.
3. The Bisection method.

A detailed discussion of these methods can be found in any good engineering numerical methods book [for example, *Numerical*

Methods for Engineers, with Personal Computer Applications, by Chapra & Canale (New York: McGraw-Hill, 1988)]. Here we'll provide only a brief description of them, because as we'll see, Mathcad has built-in methods for solving such problems.

The *Newton-Raphson method* involves rearranging the equation into the form $f(x) = 0$, so that the solution x (the unknown) will be the *root* of the equation. A guess is made for x. A tangent to $f(x)$ at this point is then constructed, and a new value of x is taken where the tangent hits the axis. The process is repeated until a solution of the desired accuracy is obtained. This process is illustrated in Figure 5.2.

In practice, this and the other methods listed are not done graphically, but a program is written in effect to do the same thing, by computing values of the function and its first derivative (to mathematically construct the tangent).

The *secant method* uses a similar geometric approach, but instead of shooting along the tangent toward a new estimate for the root, it starts with *two* guesses, say x_0 and x_1. A straight line is constructed to pass through the function values $f(x_0)$ and $f(x_1)$, and a next value for x is obtained where *this* line hits the axis. This x becomes a new x_0 (the old x_0 becomes x_1 and the old x_1 is dropped) and the procedure is repeated as often as necessary to obtain a solution. This method is a bit messier than the Newton-Raphson method but has the advantage that you don't need to obtain the derivative of what might be a complicated function $f(x)$.

The *bisection method* works on the idea that as x passes through the root, the sign of the function changes. For example, in Figure 5.2 the function changes from a negative value to a positive value as you move from left to right along the axis. In this method you need to select two values of x between which you believe there is one (and only one) root. This region of x is then bisected. Logically, *one* of these semiregions contains the root. This semiregion is the one in which the sign of $f(x)$ changes. Then this semiregion is bisected, and the procedure repeated until a value for the root is found to sufficient accuracy.

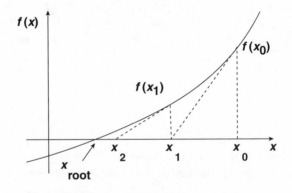

Figure 5.2

All three methods have benefits and disadvantages. All require programming in some language to actually implement.

There are also techniques available using a spreadsheet such as Microsoft Excel. Some of these techniques use the above methods. Others are special to spreadsheets, such as the Goal Seek and Solver features of Excel. For detailed descriptions of the spreadsheet approach, see, for example, *Spreadsheet Tools for Engineers,* by Gottfried (New York: McGraw-Hill, 1996).

Mathcad, as we'll soon see, provides several very attractive alternatives to all of the above techniques and methods. Mathcad not only will automatically take care of units (which none of these do!), but it has two built-in features, named *root* and *Given . . . Find,* for quickly solving a single equation. The equation can be *linear* or *nonlinear* in the single unknown. If the equation is a polynomial, Mathcad has an additional feature that can be used, called *polyroots.*

Before formally describing these features, let's solve Example 5.1 using Mathcad to illustrate both the Root and the Given . . . Find methods. Don't worry about *how* this is done yet. We'll summarize the required steps later.

Example 5.1 (Continued) Free vibration (using the root method) Let's start a new blank worksheet and enter the given data and compute the mass m_b. Also, rearrange Equation (5.1) so that you obtain a function of ω, $f(\omega)$, whose root will be the solution to the original equation.

You should have something like

Frequency of Free Vibration (using Root)

By (Your Name)

The data are:

$$\rho := 1500 \cdot \frac{kg}{m^3} \quad A := 15 \cdot ft^2 \quad l := 20 \cdot ft \quad E := 5 \cdot 10^5 \cdot psi \quad M := 10000 \cdot lb$$

The beam mass is then: $\quad m_b := \rho \cdot A \cdot l \quad m_b = 28093 \cdot lb$

The engineering equation, rearranged to be a function $f(\omega)$, is:

$$f(\omega) := \omega \cdot l \cdot \sqrt{\frac{\rho}{E}} \cdot \tan\left(\omega \cdot l \cdot \sqrt{\frac{\rho}{E}}\right) - \frac{m_b}{M}$$

Our goal is to find the root of this function. It's always a good idea (though not strictly necessary when using Mathcad to find a root) to plot the function so you have some idea of its behavior. Let's use Mathcad to plot the function over a range (chosen randomly or based on knowledge of the physical problem). In your worksheet do the following:

The function can now be plotted over a range of ω values:

$$\omega := 0 \cdot \frac{rad}{sec}, 5 \cdot \frac{rad}{sec} \; .. \; 100 \cdot \frac{rad}{sec}$$

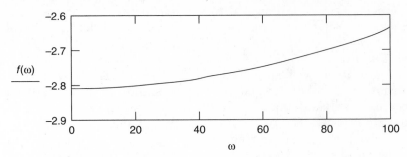

As you can see, the function does *not* have a root in the range selected. The range should be changed (perhaps by changing the ending value to a large value), and changed again, until you focus in on a range containing the root of interest. You should eventually end up with something like

A suitable range is: $\omega := 250 \cdot \frac{rad}{sec}, 251 \cdot \frac{rad}{sec} \; .. \; 300 \cdot \frac{rad}{sec}$

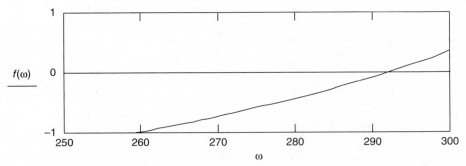

Clearly, the function has a root somewhere around 290 rad/sec.

We did all this because, as we'll see when we summarize Mathcad's methods for solving an equation, we always need to give an initial guess for the answer. It turns out that the initial guess can be pretty much any value, and Mathcad will usually find the answer you're looking for. However, if a problem has many possible solutions or roots (as is the case for Example 5.1), a random initial guess may provide you with a solution you're not interested in. Hence, it's always good practice to graph the function.

A final point about this graphing procedure: if you want just a rough idea of the root of the function, at this point you could use Mathcad's Zoom and Trace methods to focus in on the area of the root and read off a value for ω. We won't do this here, but you can review these techniques in Chapter 3.

Now let's get Mathcad to give us an accurate estimate of the solution or root. Simply type the following (we'll explain the details of what's happening later) below your previous work:

A graphical estimate for the root is: $\omega := 290 \cdot \dfrac{rad}{sec}$

Mathcad's root method can then be used: $root(f(\omega), \omega) = 292.14 \cdot \dfrac{rad}{sec}$

Mathcad took our estimate and used it to come up with a much more accurate solution (for which we inserted the rad/sec units). Note that, if you had wanted to *use* this solution later on, instead of this you could have done the following:

A graphical estimate for the root is: $\omega := 290 \cdot \dfrac{rad}{sec}$

The root is then: $\omega_{root} := root(f(\omega), \omega)$ $\qquad \omega_{root} = 292.14 \cdot \dfrac{rad}{sec}$

Let's check that this is a root: $f(\omega_{root}) = -3.036 \cdot 10^{-5}$

Strictly speaking, ω should be expressed in Hz: $\dfrac{\omega_{root}}{2 \cdot \pi} = 46.5 \cdot Hz$

Note that the function is not quite zero at the root value. This is because Mathcad uses a numerical method to find the root, so there will always be some error. However, we'll see that you can ask Mathcad to perform this Root method to pretty much any accuracy you desire.

As you can see, Mathcad's Root method is very useful and simple to use (certainly a little easier than the traditional methods involving writing code, described earlier!).

You can now save this worksheet as "Example 5.1 (using Root)" in a location of your choice.

In Example 5.1, there are actually an infinite number of roots, meaning that the system can happily vibrate at any of an infinite number of different frequencies. We have found the lowest frequency, called the *fundamental* frequency. To find others, you would keep the original worksheet and simply edit the ranges that you look at, and your initial guesses.

After we have described in detail the steps required in Mathcad to use the Root method, you might want to try finding the next root, around 900 rad/sec.

We will summarize the steps involved in this method, including when it might fail, but before doing so, let's look at the second Mathcad approach, the Given . . . Find method, for solving a single equation.

Example 5.1 (Continued) Free vibration (using the given . . . find method) Let's create a new worksheet [or, if you're comfortable doing so, edit your worksheet called Example 5.1 (using Root)] and make the first few lines look like

Frequency of Free Vibration (using Given . . . Find)

By (Your Name)

Input the given data:

$$\rho := 1500 \cdot \frac{kg}{m^3} \quad A := 15 \cdot ft^2 \quad l := 20 \cdot ft \quad E := 5 \cdot 10^5 \cdot psi \quad M := 10000 \cdot lb$$

Next we compute m_b: $\quad m_b := \rho \cdot A \cdot l \quad m_b = 28093 \cdot lb$

Save this worksheet as "Example 5.1 (using Given . . . Find)."

As with the Root method, in the Given . . . Find method you need to give Mathcad an initial guess. We'll use the value we already obtained (if we hadn't previously investigated this problem, it would be a good idea to do some graphing of the given equation).

In the Given . . . Find method you can type the given engineering equation without having to rearrange it into an $f(\omega) = 0$ format. Again, we'll summarize the Given . . . Find procedure later, but for now: enter the initial guess; type the term *Given* (which is a *math* not a *text* region!); in a region below this type the equation to be solved using the Boolean equals (you remember that one way to do this is to type **Ctrl + =**); and use the function Find as shown below.

After doing all this, you should have something like

A good initial guess is: $\quad \omega := 290 \cdot \frac{rad}{sec}$

Given $\quad \omega \cdot l \cdot \sqrt{\frac{\rho}{E}} \cdot \tan\left(\omega \cdot l \cdot \sqrt{\frac{\rho}{E}}\right) = \frac{m_b}{M} \quad$ Find$(\omega) = 292.1 \cdot \frac{rad}{sec}$

The Find function generates the value of ω that satisfies the equation. Note that it's the same answer the Root method produced, as of course it should be. Once again, if you wished to use the result later on, you would instead have done something like

$$\omega := 290 \cdot \frac{rad}{sec} \quad Given \quad \omega \cdot l \cdot \sqrt{\frac{\rho}{E}} \cdot \tan\left(\omega \cdot l \cdot \sqrt{\frac{\rho}{E}}\right) = \frac{m_b}{M}$$

$$\omega_{solution} := Find(\omega) \quad \omega_{solution} = 292.1 \cdot \frac{rad}{sec}$$

Which of the two methods we've practiced should you use for solving a single algebraic equation? To some degree it depends on personal preference, although the Root method is designed specifically for such problems, and the Given . . . Find method is designed primarily for solving sets of equations. In addition, each method uses a different numerical method to solve an equation, so if one method fails to find a solution, the other might.

The Given . . . Find method is perhaps a little more intuitive. Unlike the Root method, the equation to be solved is typed pretty much as the engineering analysis derives it, and there is no need to rearrange it into an $f(x) = 0$ format.

Now that we've seen *what* the two methods can do, let's summarize in detail the steps involved in *how* we use them.

Solving a Single Implicit Equation Using Root

We can summarize the basic steps for using the Root method to solve a single equation (you should replicate these steps on a practice worksheet):

1. Rewrite the equation to be a function of the unknown. For example: Find the solutions of $5\sin(x) = x^2 + 1$ between $x = -2$ and $x = 3$. The equation is rewritten as $f(x) = 5\sin(x) - x^2 - 1$. In Mathcad:

The function is: $f(x) := 5 \cdot \sin(x) - x^2 - 1$

2. Although not strictly necessary, it's usually a good idea to graph the function over a range that makes sense to you, to see where a root might be. Use Mathcad's Zoom and Trace as necessary. For example:

$x := -2, -1.9 .. 3$

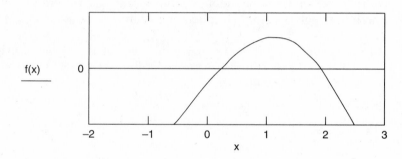

3. Based on the graph, enter an initial guess for x. (If you didn't graph the function, make an educated guess.) For example:

Let's try with the guess value: $x := 0.25$

4. Write the Root expression in the required form $\text{root}(f(x),x)$ to find the root. Check the result. For example:

$\text{root}(f(x),x) = 0.21$ or: $x := \text{root}(f(x),x)$ $x = 0.21$

Let's check that this a root: $f(x) = 3.618 \cdot 10^{-5}$

Note that you *must* enter the second argument x in the Root expression to tell Mathcad which of several possible variables in a function is the one whose root we are trying to find. For instance, you might have a function $f(x,y,z)$ and not $f(x)$, so that Mathcad needs to be told for which of x, y, and z you wish to find the root.

In the example shown above, the solution found does not quite make the function $f(x)$ zero. This is because, after all, Mathcad is using a numerical procedure to solve the problem. If more accuracy were desired, Mathcad's built-in accuracy variable TOL (whose default value is 0.001) could be reduced. See the menu item *Math . . . Options . . .* for details on this.

5. Repeat steps 2 through 4 as necessary to find other roots. For example:

Let's try with the new guess value: $x := 2$

$\text{root}(f(x),x) = 1.922$ or: $x := \text{root}(f(x),x)$ $x = 1.922$

Let's check that this is a root: $(x) = -8.52 \cdot 10^{-4}$

It goes without saying that the required format root($f(x),x$) for the Root function must always be used.

Note that, although we did not have one in this example, Mathcad easily handles equations with units. We will do several more examples from engineering using this method, but first let's summarize the procedure for using the Given . . . Find method.

5.3

Solving a Single Implicit Equation Using Given . . . Find

We can summarize the basic steps (which you should also do on the practice worksheet), which are very similar to those that were used in the Root method, for using the Given . . . Find method to solve a single implicit equation:

1. Optionally, graph the left and right sides of the equation over a range that makes sense to you. For example: Find the solutions of $5 \sin(x) = x^2 + 1$ between $x = -2$ and $x = 3$.

In Mathcad:

$x := -2, -1.95 .. 3$

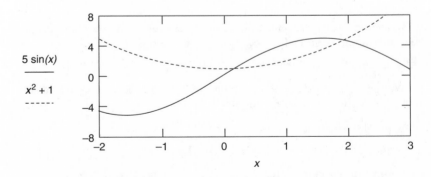

2. Based on where the two curves intersect on the graph (and after using Zoom and Trace as necessary), enter an initial guess for x. (If you don't graph the curves, make an educated guess.) For example:

Let's try with the guess value: $x := 0.2$

3. Write the Given . . . Find expression to find the root. The math expression Given *must* be typed first, followed by the equation or equations to be solved, finally followed by the Find(*x*) expression, so that Mathcad encounters them in that order.

Note that the Boolean equals (obtained using the **Ctrl + =** combination or by using the Evaluation or Boolean palette icon set) *must* be used here!

Finally, the result should be checked. For example:

Given $5 \sin(x) = x^2 + 1$ Find(*x*) = 0.21

or

Given $5 \sin(x) = x^2 + 1$ *x* := Find(*x*)   *x* = 0.21

Let's check that this is a solution: $5 \sin(x) = 1.044$ $x^2 + 1 = 1.044$

4. Repeat steps 2 through 3 as necessary to find other roots. For example:

Let's try with the new guess value: *x* := 2

Given $5 \sin(x) = x^2 + 1$ Find(*x*) = 1.922

or

Given $5 \sin(x) = x^2 + 1$ *x* := Find(*x*)   *x* = 1.922

Let's check that this is a solution: $5 \sin(x) = 4.695$ $x^2 + 1 = 4.695$

Using the Symbolic Given . . . Find

This chapter's main focus is on finding solutions to equations, when those solutions cannot be found explicitly. However, we can mention here that the Given . . . Find method can be used symbolically to see if an explicit solution exists. With enough experience in mathematics, you can often tell by inspection whether or not an equation can be explicitly solved. If, with a particular equation, you suspect that it can, but are unable to actually extract the solution, it's worthwhile to try using the symbolic Given . . . Find.

It turns out that the example equation from above (namely $5\sin(x) = x^2 + 1$) *cannot* be made explicit in the unknown (*x*), but let's try anyway!

To use the symbolic approach, you simply do everything with the Given . . . Find as before, except for two things:

1. You should not give an initial guess value for the unknown (and in fact other variables do not have to have been previously defined either).

2. You do not use the evaluation equals.

Instead of using the evaluation equals, you select only the Find expression and then use any of several methods for *symbolically evaluating* it. These methods are

1. Use the menu item *Symbolics . . . Evaluate . . . Symbolically.*

2. Use the accelerator keys **Shift + F9**.

3. Use the Symbolic Evaluation icon on the Symbolic Keyword palette (accessed from the Math palette). (Actually, for this method you don't have to enclose the entire Find expression. You can just click *anywhere* on the expression.)

4. Use the accelerator keys **Ctrl + ..** (You don't have to enclose the entire Find expression for this method either.)

The first two methods are not live, and the last two are live.

Let's try, on a new blank worksheet, using the first method on the equation. You should get something like

Given $5 \cdot \sin(x) = x^2 + 1$ Find(x)

Or, alternatively:

Given $5 \cdot \sin(x) = x^2 + 1$ $x := \text{Find}(x)$

Mathcad was unable to find a solution using either format (as we should have expected).

Just so you can see that this symbolic method *does* work sometimes, let's try it with the standard quadratic expression $ax^2 + bx + c = 0$:

Given $a \cdot x^2 + b \cdot x + c = 0$

Find (x)

$$\left[\frac{1}{(2 \cdot a)} \cdot \left(-b + \sqrt{b^2 - 4 \cdot a \cdot c}\right) \quad \frac{1}{(2 \cdot a)} \cdot \left(-b - \sqrt{b^2 - 4 \cdot a \cdot c}\right) \right]$$

Or, alternatively:

Given $a \cdot x^2 + b \cdot x + c = 0$

$x := \text{Find}(x)$

$$x := \left[\frac{1}{(2 \cdot a)} \cdot \left(-b + \sqrt{b^2 - 4 \cdot a \cdot c}\right) \quad \frac{1}{(2 \cdot a)} \cdot \left(-b - \sqrt{b^2 - 4 \cdot a \cdot c}\right) \right]$$

It does work! Mathcad gave the two solutions in matrix form. If yours didn't, you probably either selected more than or less than just the expression Find(x) before executing the symbolic math.

Let's now point out some situations where you might encounter an error using the Given . . . Find method in its nonsymbolic form.

Some Typical Errors Using Root and Given . . . Find

The most common errors associated with using the Root and Given . . . Find methods are

1. Not giving an initial guess. If you do not give an initial value for the unknown, Mathcad does not know where to begin its search for a solution. Give Mathcad its initial guess.

2. Having a units error. If the units are inconsistent, Mathcad obviously cannot proceed to a solution. Check your equation and the units of the given data.

3. Not obtaining the root you expected. If an equation has several solutions, even if your initial guess is close to the desired solution, Mathcad might converge to an unwanted solution. In this case try choosing a different initial guess, or rephrase the equation in some way.

4. The problem does not have a root, or it is not "easily found." As the Root and Given . . . Find methods are both numerical methods, there are occasions when they will not be able to find a solution. Either this means there is no solution, or you may have to restructure the entire problem and try Mathcad again.

5. The problem has complex roots, but the initial guess is real (or vice versa). This happens occasionally. To correct this, give the appropriate type of initial guess.

The third Mathcad method for solving an equation, which can occasionally be used, is the Polyroots method.

There is another Mathcad method to solve equations that are of polynomial form, that is, of the form:

$$p(x) = c_0 + c_1\,x + c_2\,x^2 + c_3\,x^3 + \cdots + c_n x^n \qquad (5.4)$$

Let's summarize the steps for this method:

1. Write a vector of the coefficients of the polynomial, with the first coefficient being c_0, the second c_1, and so on. One way to create a vector (see Chapter 6 for detailed guidance on how to create and use vectors in Mathcad) is to type **Ctrl + M** and in the window that appears enter the number of coefficients for the number of columns. You can then enter at the placeholders the values of the coefficients.

For example: Find all the roots of the equation $3x^3 - 2x^2 + 5 = 0$. In Mathcad:

The coefficient vector is: $\quad c := \begin{bmatrix} 5 \\ 0 \\ -2 \\ 3 \end{bmatrix}$

2. Write the expression for the Polyroots function in the form polyroots(c) where c is the vector containing the polynomial coefficients. Then just use the usual evaluation equals to find the solution. For example:

The expression for the roots is $\quad x_{sol} := \text{polyroots}(c)$

$$x_{sol} = \begin{bmatrix} -1 \\ 0.833 - 0.986i \\ 0.833 + 0.986i \end{bmatrix}$$

Notice in this case that the cubic equation resulted in one real and two complex conjugate roots.

3. Check the results obtained. For example:

The original equation was: $\quad p(x) := c_0 + c_1 \cdot x + c_2 \cdot x^2 + c_3 \cdot x^3$

$$\overrightarrow{p(x_{sol})} = \begin{bmatrix} -3.271 \cdot 10^{-9} \\ -3.271 \cdot 10^{-9} + 1.332 \cdot 10^{-15}i \\ -3.271 \cdot 10^{-9} + 2.22 \cdot 10^{-15}i \end{bmatrix}$$

These results are close to zero, as required.

In step 3 the three computations of $p(x)$ (one for each root) are accomplished in one step by using Mathcad's "vectorize" feature. Use Mathcad's Help to find out about this feature. Also, you can make the last result appear as zeros by changing the number format: change the default value of Zero Tolerance to some value less than 15.

As we see, the Polyroots method is very convenient for solving polynomial expressions. For example, with this method no initial guess is needed. However, there are a couple of things to be aware of when using it:

1. Care should be taken in how the elements of the coefficient are counted. Unless Mathcad's default built-in variable ORIGIN is changed, vector coefficients will be counted starting with zero, so the first element is c_0. See the menu item *Math . . . Options . . .* for details on how to change the value of ORIGIN. A common error is to assume the first element is element c_1, when it will actually be c_0 if the default ORIGIN = 0 is used.

2. Because the method works by using vector math, each coefficient of the equation must have the same units. This is not typically the case with equations derived from an engineering analysis.

Let's now do several engineering problems using the Roots and Given . . . Find methods.

Some Engineering Examples

Example 5.2 Automobile drag Consider an automobile having a certain horsepower P (hp). We wish to find the maximum speed

V (mph) of the vehicle. At any speed the vehicle will experience two kinds of resistance to its motion: *rolling resistance* due to friction in the engine, transmission, differential, tires, and so on, proportional to *V;* and *aerodynamic resistance* due to the vehicle size, the degree of streamlining, and so forth, proportional to V^2. The power consumed at speed V will then be equal to the engine power produced:

$$P = DV = (aV + bV^2)V = aV^2 + bV^3 \tag{5.5}$$

where D is the total resistance or drag and a and b are known constants. For example, consider the following data:

$$P = 150 \text{ hp}$$

$$a = 2 \frac{\text{N}}{\text{m/s}}$$

$$b = 5 \frac{\text{N}}{(\text{m/s})^2}$$

Equation (5.5) is explicit in *P:* the power required for a given speed is immediately computable (except that the mixed units make it messy!). Solving Equation (5.5) for the speed *V* for a given power *P* is trickier. This is a cubic equation for *V*. Is there an explicit equation for solving cubic equations, as there is for quadratic equations? If there is none, a traditional numerical scheme will have to be used, as described above, or we can use Mathcad's Root or Given . . . Find method. In addition to these methods, because Equation (5.5) is a cubic in *V* (a polynomial), we could try using Mathcad's Polyroots method (although we'll find that it's not convenient for this example).

You might want to try Mathcad's symbolic Given . . . Find first, to see if an analytic solution exists. If you do this on a blank worksheet, you'll get

Given $\quad P = a \cdot V^2 + b \cdot V^3$

$\qquad$ Find (V)

$$\left[\left[\frac{1}{54}\cdot\frac{(27\cdot P\cdot b^2 - 2\cdot a^3)}{b^3} + \frac{1}{18}\cdot\frac{\sqrt{3}}{b^2}\cdot\sqrt{P\cdot(27\cdot P\cdot b^2 - 4\cdot a^3)}\right]^{\frac{1}{3}} + \ldots\right]$$

The last equation was manually edited, because the full result is huge. Mathcad *could* find a symbolic solution, but its shear size makes it impractical to use.

Let's delete this material and start over again. First, let's use the Root method. You should do the following (and if you wish, save it as "Example 5.2 (using Root)":

Automobile Drag (using Root)

By (Your Name)

Input the given data $\quad P := 150 \text{ hp} \quad a := 2 \frac{\text{newton}}{\frac{\text{m}}{\text{sec}}} \quad b := 5 \frac{\text{newton}}{\left(\frac{\text{m}}{\text{sec}}\right)^2}$

Now create a function of speed V: $\qquad f(V) := P - a \cdot V^2 - b \cdot V^3$

This can now be plotted: $\qquad\qquad\qquad V := 0 \cdot mph, 1 \cdot mph \, .. \, 100 \cdot mph$

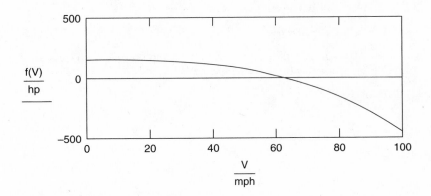

This graph leads to an initial guess. The Root method can then be applied:

A good initial guess is: $\qquad\qquad V := 65 \; mph$

Finally, the root function can be used:

$V_{150} := root(f(V), V) \qquad V_{150} = 62.7 \cdot mph$

Let's check the answer: $\qquad f(V_{150}) = 0 \cdot hp$

Note that the mph and hp units were inserted into the last two expressions, and the default value for Zero Tolerance was set to 6.

Next, let's try the Given . . . Find method (you might want to save this as "Example 5.2 (using Given . . . Find)":

__Automobile Drag (using Given . . . Find)__

By (Your Name)

Input the given data:

$$P := 150 \; hp \qquad a := 2 \, \frac{newton}{\dfrac{m}{sec}} \qquad b := 5 \, \frac{newton}{\left(\dfrac{m}{sec}\right)^2}$$

The left and right sides of the engineering equation can be plotted:

$V := 0 \cdot mph, 1 \cdot mph .. 80 \cdot mph$

The Given . . . Find method can then be used (remember to use the Boolean equals):

Based on the graph, an initial guess for the velocity is: $V := 60$ mph

We can then use Mathcad's Given . . . Find syllogism:

Given $P = a \cdot V^2 + b \cdot V^3$ $V_{sol} := Find(V)$ $V_{sol} = 62.7 \cdot mph$

Check: $a \cdot V_{sol}^2 + b \cdot V_{sol}^3 = 150 \cdot hp$

Finally, we might be tempted to use Mathcad's Polyroots method, because, as we noted, Equation (5.3) is cubic in V. Unfortunately, the Polyroots method provides the n roots of an n-degree polynomial only if the coefficients of the polynomial all have the same units. For Example 5.2, P, a, and b would have to have the same units, which they obviously do not. If you try to use this method here, Mathcad will immediately tell you that you're trying to create a vector with mismatched units. To use the Polyroots method for this problem, you would have to somehow rewrite Equation (5.5) to create coefficients that are of the same units (or take care of units yourself!) This means this method is, in practice, limited to not only polynomials, but ones which do not involve units (or ones where *you* worry about the units being correctly used!).

Example 5.3   Oxygen Depletion   Equation (5.6) gives the concentration (percent) of oxygen downstream of a water-cooled power plant:

$$c = 8 - 12\left(e^{-\frac{s}{s_0}} - e^{-\frac{5s}{s_0}}\right) \tag{5.6}$$

Here c is the oxygen concentration (initially 8 percent) and s is the distance downstream in miles ($s_0 = 10$ miles is a constant). This equation is explicit in c, so it would be easy to compute the concentration of oxygen at any point downstream. However, it is implicit in s, so that if we wish to find, say, at what point downstream the concentration is 5 percent, or the concentration is a minimum, we have some difficulty. In fact, if you tried to use any of Mathcad's symbolic methods, you'd see that there is no such explicit solution possible.

Let's use both Mathcad's Root and Given . . . Find methods to find the locations at which the concentration reaches 5 percent (you can create and save this file as "Example 5.3"):

Oxygen Depletion

By (Your Name)

Enter the data and formula:

$$s_0 := 10 \text{ mi} \qquad c(s) := 8 - 12 \cdot \left(e^{\frac{-s}{s_0}} - e^{\frac{-5s}{s_0}}\right)$$

The concentration curve can be plotted over a suitable range:

$$s := 0 \text{ mi}, 1 \text{ mi} .. 30 \text{ mi}$$

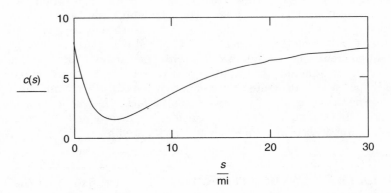

The graph (perhaps using Mathcad's Zoom feature) leads to some initial guesses.

From the graph it is clear that the concentration reaches 5 percent at approximately 1 mile and at 15 miles downstream. This suggests some initial guesses:

$s := 1$ mi

Using root: $\qquad$ root$(c(s) - 5, s) = 0.789 \cdot$mi

Using Given . . . Find $\qquad$ Given $\quad c(s) = 5 \quad$ Find$(s) = 0.789 \cdot$mi

For the second location at which the concentration is 5 percent, try a second guess:

$s := 15$ mi

Using root: $\qquad$ root$(c(s) - 5, s) = 13.823 \cdot$mi

Using Given . . . Find $\qquad$ Given $\quad c(s) = 5 \quad$ Find$(s) = 13.823 \cdot$mi

Once again both methods are in agreement.

To find the location at which the concentration reaches a minimum, we see from the graph that this is somewhere around $s = 4$ miles. This point is also where the slope of the curve is zero. One of the terrific things about Mathcad's Root and Given . . . Find methods is that they can solve an equation involving a *differential* or *integral* for a single value [do not confuse this with obtaining the solution to a differential equation by integrating it (which we'll discuss in Chapter 7)].

Let's have Mathcad find the location of minimum concentration by finding where the slope of the curve is zero:

Make a guess for the location of the minimum concentration: $\quad s := 4$ mi

Next, set up the Root and Given . . . Find methods to find where the slope of the curve attains the zero value:

$$\text{root}\left(\frac{d}{ds}c(s), s\right) = 4.023 \cdot \text{mi}$$

or: $\quad$ Given $\quad \dfrac{d}{ds}c(s) = 0 \cdot \dfrac{1}{\text{mi}} \quad$ Find$(s) = 4.024 \cdot$mi

There are a few noteworthy features of Example 5.3:

1. As we mentioned above, the Root and Given . . . Find methods can handle differentials.

2. In the Root method, instead of creating a function of which we then find the root, we can enter an *expression* as an argument of root.

3. Note that the slope of the curve was set to 0 1/mi, and not 0, because dc is dimensionless but ds has units of mi. A common error in using both methods is to have a unit mismatch.

It's interesting to note that an alternative method for finding the minimum concentration point would have been to have Mathcad *symbolically* differentiate Equation (5.6) and then you could have used the Root method to find the zero of this new function. For details on symbolic differentiation refer back to Chapter 4.

Example 5.4   RLC circuit   One of the basic circuits electrical engineers study is that consisting of a resistor, inductance, and capacitor connected in series, the resistance-inductance-capacitance (RLC) circuit. For example, suppose the circuit is open and the capacitor holds an initial charge $q_0 = 5$ coulombs. If we have the following data:

R = 500 ohm
L = 70 henry
C = 10^{-4} farad

we might be interested in how long the capacitor takes to initially discharge.

The formula for the instantaneous charge, obtained from doing a transient analysis of the circuit, is

$$q(t) = q_0 \, e^{-\frac{Rt}{2L}} \cos\left[\sqrt{\frac{1}{LC} - \left(\frac{R}{2L}\right)^2} \, t \right] \tag{5.7}$$

We need to find t in this equation when $q = 0$. Note that this consists of an oscillation and a decay. The oscillation is due to an interaction between the capacitor and inductance (similar to that between a spring and a mass in mechanics), and the decay is due to dissipation of electrical energy into heat by the resistor (similar to friction in mechanics). For example, if there is no resistor, the circuit oscillates forever, as Equation (5.7) shows when $R = 0$.

Once again, we have an implicit equation for the unknown time. Can it be made explicit in t when we set $q = 0$? On a new blank worksheet let's use a symbolic method to see if it can be done. Try to do the following (where the Solve for Variable icon in the Symbolic Keyword palette was used):

A symbolic solution is:

$$e^{\frac{-R \cdot t}{2 \cdot L}} \cdot \cos\left[\sqrt{\frac{1}{L \cdot C} - \left(\frac{R}{2 \cdot L}\right)^2} \cdot t \right] = 0 \text{ solve, } t \rightarrow$$

The exponential became colored, indicating an error. If you click on this, an explanation appears stating that you can't have anything with units in the exponent (which is true). What happened was that Mathcad used R as degrees Rankine, when all we want is symbols without units. To fix this we need to temporarily use r instead of R (in both places that it appears in the equation). Edit the expression to do this. After you do it, however, you'll *still* have an error. Mathcad has a bug here! It doesn't recognize the correction we made. What you need to do next is select the entire expression, cut it, and paste it back. You should finally get

A symbolic solution is:

$$e^{-\frac{r \cdot t}{2 \cdot L}} \cdot \cos\left[\sqrt{\frac{1}{L \cdot C} - \left(\frac{r}{2 \cdot L}\right)^2} \cdot t \right] = 0 \text{ solve, } t \rightarrow \frac{\pi}{\sqrt{\dfrac{4}{(L \cdot C)} - \dfrac{r^2}{L^2}}}$$

This time it worked, and there *is* an explicit solution possible. Let's use this solution in a new worksheet. Select and copy just the solution, and then close the worksheet without saving (we don't need it).

Let's start another worksheet (call it "Example 5.4"), in which we'll practice the Root and Given . . . Find methods and compare their results to the solution we just found. In this new worksheet, type in some text and the given data, paste in the solution we just copied, edit the r back to R, and assign it to a new variable. In other words, try and generate the following:

RLC Electric Circuit

By (Your Name)

Enter the data:

$R := 500$ ohm $L := 70$ henry $C := 10^{-4}$ farad $q_0 := 5$ coul

The exact solution to the circuit problem is:

$$t_{exact} := \frac{\pi}{\sqrt{\frac{4}{(L \cdot C)} - \frac{R^2}{L^2}}} \qquad t_{exact} = 0.138 \cdot sec$$

Now we can try the Root and Given . . . Find methods. We should graph the function to get an idea of the guess value we'll need, but here let's just use a guess of $t = 0.1$ s. For the two methods you should get

The formula for the capacitor charge is:

$$q(t) := q_0 \cdot e^{\frac{-R \cdot t}{2 \cdot L}} \cdot \cos\left[\sqrt{\frac{1}{L \cdot C} - \left(\frac{R}{2 \cdot L}\right)^2} \cdot t\right]$$

A guess value is: $t := 0.1 \cdot sec$

Then: $root(q(t), t) = 0.138 \cdot sec$

or: Given $q(t) = 0$ coul   Find$(t) = 0.138 \cdot sec$

The two methods gave the same answer as the symbolic solution. Obviously, for this problem, there is really no point in using these methods if a symbolic solution works. We did so just to get practice in their use.

A trickier problem would be to adjust the resistance R until the time for initial discharge is 0.2 second (the circuit might be part of a timing mechanism, for example). For this problem, you could try a symbolic solution, but here we'll restructure the problem so that the right-hand side of Equation (5.7) is treated as a function of R (it becomes the unknown), with time $t = 0.2$ second, a constant:

Let's set the time we wish the function to be zero: $t := 0.2$ sec

Then: $root\left[q_0 \cdot e^{\frac{-R \cdot t}{2 \cdot L}} \cdot \cos\left[\sqrt{\frac{1}{L \cdot C} - \left(\frac{R}{2 \cdot L}\right)^2} \cdot t\right], R\right] = 1261 \cdot ohm$

or

Given: $q_0 \cdot e^{\frac{-R \cdot t}{2 \cdot L}} \cdot \cos\left[\sqrt{\frac{1}{L \cdot C} - \left(\frac{R}{2 \cdot L}\right)^2} \cdot t\right] = 0 \text{ coul}$ Find$(R) = 1261 \cdot \text{ohm}$

Just by slightly changing the worksheet, we solved a different problem!

In summary, we can see that practically any engineering problem that involves solving a single equation for a single unknown can be solved with either the Root or Given . . . Find method.

We now move on to the next level of difficulty, when we have several equations and unknowns.

5.5

Simultaneous Equations Using Given . . . Find

Mathcad's Given . . . Find method, as we have seen, is an excellent tool for solving a single implicit equation. The method really comes into its own when it is used to solve a *set* of equations.

The equations to be solved could be linear or nonlinear, and could involve integrals or differentials. If the equations are linear, linear algebra methods can be used instead of the Root or Given . . . Find methods (see Chapter 6 for details on this).

The procedure for using the Given . . . Find method is as described in Section 5.4, with the following additions (which you can practice on a blank worksheet):

1. Each unknown must be given an initial guess value (based on common sense or engineering experience, or by examining the engineering problem by, for example, graphing using Mathcad). For example: Solve the set of equations shown below:

$x^2 + y = 4$ $x + y = z$ $xy = -3$

In Mathcad:

Let's try a guess for *x, y,* and *z:* $x := 0$ $y := 0$ $z := 0$

2. The set of equations to be satisfied must be placed between the Given and Find statements. Care must be taken that the equations are encountered by Mathcad *after* the Given and *before* the Find.

Note: The Boolean equals (using the **Ctrl + =** combination or the Evaluation or Boolean palette icon) *must* be used here!

For example:

Given $x^2 + y = 4$

$x + y = z$

$x \cdot y = -3$

Find $(x, y, z) = \begin{bmatrix} -1 \\ 3 \\ 2 \end{bmatrix}$

Note that the solution is given as a vector of values. Because Mathcad wants a vector to have the same units for all its elements, you *must* observe this unit's constraint when using the Given . . . Find method in this way. To use the Given . . . Find method to find, say, the time (s) and velocity (ft/s) of a problem, see the explanation on page 160.

In a similar way to the single equation problems, instead of the above output, you can define the solution as new quantities for use in a later equation. For example:

Given $x^2 + y = 4$

$\qquad x + y = z$

$\qquad x \cdot y = -3$

Ans := Find (x, y, z) $\qquad$ Ans $= \begin{bmatrix} -1 \\ 3 \\ 2 \end{bmatrix}$

In this example, because two of the equations are second degree, there are more than one solution to these equations. (How many are there?) The solution found depends on the initial guesses. For example:

Let's try a new guess for x, y, and z: $\qquad x := 1 \qquad y := 0 \qquad z := 0$

Given $x^2 + y = 4$

$\qquad x + y = z$

$\qquad x \cdot y = -3$

Find$(x, y, z) = \begin{bmatrix} 2.303 \\ -1.303 \\ 1 \end{bmatrix}$

Which solution is the desired one depends on the particular engineering problem being studied, or on your common sense.

We should add that you can sometimes *force* Mathcad to search for a particular solution by adding an additional constraint equation (for example $x > 0$). (Use Mathcad's Evaluation or Boolean Palette icon.)

This Given . . . Find method is numeric (it gives you numbers), but it can sometimes be used symbolically.

Using the Symbolic Given . . . Find

Occasionally a set of equations will have a symbolic solution. To do this with Mathcad you follow the procedure described above, but you should not provide initial guesses for the unknowns, and instead of the evaluation equals you can use any of the symbolic operators (such as the accelerator keys **Ctrl + .**) we have previously used. For example, solving the same set of equations symbolically (try it):

Given $\quad x^2 + y = 4 \qquad x + y = z \qquad x{\cdot}y = -3$

$$\text{Find}(x, y, z) \rightarrow \begin{bmatrix} -1 & \dfrac{1}{2} + \dfrac{1}{2}{\cdot}\sqrt{13} & \dfrac{1}{2} - \dfrac{1}{2}{\cdot}\sqrt{13} \\[2mm] 3 & \dfrac{1}{2} - \dfrac{1}{2}{\cdot}\sqrt{13} & \dfrac{1}{2} + \dfrac{1}{2}{\cdot}\sqrt{13} \\[2mm] 2 & 1 & 1 \end{bmatrix}$$

This multiple solution (where each of the three columns is a solution) is symbolic (suggested by the appearance of the roots).

If instead of **Ctrl + .** you select the entire Find expression and use the menu item *Symbolics . . . Evaluate . . . Floating Point* (with a Floating Point Precision of 3), you get

Given $\quad x^2 + y = 4 \qquad x + y = z \qquad x{\cdot}y = -3$

Find(x, y, z)

$$\begin{bmatrix} -1. & 2.31 & -1.31 \\ 3. & -1.31 & 2.31 \\ 2. & 1. & 1. \end{bmatrix}$$

These two answers produced numbers rather than symbols because of the nature of the three equations. If the equations had been written with variable names (a, b, etc.), you would have obtained a symbolic solution using these variable names.

Let's now list some of the typical errors in using the numerical Given . . . Find method.

Some Typical Errors Using Given . . . Find

1. There are an insufficient number of equations. For each unknown, one independent equation must be given. If you did not provide enough equations, check the engineering problem for conceptual errors.

2. The unknowns have different units and you have defined a variable (e.g. "Ans") to be equal to the Find, or tried to directly evaluate the Find. If you wish to use units here, you *must* define a column vector of the unknowns to be equal to the Find, and then *individually* evaluate the unknowns obtained. Alternatively, you can somehow restructure the problem so that all the unknowns have no dimensions, or take care of units yourself.

3. The initial guesses do not lead to a solution, or lead to an unwanted solution. Because this is a numerical method, occasionally the method will fail, even if the problem is "well-posed." If this occurs, the only options are to try different initial conditions or to add an additional constraint equation.

Example 5.5 DC circuit

A common problem in DC circuit analysis is to find the currents flowing in each branch of a network of resistors. For example, consider the circuit shown in Figure 5.3. We wish to find the values of the currents I_1, I_2, and I_3. In this circuit R_1, R_2, and R_3 are 25, 10, and 5 ohms and the voltages V_1 and V_2 are 165 and 70 volts.

The three equations required for three unknowns can be obtained from applying Kirchhoff's Law and by summing voltage drops across nodes:

$$
\begin{aligned}
I_1 + \quad I_2 - \quad I_3 &= 0 \text{ amp} \\
R_1 I_1 \qquad\qquad + R_3 I_3 &= V_1 \qquad\qquad (5.8) \\
R_2 I_2 + R_3 I_3 &= V_2
\end{aligned}
$$

First of all, it turns out that these equations can be solved symbolically. On a blank worksheet, type in the Given expression and then the equations (the right of the first equation should be typed without the amp unit). Then define a variable called *Solution* to be equal to the appropriate Find. You'll find when you do this that some of the expression will be colored, because the resistors have not been defined and initial guesses have not been provided. Let's proceed anyway, by selecting just the Find and using the menu item *Symbolics . . . Evaluate Symbolically*. You should end up with

Given $\quad I_1 + I_2 - I_3 = 0 \qquad R_1 \cdot I_1 + R_3 \cdot I_3 = V_1 \qquad R_2 \cdot I_2 + R_3 \cdot I_3 = V_2$

Solution := Find(I_1, I_2, I_3)

$$
\text{\textit{Solution}} := \begin{bmatrix} \dfrac{(-R_3 \cdot V_2 + R_2 \cdot V_1 + V_1 \cdot R_3)}{(R_1 \cdot R_2 + R_1 \cdot R_3 + R_2 \cdot R_3)} \\[2ex] \dfrac{(R_3 \cdot V_2 - V_1 \cdot R_3 + R_1 \cdot V_2)}{(R_1 \cdot R_2 + R_1 \cdot R_3 + R_2 \cdot R_3)} \\[2ex] \dfrac{(R_2 \cdot V_1 + R_1 \cdot V_2)}{(R_1 \cdot R_2 + R_1 \cdot R_3 + R_2 \cdot R_3)} \end{bmatrix}
$$

Mathcad was able to *symbolically* solve this set of equations. If you wished, you could rearrange these equations and add definitions of the values of the resistors and voltages to get numerical values of the currents.

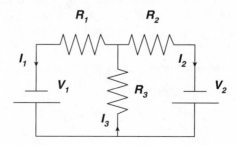

Figure 5.3

Let's delete all this and start over to *numerically* solve the set of equations. First, we should provide a title and enter the given data for the problem and initial guesses for the currents (call this worksheet "Example 5.5"):

<u>DC Network</u>

By (Your Name)

The resistances and voltages are:

$R_1 := 25 \cdot \text{ohm}$ $R_2 := 10 \cdot \text{ohm}$ $R_3 := 5 \cdot \text{ohm}$

$V_1 := 165 \cdot \text{volt}$ $V_2 := 70 \cdot \text{volt}$

Let's try the following initial guesses:

$I_1 := 0 \cdot \text{amp}$ $I_2 := 0 \cdot \text{amp}$ $I_3 := 0 \cdot \text{amp}$

The three equations can then be entered between the Given and Find statements. The output equation was created by starting with a vector generated, for example, by starting with **Ctrl + M**:

The engineering equations are:

Given

$$I_1 + I_2 - I_3 = 0 \cdot \text{amp} \qquad R_1 \cdot I_1 + R_3 \cdot I_3 = V_1 \qquad R_2 \cdot I_2 + R_3 \cdot I_3 = V_2$$

$$\begin{bmatrix} I_1 \\ I_2 \\ I_3 \end{bmatrix} := \text{Find}(I_1, I_2, I_3) \qquad \begin{bmatrix} I_1 \\ I_2 \\ I_3 \end{bmatrix} = \begin{bmatrix} 5 \\ 3 \\ 8 \end{bmatrix} \cdot \text{amp}$$

Note that Mathcad not only solved the problem but, as we have repeatedly indicated, it successfully handled the units. Let's make sure the values obtained are correct:

Checking with the original equations:

$$I_1 + I_2 - I_3 = 0 \cdot \text{amp}$$

$$R_1 \cdot I_1 + R_3 \cdot I_3 = 165 \cdot \text{volt}$$

$$R_2 \cdot I_2 + R_3 \cdot I_3 = 70 \cdot \text{volt}$$

The worksheet is also live, so you could now change the values of any of the inputs and get a new solution. For example, by judicious choice of values, you could see what the current is if you have a single battery and resistor:

The resistances and voltages are:

$R_1 := 25 \cdot \text{ohm}$ $R_2 := 0 \cdot \text{ohm}$ $R_3 := 1 \cdot \text{ohm}$

$V_1 := 165 \cdot \text{volt}$ $V_2 := 0 \cdot \text{volt}$

Let's try the following initial guesses:

$I_1 := 0 \cdot amp \qquad I_2 := 0 \cdot amp \qquad I_3 := 0 \cdot amp$

The engineering equations are:

Given

$I_1 + I_2 - I_3 = 0 \cdot amp \qquad R_1 \cdot I_1 + R_3 \cdot I_3 = V_1 \qquad R_2 \cdot I_2 + R_3 \cdot I_3 = V_2$

$$\begin{bmatrix} I_1 \\ I_2 \\ I_3 \end{bmatrix} := \text{Find}(I_1, I_2, I_3) \qquad \begin{bmatrix} I_1 \\ I_2 \\ I_3 \end{bmatrix} = \begin{bmatrix} 6.6 \\ -6.6 \\ 0 \end{bmatrix} \cdot amp$$

The values of R_2 and R_3 were chosen here so that the right-hand branch of the circuit becomes a nul circuit (essentially, $R_2 = 0$ ohm short-circuits the branch so that R_3 can be anything). As you might expect, $I_1 = -I_2 = V_1/R_1$.

As we mentioned earlier, Mathcad has another approach, namely its linear algebra capability, available for solving *linear* equation sets, such as this example. For details on this see Chapter 6.

Example 5.6 Sphere collision

Consider two spheres undergoing a direct collision, as shown in Figure 5.4. We wish to find the velocities v'_1 and v'_2 after the collision. These depend not only on the two masses m_1 and m_2, and two velocities v_1 and v_2, but also on the *coefficient of restitution e* between the two masses. This coefficient is a measure of the amount of elasticity in the spheres: a value of 1 indicates that the spheres are *perfectly elastic,* so that no energy is lost to collision deformations; a value of 0 indicates 100 percent *plastic* deformation, when all the energy of collision deformation is lost. Any value of e between 0 and 1 indicates *inelastic* behavior. The value of e obviously has a large effect on the resulting velocities.

The two equations required for two unknowns are the momentum conservation law and the equation allowing for the coefficient of restitution:

$$m_1 v_1 + m_2 v_2 = m_1 v'_1 + m_2 v'_2 \qquad (5.9)$$

$$v'_1 - v'_2 = e(v_2 - v_1) \qquad (5.10)$$

In Equations (5.9) and (5.10) it's important to note that all velocities are positive to the right, negative to the left.

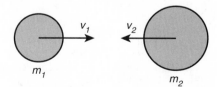

Figure 5.4

Let's have Mathcad tackle this problem with the following (mixed unit!) data:

$$m_1 = 1\,\text{lb} \quad v_1 = 2\,\frac{\text{m}}{\text{sec}}$$

$$m_2 = 3\,\text{lb} \quad v_2 = -1\,\frac{\text{m}}{\text{sec}}$$

We wish to know the velocities after the collision assuming both completely elastic ($e = 1$) and completely plastic ($e = 0$) spheres.

Once again it turns out that Equations (5.9) and (5.10) can be solved symbolically, but we will not do that here.

Let's create another worksheet (call it "Example 5.6"). Note that to create a *prime* in Mathcad you should use the *back-prime* key (`` ` ``) and *not* the normal prime key ('), because the latter is used by Mathcad to generate parentheses.

You should be able to do the following:

Sphere Collision

By (Your Name)

Enter the given data:

$$m_1 := 1\,\text{lb} \quad v_1 := 2\,\frac{\text{m}}{\text{sec}} \quad m_2 := 3\,\text{lb} \quad v_2 := -1\,\frac{\text{m}}{\text{sec}}$$

Provide initial guesses, and the value of *e*:

$$v'_1 := v_1 \qquad v'_2 := v_2 \qquad e := 1$$

Given $\quad m_1 \cdot v_1 + m_2 \cdot v_2 = m_1 \cdot v'_1 + m_2 \cdot v'_2$

$$v'_1 - v'_2 = e \cdot (v_2 - v_1)$$

$$\begin{bmatrix} v'_1 \\ v'_2 \end{bmatrix} := \text{Find}(v'_1, v'_2) \qquad \begin{bmatrix} v'_1 \\ v'_2 \end{bmatrix} = \begin{bmatrix} -2.5 \\ 0.5 \end{bmatrix} \cdot \frac{\text{m}}{\text{sec}}$$

Of course, you should check that these results are correct.

What about the loss of energy? It's easy to compute:

We can compute the loss of energy in the collision:

$$E_{\text{Loss}} := \left(\frac{1}{2} \cdot m_1 \cdot v_1^2 + \frac{1}{2} \cdot m_2 \cdot v_2^2 \right) - \left(\frac{1}{2} m_1 \cdot v'^2_1 + \frac{1}{2} \cdot m_2 \cdot v'^2_2 \right)$$

$$E_{\text{Loss}} = 0 \cdot \text{joule}$$

As expected, there is no loss of energy for the perfectly elastic collision. If we change the value of *e* to zero, so that the collision is 100 percent plastic, we can immediately see the new results:

$$\begin{bmatrix} v'_1 \\ v'_2 \end{bmatrix} = \begin{bmatrix} -0.25 \\ -0.25 \end{bmatrix} \cdot \frac{m}{\text{sec}}$$

$$E_{\text{Loss}} := \left(\frac{1}{2} \cdot m_1 \cdot v_1^2 + \frac{1}{2} \cdot m_2 \cdot v_2^2 \right) - \left(\frac{1}{2} \cdot m_1 \cdot v'_1^2 + \frac{1}{2} \cdot m_2 \cdot v'_2^2 \right)$$

$E_{\text{Loss}} = 1.531 \cdot \text{joule}$

As we can see, for plastic collisions the two bodies coalesce, and there is significant loss of mechanical energy to heat. Note that the Given . . . Find method allows unknowns on either or both sides of equations.

In Example 5.6 Mathcad's linear algebra capability could once again have been used.

Example 5.7 Wing design

When an airplane is cruising in air (density ρ) at constant speed V, the forces acting on it will be in balance. The *thrust* of the engines will be equal to the *drag* of the fuselage and wings, and the *weight* of the airplane will be balanced by the *lift* produced by the wings. These forces are shown in Figure 5.5.

The lift L and drag D are given by

$$L = \frac{1}{2} \rho A V^2 C_{\text{L}} \tag{5.11}$$

$$D = \frac{1}{2} \rho \left[A \left(C_{\text{D}} + \frac{C_{\text{L}}^2}{\pi \, ar} \right) + k \right] V^2 \tag{5.12}$$

In Equations (5.11) and (5.12) A is the wing plan area, ar is the wing aspect ratio (defined below), k is the fuselage drag-area, and C_{L} and C_{D} are the wing lift and drag coefficients.

The overall size of a wing is given by its chord c (the distance from the leading edge to the trailing edge) and span s (the distance from the wing base to wing tip). The wing area $A = sc$, and the aspect ratio $ar = s/c$ (indicating whether the wing is short and "stubby" or long and slender).

In designing a wing for a given airplane, once the wing profile (i.e., the cross-section shape, allowing for such things as wing thickness, curve, or camber, etc.) has been chosen, the only free parameters left are the overall size of the wing, given by c and s. To determine these parameters, we need to solve Equations (5.11) and (5.12), in which c and s are buried in the wing area A and aspect ratio ar.

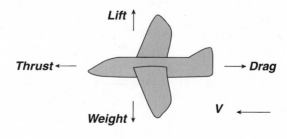

Figure 5.5

Consider the following data:

Thrust $= 3.5 \times 10^5$ lbf   Weight $= 2 \times 10^6$ lbf

$k = 2.5$ m^2 $\rho = 1.2$ kg/m^3

$C_L = 5$ $C_D = 0.5$

Given this data, let's find the wing size [c and s (both in ft)] if the cruising speed is $V = 250$ mph.

First of all, could this be solved symbolically? We'll leave the answer to this question as an exercise and proceed to the numerical Given . . . Find solution.

Let's call this worksheet "Example 5.7." Try to do the following:

<u>Wing Design</u>

By (Your Name)

Enter the known data: $k := 2.5$ m^2 $\rho := 1.2 \dfrac{\text{kg}}{\text{m}^3}$ $V := 250$ mph

Enter the desired performance:

$Thrust := 3.5 \cdot 10^5 \cdot \text{lbf}$ $Drag := Thrust$ $C_D := .5$

$Weight := 2.0 \cdot 10^6 \cdot \text{lbf}$ $Lift := Weight$ $C_L := 5$

Define the wing properties: $A(c, s) := c \cdot s$ $ar(c, s) := \dfrac{s}{c}$

We can now provide initial guesses for the unknowns:

Estimate the wing dimensions: $c := 3.3$ m $s := 100$ m

Finally, we can set up the Given . . . Find system:

Given

$$Lift = \frac{1}{2} \cdot \rho \cdot A(c, s) \cdot V^2 \cdot C_L \qquad Drag = \frac{1}{2} \cdot \rho \cdot \left[A(c, s) \cdot \left(C_D + \frac{C_L^2}{\pi \cdot ar(c, s)} \right) + k \right] \cdot V^2$$

$$\begin{bmatrix} c \\ s \end{bmatrix} := \text{Find}(c, s) \quad \text{Hence:} \quad c = 10.8 \cdot \text{ft} \quad s = 236.2 \cdot \text{ft}$$

Let's check the results:

$$\frac{1}{2} \cdot \rho \cdot A(c, s) \cdot V^2 \cdot C_L = 2 \cdot 10^6 \cdot \text{lbf}$$

$$\frac{1}{2} \cdot \rho \cdot \left[A(c, s) \cdot \left(C_D + \frac{C_L^2}{\pi \cdot ar(c, s)} \right) + k \right] \cdot V^2 = 3.5 \cdot 10^5 \cdot \text{lbf}$$

Mathcad once again does the job.

There are two important new features in this example:

1. We have included in the Given . . . Find loop two *user-defined* functions $A(c,s)$ and $ar(c,s)$.

2. The equations to be solved are *nonlinear* in the unknowns.

Comments and Summary

We've seen that Mathcad's symbolic Solve feature and its symbolic and numeric Given . . . Find and Root features are extremely powerful for solving one or more equations.

In Chapter 6 we'll look at other methods for solving sets of equations when those equations are linear, using concepts from linear algebra.

Where to Find More

For a more comprehensive description of all of the methods reviewed in this chapter, see the Mathcad *User's Guide* included in the Mathcad 7 package. Here you will find information on

1. Why the methods might fail, and hints on improving the likelihood of success.

2. Use of these methods to automatically and repeatedly solve equations.

3. Use of inequalities between the Given and Find statements.

4. Use of Mathcad's Minerr method, which is similar to Find except that it will give a "solution" even if the equations are not fully satisfied.

5. Details on how the various methods work.

In addition, Mathcad 7 has the *Resource Center* (found either under the Help menu or by clicking on its icon), shown in Figure 2.17.

Clicking on the *Treasury Guide to Programming* leads to the *Treasury Guide to Solving,* shown in Figure 5.6. This help section has more information on this chapter's material. Finally, don't overlook Mathcad's Web site at http: //www.mathsoft.com.

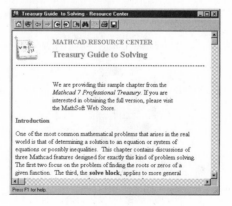

Figure 5.6

Exercises

5.1 A cantilever beam as shown in Figure 5.7 has a load placed at its end. Find the position x (in.) along the beam where the deflection y is 0.01 in. The equation for the beam deflection is

$$y = \frac{F}{EI}\left(\frac{lx^2}{2} - \frac{x^3}{6}\right) \tag{5.13}$$

where $F = 20$ lbf, the length of the beam is $l = 1$ ft, the moment of inertia of the beam cross section is $I = 0.075$ in^4, and Young's Modulus of the beam is $E = 10 \times 10^6$ psi.

5.2 A space vehicle is launched by firing a rocket engine that produces an exhaust with a velocity of $v_{ex} = 2,000$ m/s. The rocket consumes $Q = 3,000$ kg/s of fuel, and the initial mass of the entire system is $M_0 = 100,000$ kg. It can be shown that the equation for the speed of the rocket at any time t is

$$V = v_{ex} \ln\left(\frac{M_0}{M_0 - Qt}\right) - gt \tag{5.14}$$

This equation allows for the fact that as the motion proceeds, the system mass is constantly decreasing as fuel is consumed. Find how long it takes the rocket to reach a speed of 2,000 m/s.

5.3 The column shown in Figure 5.8 is supporting an eccentrically placed load. It will fail (collapse) depending on the magnitude of the load and the load eccentricity (the larger the load and eccentricity, the more likely the column is to fail). Consider a column of rectangular

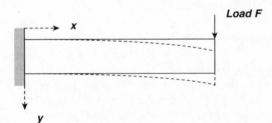

Figure 5.7

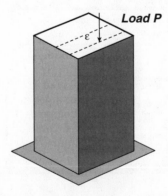

Figure 5.8

cross section $b = 5$ in. and $d = 3$ in., and height $L = 3$ ft. The material properties of the beam are Young's Modulus $E = 10 \times 10^6$ psi and maximum sustainable stress of $\sigma_{max} = 45{,}000$ psi.

There are two design criteria for this problem: First, we need to know the maximum eccentricity ε_{max} (in.) at which a load of $P = 2 \times 10^5$ lbf can be placed. Second, we wish to know what the maximum load P_{max} (lbf) is if the eccentricity is $\varepsilon = 1$ in.

The well-known secant formula can be used:

$$\frac{P}{A} = \frac{\sigma_{max}}{1 + \dfrac{\varepsilon c}{r^2}\sec\left(\dfrac{L}{2r}\sqrt{\dfrac{P}{EA}}\right)} \tag{5.15}$$

Here $I = \dfrac{bd^3}{12}$ (in^4) is the *minimum* moment of inertia of the cross section, $r = \sqrt{\dfrac{I}{A}}$ (in.) is the corresponding radius of gyration [$A = bd$ (in^2) is the cross-sectional area], and $c = \dfrac{d}{2}$ is the distance from the neutral axis to the outermost column fiber. For example, if the load is *not* placed eccentrically ($\varepsilon = 0$ in.), the equation leads to $\dfrac{P}{A} = \sigma_{max}$, as we might expect.

Use the Root and Given . . . Find methods to find ε_{max} (in.) and P_{max} (lbf).

5.4 Compare the specific volume v (m^3/kg) of ammonia at temperature $T = 600$ K and pressure $p = 2 \times 10^6$ Pa obtained using:

(*a*) The ideal gas equation.
(*b*) The van der Waals equation.
Use both the Root and Given . . . Find methods.
The ideal gas equation is

$$p\,v = R\,T \tag{5.16}$$

where $R = 488.2$ joule/kg-K is the gas constant for ammonia.

The van der Waals equation is

$$\left(p + \frac{a}{v^2}\right)(v - b) = R\,T \tag{5.17}$$

The constant a allows for the fact that molecules tend to attract one another, reducing the pressure of the gas. The constant b allows for the fact that the (incompressible) molecules themselves take up some volume, setting a theoretical lower limit on the gas volume. Note that the ideal gas equation assumes $a = 0$ (no intermolecular attraction) and $b = 0$ (the molecules are "point masses," having no inherent volume). These constants are obtained from

$$a = \frac{27 R^2 T_{cr}^{\,2}}{64 p_{cr}} \tag{5.18}$$

and

$$b = \frac{RT_{cr}}{8p_{cr}} \tag{5.19}$$

Here $T_{cr} = 405.5$ K and $p_{cr} = 11.26 \times 10^6$ Pa are the critical temperature and pressure of ammonia.

Note: Don't use the symbol R for the gas constant R or your units won't work!

5.5 The volume of a circular cylinder is $V = 0.025$ m^3, and its total surface area is $A = 1$ m^2. What are the radius r and height h of this cylinder?

The equations for the volume and area are

$$V = \pi r^2 l$$

$$A = 2\pi r(r + l) \tag{5.20}$$

5.6 Find the two points on a circle of radius 5 (centered at the origin) at which a straight line of slope −1 and intercept 2 passes through it.

5.7 Find the value of x at which the function $y(x) = x^3 - 2x + 6$ is equal to its own slope. To do this, define the function $y(x)$; guess a value of x; and then, between the Given and Find, define an equation (using, of course, the Boolean equals) in which the derivative of $y(x)$ equals $y(x)$.

5.8 Solve the following set of equations:

$$
\begin{aligned}
3x_1 + 5x_2 - 7x_3 - 5x_4 &= 24 \\
x_1 - 7x_2 \qquad\quad + x_4 &= -38 \\
x_1 + x_2 + x_3 + x_4 &= 2 \\
5x_1 \qquad\qquad\quad - 7x_4 &= -3
\end{aligned}
\tag{5.21}
$$

5.9 Suppose you have a cylindrical gasoline storage tank of diameter $D = 4$ m and length $L = 7$ m, as shown in Figure 5.9. What will the depth h (m) be if you put 22,000 gal of gasoline in the tank?

Hint: The equation for the volume V of fluid in the tank filled to a depth h can be shown to be

$$V(h) = 2L \int_0^h \sqrt{\left(\frac{D}{2}\right)^2 - \left(x - \frac{D}{2}\right)^2}\, dx \tag{5.22}$$

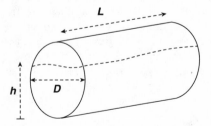

Figure 5.9

5.10 The probability density distribution for the *normal* (or *Gauss*) distribution or population is

$$f(x) = \frac{1}{\sigma\sqrt{2\pi}}e^{-\frac{1}{2}\left(\frac{x-\mu}{\sigma}\right)^2} \qquad (5.23)$$

where μ is the *mean* and σ is the *standard deviation*. As we discussed in Exercise 4.14, the mean is the average of the population, and the standard deviation measures how much spread there is in the population; a distribution which is very spread out will have a large value for σ. To find the percentage of a population x that is between the limits a and b, $f(x)$ must be integrated:

$$F(x) = \int_a^b f(x)dx \qquad (5.24)$$

If the distribution of heights of a population of adult males is normal, with $\mu = 5'9''$ (5.75') and $\sigma = 4''$, find the lower and upper heights (ft) within which 95%, 99%, and 99.5% of the population fits. Also, find the results in terms of $\pm\ \sigma$ values (in other words, how many σ values above and below the mean do you need to include 95%, 99%, and 99.5% of the population). To do this, first define the values of μ and σ. Then provide an initial guess for δ (e.g., try 1 ft), the height to be added to and subtracted from μ to compute the upper and lower limits. Define the function $f(x)$. Finally, you can use a *Given . . . Find* to solve

$$\int_{\mu-\delta}^{\mu+\delta} f(x)dx = 95\cdot\% \qquad (5.25)$$

for the correct value of δ for 95% of the population, and so on. All you need to do is use this value δ to compute $\mu - \delta$ and $\mu + \delta$. The results in terms of $\pm\ \sigma$ values will simply be given by the value of δ/σ. The results you obtain are well known in statistical analysis (look them up in any book on statistics). As we'll see in Chapter 8, equations (5.23) and (5.24) are built into Mathcad as *pnorm* and *dnorm*.

5.11 Figure 5.10 shows the circuit diagram discussed in Chapter 1. It can be shown that the equations describing this circuit are

$$
\begin{aligned}
V_1 - I_1(R_1 + R_2 + R_3) + I_3R_3 + I_2R_2 &= 0 \\
V_2 - I_2(R_2 + R_6) + I_1R_2 - V_3 &= 0 \\
V_3 - I_3(R_3 + R_5) + I_1R_3 + I_4R_5 &= 0 \\
-V_4 - I_4(R_4 + R_5) + I_3R_5 &= 0
\end{aligned}
\qquad (5.26)
$$

If all the voltages are 100 volts, and all the resistors are 10 ohms, find the four loop currents I_1, I_2, I_3, and I_4 (in amps). Suppose you now want all the currents to be 1 amp. Find the voltages V_1, V_2, V_3, and V_4 (in volts) required to achieve this.

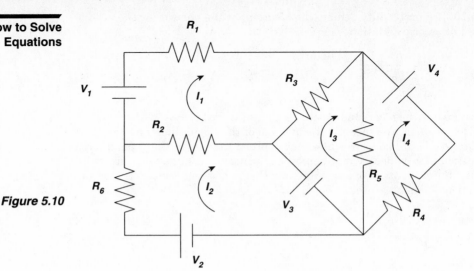

Figure 5.10

Hint: Use literal subscripts throughout. Because the unknowns in each part of the question have the same units (in one case all amps, in the other all volts), you can use units in this problem.

5.12 You want to buy a new car, and you decide to take out a loan of $21,000 repayable over four years. You need to find an interest rate so that your monthly payment will be no more than $500? What interest rate will you have to look for?

Hint: One formula for this is

$$A = P \left[\frac{\frac{i}{12}\left(1 + \frac{i}{12}\right)^n}{\left(1 + \frac{i}{12}\right)^n - 1} \right] \tag{5.27}$$

where A is the monthly payment, P is the loan amount, n is the total number of monthly payments, and i is the interest rate (and note that % can be treated as a "unit" in Mathcad). Mathcad does not have a "unit" for dollars, so just treat dollar amounts as numbers.

5.13 A supersonic airplane will have an *oblique shock* attached to it. Essentially what happens is that the air suddenly changes direction across the shock, and slows down. The pressure, temperature, and density of the air all rise dramatically. The strength of the shock depends on the shape of the front of the airplane; the smaller the angle θ, as shown schematically in Figure 5.11, the smaller the angle of the shock, and the weaker it will be. The idea behind *supersonic streamlining* is that the more "pointed" an airplane is, the weaker the shock and therefore the smaller the pressure rise, making it easier for the airplane to move through the air.

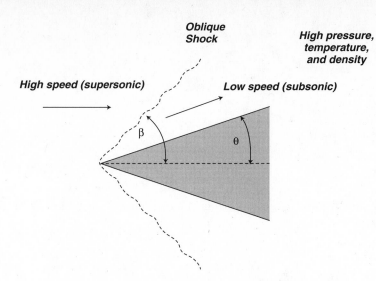

Oblique Shock

High pressure, temperature, and density

High speed (supersonic)

Low speed (subsonic)

β

θ

Figure 5.11

It is known that the equation for the oblique shock angle β is given by

$$\tan(\theta) = 2\cot(\beta)\left[\frac{M^2\sin^2(\beta) - 1}{M^2(k + \cos(2\beta)) + 2}\right] \tag{5.28}$$

where M is the *Mach number* before the shock and $k = 1.4$ is the ratio of specific heats for air. The Mach number for a flow is given by

$$M = \frac{V}{\sqrt{kR_{\text{air}}T}} \tag{5.29}$$

where V is the airplane speed, $R_{\text{air}} = 287$ joule/kg-K is the gas constant for air, and $T = 20°F$ (480 R) is the atmospheric temperature. The pressure after the shock is given by

$$p = p_{\text{atm}}\left[1 + \frac{2k}{k+1}(M^2\sin^2(\beta) - 1)\right] \tag{5.30}$$

where $p_{\text{atm}} = 14.7$ psi is the atmospheric pressure. Find the pressure (psi) after the shock if the speed is 1,500 mph and $\theta = 10°$. To do this, you'll first have to solve Equation (5.28) for β. See what happens to this pressure, and to the shock angle β (deg), as you increase the speed to 1750 mph and 2000 mph. Do these results make sense?

5.14 Refer back to Figure 4.9 of Exercise 4.21, which shows a cantilever beam of length $L = 5$ ft built in at the left end, with two loads $F_1 = -400$ lbf (negative because it is upwards) and $F_2 = 100$ lbf acting on it. The distance $a = 2$ ft, the beam moment of inertia is $I = 0.125$ in^4, and Young's modulus is $E = 30 \times 10^6$ psi. Change the position a of load F_1 so that the end deflection becomes zero. Also, find the position of the load if the end deflection is to be -1 in and 1 in.

Hint: It can be shown that the end deflection, written as a function of a, is

$$y_{\text{end}}(a) = \frac{1}{EI}\left[-(F_1a + F_2L)\frac{L^2}{2} + (F_1 + F_2)\frac{L^3}{6} - F_1\frac{(L-a)^3}{6}\right] \tag{5.31}$$

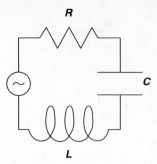

Figure 5.12

5.15 The RMS current I_{RMS} (amps) in the *RLC* circuit shown in Figure 5.12 is given by

$$I_{\text{RMS}}(\omega) = \frac{V_{\text{RMS}}}{\sqrt{R^2 + \left(\omega L - \dfrac{1}{\omega C}\right)^2}} \tag{5.32}$$

where ω is frequency in rad/sec of the applied voltage. The RMS value of the voltage is $V_{\text{RMS}} = 10$ volts, the resistor is $R = 25$ ohm, the inductor is $L = 300$ mH, and the capacitor is $C = 55$ μF.

Find the frequency f(Hz) at which the circuit current will be maximized and give the magnitude of this current. This will be when the circuit is "tuned" or is "at resonance," illustrating the basic idea behind the way a radio works when it tunes in to a particular radio station. The frequency f is obtained from ω by dividing by 2π.

Hint: You should definitely plot this function so that you can see where the peak occurs because, depending on your initial guess, the *Given . . . Find* could find ω to be either zero or infinite, instead of a reasonable value! Note that the derivative of I_{RMS} with respect to ω has units of coulombs. Finally, if you do more analysis in the worksheet, be sure to redefine R as degrees Rankine ($R = \dfrac{5}{9} \cdot K$).

5.16 The temperature distribution in a rod of length $l = 1$ in is given by

$$T(x) = T_0\left(\sin\left(\frac{2\pi x}{l}\right) + \sin\left(\frac{4\pi x}{l}\right)\right) \tag{5.33}$$

where $T_0 = 500$ R. Find the location at which the temperature is highest.

Hint: You should plot this function so that you can see where the peak occurs because, depending on your initial guess, the *Given . . . Find* could find where the rod is coldest or give a value for x outside the range of the rod dimensions (and be careful to use the correct units for the derivative of temperature).

5.17 In the kinetic theory of gases, one of the interesting concepts is the *Maxwell Boltzmann* distribution given by

$$f(v) = 4\pi v^2\left(\frac{mass}{2\pi k_b T}\right)^{\frac{3}{2}} e^{-\left(\frac{mass\, v^2}{2k_b T}\right)} \tag{5.34}$$

This function gives the probability that an individual molecule of a gas at temperature T (K) will have a velocity v. The *mass* is the molecule mass and k_b is Boltzmann's constant. Use Equation (5.34) to find the velocity (m/sec) of molecules of Helium at 25°C (298 K) that has the highest probability of occurring. If you increase the temperature by 200 degrees, what will the new most probable velocity be?

Hint: The mass of a molecule is given by

$$mass = \frac{nM}{N_A} \tag{5.35}$$

where n is the number of atoms in a molecule of the gas (for Helium this will be two), M is the atomic mass of Helium, and N_A is Avogadro's number. These last two terms, as well as Boltzmann's constant, can be obtained from Mathcad's *Resource Center Reference Tables* (except that you should insert the units gm/mole to the definition of M).

5.18 Sometimes engineers need to investigate the phenomenon of "resonance." An example of this is an automobile whose engine will run through a range of speeds (ω values) from 0 to 3,000 rpm. If the natural frequency of vibration of a door panel of this car is 20 Hz, when the engine runs at close to that speed (where 1 rpm = 60 Hz) the door might begin to vibrate in an annoying manner. Find the lower and higher engine speeds (rpm) at which the normalized amplitude of vibration of the door exceeds 2. The normalized amplitude is simply a relative measure of how much the door is vibrating, and is given by

$$A(\omega) = \frac{1}{\sqrt{\left(1 - \left(\frac{\omega}{\Omega}\right)^2\right)^2 + c^2\left(\frac{\omega}{\Omega}\right)^2}} \tag{5.36}$$

where $c = 0.15$ is a coefficient that determines the amount of *damping* (or friction) in the door and Ω is the natural frequency of the door.

Hint: To obtain the two values of ω at which $A(\omega) = 2$ you should use a constraint on ω as necessary to make Mathcad give you the frequency you want (and of course you should plot $A(\omega)$ against ω first).

5.19 A jogging track is designed to be elliptical in shape. The design constraints are that the maximum dimension a must be 100 m, and the total length or perimeter P of the track must be 2,000 ft. Find the minimum dimension b (m) then set b equal to this value. Next, find the angle ϕ (deg) around the track at which a runner will have traveled 100 yards. It can be shown that the equation for the perimeter of an ellipse is

$$P = \int_0^{2\pi} a\sqrt{1 - \left(\frac{a^2 - b^2}{a^2}\right)\sin^2(\phi)}\, d\phi \tag{5.37}$$

where ϕ is the angle measured around the ellipse.

Hint: Define a and a guess value for b. Then just place the integral (the right side of Equation (5.37)), set equal to 2,000 ft in the *Given . . . Find*, and you can ask for the correct value of b. For the second part, set ϕ as the upper limit in the integral, which should now be set equal to 100 yd, and you can then ask Mathcad to give you the correct value for ϕ.

5.20 In Exercise 5.13 we computed the pressure after an oblique shock, which is the kind of shock you get when an airplane has supersonic streamlining. Now consider a non-streamlined supersonic object. This is an object which is blunt or rounded at the front rather than sharp or pointed. In this case there will be a powerful *normal shock* sitting in front of the object, across which the pressure, temperature, and density of the air experience very large increases. The pressure rise leads to very high drag on a blunt object. It is known that the conditions before the shock (state 1) and after the shock (state 2) can be related using the appropriate laws of physics: mass conservation; Newton's second law; the ideal gas equation; and the first law of thermodynamics. These laws take on the following form for this problem:

$$\rho_1 V_1 = \rho_2 V_2$$

$$p_1 + \rho_1 V_1^2 = p_2 + \rho_2 V_2^2$$

$$\frac{p_1}{\rho_1 T_1} = \frac{p_2}{\rho_2 T_2} \tag{5.38}$$

$$c_\mathrm{p} T_1 + \frac{1}{2} V_1^2 = c_\mathrm{p} T_2 + \frac{1}{2} V^2$$

where p_1, ρ_1, T_1, and V_1, are the pressure, density, temperature, and velocity before the shock, p_2, ρ_2, T_2, and V_2, are the pressure, density, temperature and velocity after the shock, and $c_\mathrm{p} = 1000$ joule/kg-K is the specific heat of air. Find the pressure, density, temperature, and velocity after the shock if $p_1 = 100 \times 10^3$ Pa, $\rho_1 = 1.318$ kg/m^3, $T_1 = 267$ K, and $V_2 = 670$ m/sec. Then copy and paste the value you obtain for p_2 and redefine p_2 to be equal to this value multiplied by Pa. Evaluate p_2 and insert units of psi. This last procedure is simply a way to obtain p_2 in psi. Compare this pressure in psi to that of Exercise 5.13 (the pre-shock data here are essentially the SI values of those in Exercise 5.13). Which pressure is higher? Can you think why?

Hint: Do not use units here. If you do, the *Given . . . Find* method will fail in its attempt to give you a vector for the values of p_2, ρ_2, T_2, and V_2 (remember that a vector must have the same units for all its elements). Also, depending on the guess values for p_2, ρ_2, T_2, and V_2, you might get a "solution" setting them equal to the values of p_1, ρ_1, T_1, and V_1. If this happens, choose a different guess value. What should you choose for your four guess values? One approach would be to let all the unknowns equal their corresponding values before the shock, except V_1, which you could set to, for example, a low value. If you wish to use units, see the instructions on page 160.

Vectors, Matrices, and More

In this chapter we'll use Mathcad to explore the topic of linear algebra. This topic is a very large one and cannot be discussed in much detail here. For a comprehensive description, see any good engineering analysis text [for example, *Advanced Engineering Mathematics,* by Kreyszig (New York: Wiley, 1993)]. The topic can be considered to have two aspects: *concepts*, in which, for example, general properties and categories of matrices are studied; and *solution methods*, in which numerical methods for solving problems are developed. Here we will occasionally refer to the former, but mainly focus on using Mathcad to solve engineering problems. Of course, these two aspects are not separate: you should have an understanding of the basic concepts of matrix properties so that, for example, when incorrect results occur, you will understand why this happened, and hopefully what to do to remedy the situation.

In addition to linear algebra, we'll use Mathcad as a tool for performing vector arithmetic such as scalar and vector products, and so on. We'll see that Mathcad is an excellent tool for analyzing problems involving vectors and matrices.

Before describing some basics of linear algebra and vector math and learning how to use Mathcad to solve problems, let's consider an example in which linear algebra is needed.

Example 6.1 Material analysis Companies often need to compute how much material is needed to complete a job. For example, consider the following table, which shows five different apartment construction sites and how many each site has of four different apartment styles:

	Site 1	Site 2	Site 3	Site 4	Site 5
Style A	10	5	2	8	4
Style B	14	7	3	3	2
Style C	12	6	4	5	5
Style D	6	3	2	6	3

From this table we can easily see, for example, that there are 10 + 5 + 2 + 8 + 4 = 29 apartments of Style A, or that the total number of apartments on Site 3 is 2 + 3 + 4 + 2 = 11.

To add complexity, consider the additional information: each style requires different amounts of paint, as shown in the table below:

	Style A	Style B	Style C	Style D
Enamel	2	0	2	3
Semigloss	4	3	1	5
Exterior flat	7	5	6	2
Interior flat	5	2	4	3
White trim	3	1	2	3
Black trim	5	4	3	4

Suppose we wish to arrange paint delivery. We will need to know, for example, the amount of enamel paint for Site 1. To obtain this number we need to multiply each of the numbers in the first row of the paint–style table by the numbers in the first column of the style–site table: the result is that $(10 \times 2 + 14 \times 0 + 12 \times 2 + 6 \times 3) = 62$ cans of enamel paint are needed for Site 1. There are 30 such calculations needed (five sites × six paints). Imagine the work involved if we had 300 sites, 50 styles, and 30 kinds of paint. This becomes a very tedious set of computations!

The efficient way to compute this is to use linear algebra. All of these 30 calculations can be symbolized as

$$C = A \cdot B \tag{6.1}$$

where:

$$A = \begin{bmatrix} 2 & 0 & 2 & 3 \\ 4 & 3 & 1 & 5 \\ 7 & 5 & 6 & 2 \\ 5 & 2 & 4 & 3 \\ 3 & 1 & 2 & 3 \\ 5 & 4 & 3 & 4 \end{bmatrix} \tag{6.2}$$

is the paint–style matrix and

$$B = \begin{bmatrix} 10 & 5 & 2 & 8 & 4 \\ 14 & 7 & 3 & 3 & 2 \\ 12 & 6 & 4 & 5 & 5 \\ 6 & 3 & 2 & 6 & 3 \end{bmatrix} \tag{6.3}$$

is the style–site matrix.

Equation (6.1) is an example of *matrix multiplication*. To perform this matrix multiplication, the numbers in each element of the *rows* of A are "multiplied into" the numbers in each element of the *columns* of B (just as we demonstrated in obtaining the amount of enamel paint for Site 1), yielding the matrix C for the amount of paint needed at each site:

$$C = \begin{bmatrix} 62 & 31 & 18 & 44 & 27 \\ 124 & 62 & 31 & 76 & 42 \\ 224 & 112 & 57 & 113 & 74 \\ 144 & 72 & 38 & 84 & 53 \\ 86 & 43 & 23 & 55 & 33 \\ 166 & 83 & 42 & 91 & 55 \end{bmatrix} \qquad (6.4)$$

It would be quite a task to manually obtain Equation (6.4). Before formally summarizing Mathcad's matrix methods, let's immediately get to work using Mathcad. Start a new worksheet called "Example 6.1" and enter some explanatory text. Then define the two matrices A and B. We'll look at alternative ways to create a matrix in Mathcad later, but for now you recall from Chapter 2 that you can use the accelerator keys **Ctrl + M**. Then, all you need to do is enter the data in the matrix cells (and you can jump from cell to cell using the **Tab** key or by using the mouse or arrow keys). Try to get something like

Material Analysis

By (Your Name)

The Paint-Style and Style-Site matrices are:

$$A := \begin{bmatrix} 2 & 0 & 2 & 3 \\ 4 & 3 & 1 & 5 \\ 7 & 5 & 6 & 2 \\ 5 & 2 & 4 & 3 \\ 3 & 1 & 2 & 3 \\ 5 & 4 & 3 & 4 \end{bmatrix} \quad \text{and} \quad B := \begin{bmatrix} 10 & 5 & 2 & 8 & 4 \\ 14 & 7 & 3 & 3 & 2 \\ 12 & 6 & 4 & 5 & 5 \\ 6 & 3 & 2 & 6 & 3 \end{bmatrix}$$

Once you've defined the two matrices, to get the product you simply use the product key (*). Try it:

Then the Paint-Site matrix is: $C := A \cdot B$ $\quad C = \begin{bmatrix} 62 & 31 & 18 & 44 & 27 \\ 124 & 62 & 31 & 76 & 42 \\ 224 & 112 & 57 & 113 & 74 \\ 144 & 72 & 38 & 84 & 53 \\ 86 & 43 & 23 & 55 & 33 \\ 166 & 83 & 42 & 91 & 55 \end{bmatrix}$

Rewriting the matrix C as a table leads to

	Site 1	Site 2	Site 3	Site 4	Site 5
Enamel	62	31	18	44	27
Semigloss	124	62	31	76	42
Exterior flat	224	112	57	113	74
Interior flat	144	72	38	84	53
White trim	86	43	23	55	33
Black trim	166	83	42	91	55

Notice that the first entry, the amount of enamel paint at Site 1, is 62, as we predicted.

Now that we've seen a quick demonstration, we're ready to summarize the ways that matrices and vectors are created in Mathcad.

6.1

How to Create Matrices and Vectors in Mathcad

We've already introduced how to create matrices and vectors in Mathcad in previous chapters. Let's now review all the details of how to do this.

There are two ways to create matrices or vectors (which are simply matrices with a single column):

1. Use the Insert Matrix dialog box shown in Figure 6.1. To access this box, as in most Windows applications, there are three methods: using the menu item *Insert . . . Matrix . . .*; using the accelerator keys **Ctrl + M**; or using the Matrix or Vector icon on the Vector and Matrix palette (available from the Math palette). Once you have this dialog box, simply select the desired row and column size of the matrix (for example, a vector will have one column).

2. Use Mathcad's *subscript* notation. This is tricky until you get used to it, because there are a couple of errors that beginners frequently make. Let's discuss this approach in detail.

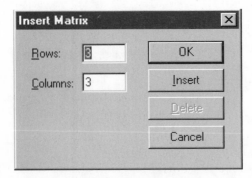

Figure 6.1

Mathcad's Subscript Notations

It's very important to be clear about what kind of subscript you wish to create. There are two different kinds, both of which we've already seen in previous chapters. Nevertheless, let's review in detail what these are (for extra practice, you might want to replicate what follows in a practice worksheet):

1. *Literal* subscripts. As we saw in Chapter 2, these are subscripts you create for your own convenience in naming constants or variables. To create these you must type a *period* (.).

For example, in Mathcad you would type $x.2$ and $y.max$ to get

x_2 y_{max}

2. *Vector* or *Array* subscripts. These are subscripts used for creating or evaluating vector or matrix elements. They are created by typing a *left square bracket* ([).

For example, in Mathcad you would type $x[2$, $y[max$, and $z[i,j$ to get

x_2 y_{max} $z_{i,j}$

This somewhat quirky use of the period and square bracket is a convention unique to Mathcad. It is, at first glance, a bit odd, until you realize that there are only a limited number of typewriter keys, and lots of accelerator-key combinations are already spoken for by Windows. If you wish to use this subscript notation, you just have to memorize these particular keystrokes. The last example, $z[i,j$, is the format you would use for specifying the cell in row i and column j (or, as we will see, for creating a matrix with $i + 1$ rows and $j + 1$ columns) of a matrix z.

Unless you have very young eyes, it's quite difficult (depending on the fonts you use in Mathcad) to visually distinguish between literal and vector subscripts. However, they have completely different meanings: the literal subscript is simply a way to label variables so that, for example, it would be convenient to call the maximum height reached by a projectile y_{max}; the vector subscript indicates which cell of a vector or matrix is being referred to, so x_2 refers to the *third* cell in a vector x.

That last statement was not an error: Mathcad counts elements in a vector or matrix starting with *zero,* unless you specifically override this default and set the built-in variable ORIGIN to, say, one. Let's verify this default on this practice worksheet by asking Mathcad to give us what it understands ORIGIN to be:

The current value of ORIGIN is: ORIGIN = 0

To change this to unity, simply type in Mathcad

ORIGIN := 1   ORIGIN = 1

Perhaps more elegantly (and invisibly as far as the worksheet is concerned), we can change ORIGIN by using the menu item *Math . . . Options.* It is obviously essential to always be aware of the value of ORIGIN for a particular worksheet, because it determines the value at which default counting begins.

There's one final quirk in how Mathcad handles vectors and matrices. To see this, use the Vector or Array subscript to define a value for a variable x_2 (where we have chosen to give the element units):

The value of a quantity is defined as: $x_2 := 5 \cdot \text{psi}$

It turns out that you have not only given the element x_2 the value of 5 psi, but you have *also* specified that the *last* element in a *new* vector x is element x_2 and that the previous elements are, unless previously defined, zero!

Let's create and evaluate some vectors and matrices using Mathcad, to illustrate these ideas. Try typing the following in the practice worksheet (but first edit and delete some of what you typed above so you end up with what is shown below):

Using the default of: ORIGIN = 0

$x_2 := 5 \text{ psi}$ $\alpha := 3$ $v_\alpha := -\pi$ $Cost_{2,3} := 2$

so that $x = \begin{bmatrix} 0 \\ 0 \\ 5 \end{bmatrix} \cdot \text{psi}$ $v = \begin{bmatrix} 0 \\ 0 \\ 0 \\ -1 \end{bmatrix} \cdot \pi$ $Cost = \begin{bmatrix} 0 & 0 & 0 & 0 \\ 0 & 0 & 0 & 0 \\ 0 & 0 & 0 & 2 \end{bmatrix}$

Note that in defining x_2 we created a 3-D vector (where we inserted the psi units in the answer), setting $\alpha = 3$ created a 4-D vector v_α (the output was multiplied by π), and defining $Cost_{2,3}$ created a 3×4 matrix.

Look what happens here if ORIGIN is now changed to unity (try it):

Setting a new ORIGIN value: ORIGIN := 1

$x_2 := 5 \text{ psi}$ $\alpha := 3$ $v_\alpha := -\pi$ $Cost_{2,3} := 2$

so that $x = \begin{bmatrix} 0 \\ 5 \end{bmatrix} \cdot \text{psi}$ $v = \begin{bmatrix} 0 \\ 0 \\ -1 \end{bmatrix} \cdot \pi$ $Cost = \begin{bmatrix} 0 & 0 & 0 \\ 0 & 0 & 2 \end{bmatrix}$

Notice how the size of each vector or matrix was decreased by changing the ORIGIN value to unity. For instance, now that we start counting at unity, the vector x is 2-D.

This demonstrates the effect of the ORIGIN value! You should *always* be aware of the value of ORIGIN in each of your worksheets, and you should not change it in the middle of any worksheet unless you have some very unusual reason for doing so.

This is a good place to review Mathcad's notation for creating and using *range variables*.

Range Variables

We have seen in Chapter 3 that range variables are used, for example, in setting up how graphs are to be plotted. Here we will see that they are useful in working with vectors and matrices.

This is best demonstrated by giving a few examples in Mathcad, which you should replicate as an exercise:

Let's set ORIGIN to unity, and create a vector and matrix using two ranges:

ORIGIN := 1

$$i := 1 .. 4 \qquad v_i := 2 + i \qquad v = \begin{bmatrix} 3 \\ 4 \\ 5 \\ 6 \end{bmatrix}$$

$$j := 1 .. 3 \qquad M_{i,j} := i^2 - j^2 \qquad M = \begin{bmatrix} 0 & -3 & -8 \\ 3 & 0 & -5 \\ 8 & 5 & 0 \\ 15 & 12 & 7 \end{bmatrix}$$

You recall from Chapter 2 that, if a range variable is defined using the $a .. b$ notation, where a is the first value and b is the last value, Mathcad automatically assumes the step size is one. This will normally be desired when using range variables to create vectors or matrices. Also, for this use, a and b should obviously be integers (a matrix element could not be defined as, for example, $v_{1.5}$).

Now that we know various ways to create vectors and matrices, we can summarize the basics of vector and matrix mathematics.

Vector Arithmetic

Let's illustrate vector addition, subtraction, and multiplication by example, using some 3-D vectors. Try doing the following in Mathcad (using the Vector and Matrix palette as described in Chapter 2):

In these examples, we have set the ORIGIN: ORIGIN = 1

Let's create three 3-D vectors: $\quad a := \begin{bmatrix} 1 \\ -2 \\ 3 \end{bmatrix} \quad b := \begin{bmatrix} 2 \\ 2 \\ 1 \end{bmatrix} \quad c := \begin{bmatrix} -1 \\ 2 \\ 1 \end{bmatrix}$

We can add and subtract:

$$a + b = \begin{bmatrix} 3 \\ 0 \\ 4 \end{bmatrix} \qquad b - c = \begin{bmatrix} 3 \\ 0 \\ 0 \end{bmatrix}$$

We can perform scalar and vector products:

$$a \cdot b = 1 \qquad b \times c = \begin{bmatrix} 0 \\ -3 \\ 6 \end{bmatrix} \qquad a \cdot a = 14 \qquad 5 \cdot b = \begin{bmatrix} 10 \\ 10 \\ 5 \end{bmatrix}$$

$$a \times b \cdot c = 24 \qquad a \cdot b \times c = \qquad a \cdot (b \times c) = 24$$

The scalar product is produced using the regular multiply key (*) or by clicking on the Dot Product icon on the Vector and Matrix palette. The vector product is accessed either by using the accelerator keys **Ctrl + 8** or the Cross Product icon.

Note that the next-to-last equation did not compute, because Mathcad evaluates a sequence of products from left to right, and therefore computed the scalar first, which, of course, could not be used in the following vector product. The solution to such a problem is to use parentheses, as shown in the last expression.

Mathcad also performs the *transpose* (accessed through the Vector and Matrix palette or by using the accelerator keys **Ctrl + 1**):

$$a^T = [1 \ -2 \ 3] \qquad a^T \cdot a = 14 \qquad a \cdot a^T = \begin{bmatrix} 1 & -2 & 3 \\ -2 & 4 & -6 \\ 3 & -6 & 9 \end{bmatrix}$$

Notice the radically different results in the last two examples (do you know why?).

Finally, consider the following:

$$a_2 = -2 \qquad |a| = 3.742 \qquad 3 + a = \begin{bmatrix} 4 \\ 1 \\ 6 \end{bmatrix}$$

The first equation shows that, because we set ORIGIN equal to unity, a_2 asks for the *second* element of the 3-D vector **a**.

The last equation demonstrates an unorthodox feature of Mathcad: conventionally, a scalar cannot be added to a vector, but, as a convenience, Mathcad allows this, interpreting it to mean the scalar is added to *all* elements of the vector.

Matrix Arithmetic

Let's demonstrate how Mathcad performs various matrix computations. Try to do the following (once again, we've set ORIGIN to unity):

Next, let's define some matrices:

$$A := \begin{bmatrix} 1 & 0 & 2 \\ 1 & 4 & 0 \end{bmatrix} \qquad B := \begin{bmatrix} 1 & 2 \\ 3 & 1 \end{bmatrix} \qquad C := \begin{bmatrix} 1 & -2 & 1 \\ 2 & 3 & 0 \\ 0 & 2 & 4 \end{bmatrix}$$

Then: $A^T = \begin{bmatrix} 1 & 1 \\ 0 & 4 \\ 2 & 0 \end{bmatrix}$ $|C| = 32$ $A \cdot B =$

$$B \cdot A = \begin{bmatrix} 3 & 8 & 2 \\ 4 & 4 & 6 \end{bmatrix} \qquad C \cdot A^T = \begin{bmatrix} 3 & -7 \\ 2 & 14 \\ 8 & 8 \end{bmatrix} \qquad B \cdot A \cdot C = \begin{bmatrix} 19 & 22 & 11 \\ 12 & 16 & 28 \end{bmatrix}$$

$$A^{-1} = \qquad B^{-1} = \begin{bmatrix} -0.2 & 0.4 \\ 0.6 & -0.2 \end{bmatrix} \qquad C^{-1} = \begin{bmatrix} 0.375 & 0.313 & -0.094 \\ -0.25 & 0.125 & 0.063 \\ 0.125 & -0.063 & 0.219 \end{bmatrix}$$

The inverse is typed using $^\wedge - 1$, just as for scalars. Note that the rules for matrix multiplication are obeyed. For example, the product of A and B cannot be computed, because for matrix multiplication the number of columns in A must equal the number of rows in B. Further, the inverse of A cannot be computed because it is not square, whereas those of B and C can be computed.

Finally, we note some special notation of Mathcad:

$$C_{3,2} = 2 \qquad C^{<2>} = \begin{bmatrix} -2 \\ 3 \\ 2 \end{bmatrix} \qquad 3 - A = \begin{bmatrix} 2 & 3 & 1 \\ 2 & -1 & 3 \end{bmatrix}$$

Here, the first equation produces the element in row 3, column 2, because ORIGIN = 1; the second (where the special superscript is obtained by using the Matrix Column icon in the Vector and Matrix palette, or by using the accelerator keys **Ctrl + 6**) produces the vector equal to column 2; the last equation (which strictly speaking violates the linear algebra convention that a scalar cannot be added to a matrix) shows that Mathcad allows you to add a scalar to each element of a matrix.

Don't get concerned about the plethora of accelerator keys beginning with **Ctrl + . . .** in the last few pages. Most people don't bother to memorize them, unless they are doing a *lot* of linear algebra with Mathcad.

Symbolic Vector and Matrix Math

Most of the operations with vectors and matrices described above can be done symbolically. To review the various techniques to invoke symbolic math (in other words, using the menu system, using icons in the Symbolic Keyword palette, or using accelerator keys), refer back to Chapter 2. Let's do a few examples on a practice worksheet (which you can then close without saving), using the accelerator keys **Ctrl + .** (you remember that this is used instead of the evaluation equals).

Let's create three 3-D vectors: $a := \begin{bmatrix} p \\ q \\ r \end{bmatrix}$ $b := \begin{bmatrix} x \\ y \\ z \end{bmatrix}$

We can add and subtract: $a + b \rightarrow \begin{bmatrix} p + x \\ q + y \\ r + z \end{bmatrix}$ $b - c \rightarrow \begin{bmatrix} x - c \\ y - c \\ z - c \end{bmatrix}$

The magnitude of a vector is: $|a| \rightarrow \sqrt{(|p|)^2 + (|q|)^2 + (|r|)^2}$

We can perform scalar and vector products:

$a \cdot b \rightarrow p \cdot x + q \cdot y + r \cdot z$ $a \times b \rightarrow \begin{bmatrix} q \cdot z - r \cdot y \\ r \cdot x - p \cdot z \\ p \cdot y - q \cdot x \end{bmatrix}$

We haven't shown it here, but you can do symbolic manipulations with matrices too, although the results are often too large and unwieldy to be useful.

Let's now do a few engineering examples using these concepts.

Some Engineering Examples

Example 6.2 Torque   Find the torque produced by the force F acting on the lever shown in Figure 6.2. The data for the problem is that $l = 1$ ft, $F = 100$ lbf, $\theta = 60°$, and $\alpha = 25°$. Let's construct two vectors l and F for the arm and the force, so that the torque will be

$$T = l \times F \tag{6.5}$$

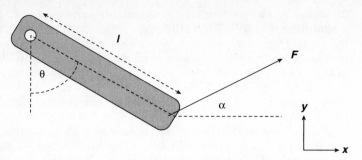

Figure 6.2

Create a new worksheet (and save it as "Example 6.2") and try to do the following:

<u>Torque</u>

By (Your Name)

Input the given data: $l := 1 \cdot ft$ $F := 100 \cdot lbf$ $\theta := 60 \cdot deg$ $\alpha := 25 \cdot deg$

The two vectors will then be: $\mathbf{l} := l \cdot \begin{bmatrix} \sin(\theta) \\ -\cos(\theta) \\ 0 \end{bmatrix}$ $\mathbf{l} = \begin{bmatrix} 0.866 \\ -0.5 \\ 0 \end{bmatrix} \cdot ft$

$$\mathbf{F} := F \cdot \begin{bmatrix} \cos(\alpha) \\ \sin(\alpha) \\ 0 \end{bmatrix} \quad \mathbf{F} = \begin{bmatrix} 90.631 \\ 42.262 \\ 0 \end{bmatrix} \cdot lbf$$

$$\mathbf{T} := \mathbf{l} \times \mathbf{F} \quad \mathbf{T} = \begin{bmatrix} 0 \\ 0 \\ 81.915 \end{bmatrix} \cdot ft \cdot lbf$$

There are some interesting things about this worksheet:

1. We created 3-D vectors even though the problem is only 2-D. This is because you can only perform vector products on 3-D vectors.

2. We created a new *font tag* to distinguish *vectors* (*l* and *F*) from their magnitudes (*l* and *F*). To do this, type *l* and then immediately click on the Format Bar Style window. Select User 1, and then click on the Bold button. What you will have done is create a new style, initially with the default style properties. When you clicked on the Bold button, you modified this new style to be bold. If you wish you can rename this style from User 1 to, say, Vectors. For guidance on this, see the Mathcad *User's Guide* or use Help.

Once you have this new style, when you wish to apply it to a new variable (e.g., *F*) all you need to do is type the variable (e.g., *F*) in the regular way and then just select the User 1 style from the Format Bar Style window. Note that Mathcad recognizes the *same* letter or phrase (in this case *F*) as *different* variables when it has a different style assigned to it.

As you might have expected, the torque is a vector acting purely along the *z* axis (perpendicular to the paper in Figure 6.2).

Example 6.3 Airplane relative motion

An airplane in flight will sometimes appear to an observer on the ground that it's flying askew. That is, it appears not to be flying directly forward, so that its velocity seems not to be parallel to the fuselage axis. This is because an airplane orients itself so that it's flying directly into the air, or, in other words, so that the *airflow* is parallel to the fuselage axis. This is illustrated in Figure 6.3. The velocity of the airplane with respect to the ground is V_p. The velocity of the wind with respect to the ground is V_w. Hence, the velocity of the airplane relative to the air is V_{prelw} and is given by the vector difference between the two other velocities, as shown in the figure.

Suppose a pilot knows she is traveling at 400 mph directly east. A weather report indicates that the prevailing wind is moving at 60 knots, coming directly from the northeast. Find the speed of the wind in mph and the relative velocity of the plane relative to the air.

To solve this problem, we need to look up the value of a *knot* and define it as a new unit. We also need to construct the 2-D vectors V_p and V_w. We can then subtract one from the other to find V_{prelw}, and then use the vector magnitude keystroke (|) to obtain vector magnitudes.

See if you can replicate the following (where we have defined a User 1 style as we did in Example 6.2):

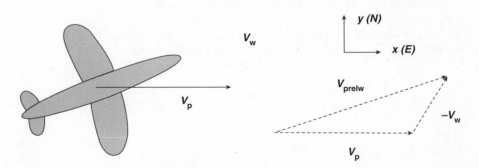

Figure 6.3

Airplane Relative Motion

By (Your Name)

We need to define a new unit: $knot := 1.15 \cdot mph$

Input the given data:

$$V_p := \begin{bmatrix} 400 \\ 0 \end{bmatrix} \cdot mph \qquad V_w := - \begin{bmatrix} \cos(45 \cdot deg) \\ \sin(45 \cdot deg) \end{bmatrix} \cdot 60 \cdot knot$$

The motion can then be analyzed:

$$V_{prelw} := V_p - V_w$$

$$|V_w| = 69 \cdot mph \qquad |V_{prelw}| = 451.4 \cdot mph$$

You can see that the airplane speed in the air (451 mph) is somewhat higher than that relative to the ground (400 mph), because in this example the plane is experiencing a *headwind*.

Example 6.4   DC circuit

In electrical circuit analysis we sometimes have an arrangement of resistors and voltage sources (e.g., batteries) and need to determine the various currents. For example, consider the circuit shown in Figure 6.4.

Three equations for the unknown currents can be obtained by summing up currents at the nodes and by computing voltage drops over resistors:

$$
\begin{aligned}
I_1 - I_2 + I_3 &= 0 \\
20I_1 + 5I_2 \qquad &= 80 \\
5I_2 + 25I_3 &= 45
\end{aligned}
\qquad (6.6)
$$

This gives us three equations for the three unknown currents. The equations can be represented as

$$A \cdot x = b \qquad (6.7)$$

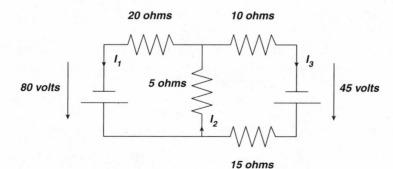

Figure 6.4

where:

$$A = \begin{bmatrix} 1 & -1 & 1 \\ 20 & 5 & 0 \\ 0 & 5 & 25 \end{bmatrix} \qquad b = \begin{bmatrix} 0 \\ 80 \\ 45 \end{bmatrix} \qquad x = \begin{bmatrix} I_1 \\ I_2 \\ I_3 \end{bmatrix} \qquad (6.8)$$

Note that we didn't use I for the unknown current vector, because in linear algebra this is usually used for the *identity* matrix (the matrix equivalent of the scalar number one).

The solution to Equation (6.7) is

$$x = A^{-1} \cdot b \qquad\qquad (6.9)$$

This is an example of inverting and multiplying matrices. Let's have Mathcad do it for us. See if you can do the following (and save the worksheet as "Example 6.4"):

DC Circuit

By (Your Name)

The three equations can be represented as $Ax = b$, where:

$$A := \begin{bmatrix} 1 & -1 & 1 \\ 20 & 5 & 0 \\ 0 & 5 & 25 \end{bmatrix} \qquad b := \begin{bmatrix} 0 \\ 80 \\ 45 \end{bmatrix}$$

Then x will be given by: $\qquad x := A^{-1} \cdot b \qquad x = \begin{bmatrix} 3 \\ 4 \\ 1 \end{bmatrix}$

There's nothing particularly tricky about this example, except that we didn't use units here because if we had, the vectors and matrix would have had inconsistent units: the first row of each would be amps, and the second and third would be volts. You recall that you cannot define a vector or matrix that has differing dimensions for its elements.

This problem can also be solved symbolically. Suppose we replaced the resistor values of 20, 5, and (10 + 15) ohms with R_1, R_2, and R_3, and the voltages of 80 and 45 volts with V_1 and V_2. We end up with the following replacements for Equations (6.6):

$$\begin{aligned} I_1 - I_2 + I_3 &= 0 \\ R_1 I_1 + R_2 I_2 \qquad &= V_1 \\ R_2 I_2 + R_3 I_3 &= V_2 \end{aligned} \qquad (6.10)$$

On a new practice worksheet, try symbolically solving this problem, as shown below (using literal subscripts):

$$A := \begin{bmatrix} 1 & -1 & 1 \\ R_1 & R_2 & 0 \\ 0 & R_2 & R_3 \end{bmatrix} \qquad b := \begin{bmatrix} 0 \\ V_1 \\ V_2 \end{bmatrix}$$

Then x will be given by: $x := A^{-1} \cdot b$

$$x := \begin{bmatrix} \dfrac{(V_1 \cdot R_3 + R_2 \cdot V_1 - R_2 \cdot V_2)}{(R_1 \cdot R_2 + R_1 \cdot R_3 + R_2 \cdot R_3)} \\[3ex] \dfrac{(V_1 \cdot R_3 + R_1 \cdot V_2)}{(R_1 \cdot R_2 + R_1 \cdot R_3 + R_2 \cdot R_3)} \\[3ex] \dfrac{(-R_2 \cdot V_1 + R_2 \cdot V_2 + R_1 \cdot V_2)}{(R_1 \cdot R_2 + R_1 \cdot R_3 + R_2 \cdot R_3)} \end{bmatrix}$$

The last result was obtained by selecting just the expression $A^{-1}b$ and using the accelerator keys **Shift + F9.** As we mentioned earlier, symbolic results are often a bit cumbersome.

Other Ways to Do Linear Algebra

In doing these examples, you can see that performing vector and matrix computations using Mathcad is little more difficult than being able to type in the expressions. Other applications (Maple, Mathematica, and especially MATLAB) can also perform such computations.

Note also that spreadsheets are excellent tools for inverting matrices and solving sets of linear equations. For details on this, see, for example, *Spreadsheet Tools for Engineers,* by Gottried (New York: McGraw-Hill, 1996).

Prior to the advent of these math packages and spreadsheets, engineers solved linear algebra problems using traditional programming methods.

As we saw in Example 6.4, solving matrix problems often involves evaluating the inverse of a matrix. Traditional matrix inversion processes are often rather laborious to do manually or to program. We won't need to use these methods here because, as we've seen, Mathcad can easily invert matrices, but there are several such techniques. The most commonly used ones are

1. The Gauss-Jordan method.
2. The LU factorization method.

The *Gauss-Jordan* method essentially involves performing *row operations* (adding and subtracting multiples of rows of the *A* matrix and an identity matrix, equivalent to adding and subtracting multiples of the original equations) to obtain an inverse. The *LU factorization* method involves breaking up the matrix *A* into a *lower triangular* matrix and *upper triangular* matrix, which enables various solution techniques to be applied. Implementing either of these, or other, methods involves writing code in, for example, BASIC, Fortran, or Pascal.

In addition, several techniques have been developed to solve sets of linear equations like Equation (6.6) without first finding the inverse of *A,* such as

1. Cramer's rule.
2. The Gauss elimination method.
3. The Gauss-Seidel method.

Cramer's rule involves recasting the solutions of equations to be solved in terms of *determinants* of various matrices. The *Gauss elimination* method uses row techniques similar to those employed in the Gauss-Jordan matrix inverting method. This method does not invert matrix *A* but instead simplifies the original equations to a simpler (solvable) form. The *Gauss-Seidel* method involves restructuring the equations so that a guess for each of the unknowns, entered on the right of each equation, leads to new values for the unknowns, which are in turn fed back into the right-hand sides, and so on, until (hopefully) convergence to a solution occurs. This last method is an example of an *iteration* technique.

For details on all of these methods, see any good numerical methods text, such as *Numerical Methods for Engineers,* by Chapra & Canale (New York: McGraw-Hill, 1988).

6.3

Eigenvalues and Eigenvectors

In Chapter 3 we looked at the vibration of an elastic membrane and discussed the idea of *eigenvalues* and *eigenvectors*. In that example, the eigenvectors were the *shapes* with which the membrane could vibrate and the corresponding eigenvalues (which we didn't look at) would be the frequency at which that vibration took place. We didn't go into the details of what it means to call something an eigenvalue or eigenvector, and we will not do so here either, except to say that these are the *appropriate* or *correct* values of something that makes the solution work. In the case of the vibration of the membrane, it can only vibrate at certain specific values of the frequency.

If you wish to learn about this topic, consult any good analysis text, such as *Advanced Engineering Mathematics,* by Kreyszig (New York, Wiley, 1993).

Eigenvalues and eigenvectors occur also in linear algebra. In fact, one common application of matrix mathematics is in solving the vibration of a system of discrete masses connected with springs, as shown in Figure 6.5. This system could be a simple representation of a building, so that each mass represents a floor of the building and each spring represents the structural elements of the building. It turns out that applying Newton's second law of motion to each mass leads to a set of differential

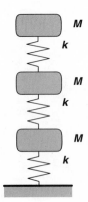

Figure 6.5

equations, the solution of which leads to an eigenvalue matrix problem for the unknown natural frequencies of the system.

Instead of *this* example of an eigenvalue matrix problem, we'll look at a different application. It turns out that the same kind of eigenvalue matrix mathematics arises in the study of stresses in a solid. Let's do an example to illustrate this.

Example 6.5   The stress tensor   Consider a cantilever beam with a load resting on its free end, as shown in Figure 6.6. This load will generate stresses at each point in the beam. The stresses at any point can be represented with the *stress tensor*. For example, in a beam with a given load, we might have the following stresses at some point in the beam:

$$\tau = \begin{bmatrix} \tau_{xx} & \tau_{xy} & \tau_{xz} \\ \tau_{yx} & \tau_{yy} & \tau_{yz} \\ \tau_{zx} & \tau_{zy} & \tau_{zz} \end{bmatrix} = \begin{bmatrix} 1 & 2 & 1 \\ 2 & 6 & 2 \\ 1 & 2 & 6 \end{bmatrix} \times 10^3 \text{ psi} \qquad (6.11)$$

Here the diagonal stresses represent *normal* stresses (in this example, all tensile, because they are positive), and the off-diagonals represent *shear* stresses. Note that, for physical reasons, the stress tensor is always symmetric.

These are not the only stresses at that point. If we had chosen a different orientation of the infinitesimal cube at that point, we would have obtained different stress values. What are the "real" stresses at the point? They all are! For example, consider pulling on a piece of material, and imagining two different infinitesimal squares, as shown in Figure 6.7. The one on the left will have only tension (*normal* stress) on its upper and lower faces, but the one on the right, *with the same applied forces,* will have only *shear* stress on its faces.

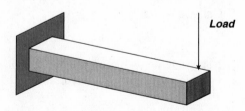

Load

Figure 6.6

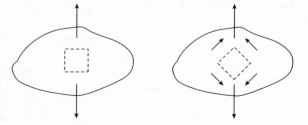

Figure 6.7

We could then ask, given the above stress tensor: Will a particular material, which is known to crack if the tension in it exceeds 7,000 psi, in fact crack? The answer appears to be no (the largest applied tension is 6,000 psi), but in fact it turns out that the above stress tensor means that the point also has the following stresses:

$$\tau = \begin{bmatrix} 0.282 & 0 & 0 \\ 0 & 8.60 & 0 \\ 0 & 0 & 4.12 \end{bmatrix} \times 10^3 \text{ psi} \qquad (6.12)$$

Hence, in fact, the material *does* fail, because we have a tensile stress of 8,600 psi!

Where does this second matrix come from? It is an example of eigenvalue/eigenvector analysis (and, in solid mechanics, the stresses obtained are called the *principal stresses*). These eigenvalues represent pure normal stresses (in this example, all tensile). Eigenvalue analysis of the stress tensor leads to the result that whatever combination of shear and normal stresses is applied at a point, it can *always* be represented as three normal stresses (the shear stresses will be zero). In terms of geometry, what this analysis does is mathematically rotate the axes of the infinitesimal cube on which the stresses act until the stresses become purely normal. Just as these stresses are called the *principal stresses,* the axes are called the *principal axes.*

Mathcad has a built-in eigenvalue/eigenvector capability for doing all this. Let's start a new worksheet called "Example 6.5" and enter the basic data for the problem:

The Stress Tensor

By (Your Name)

The stress tensor is: $\tau := \begin{bmatrix} 1 & 2 & 1 \\ 2 & 6 & 2 \\ 1 & 2 & 6 \end{bmatrix} \cdot 10^3 \cdot \text{psi}$

Note that we've actually created a matrix with dimensions. This is acceptable whenever all cells of a matrix have the same dimensions (as in this case).

To find the eigenvalues for this matrix, we simply need to use Mathcad's *eigenvals* function (and in the worksheet below, τ_{Eigen} is created using the *literal* subscript):

The eigenvalues are: $\tau_{\text{Eigen}} := \text{eigenvals}(\tau)$

$$\tau_{\text{Eigen}} = \begin{bmatrix} 1.308 \cdot 10^6 \\ 3.985 \cdot 10^7 \\ 1.907 \cdot 10^7 \end{bmatrix} \cdot \text{lb} \cdot \text{ft}^{-1} \cdot \text{sec}^{-2}$$

The only remaining thing to do is format the answer so that it looks like the input data. Double-click on the answer and see if you can do the following:

The eigenvalues are: $\tau_{Eigen} := eigenvals(\tau)$

$$\tau_{Eigen} = \begin{bmatrix} 0.282 \\ 8.601 \\ 4.117 \end{bmatrix} \cdot 10^3 \cdot psi$$

In addition to the eigenvalues, we can compute the eigenvectors. Try to do the following (where V_0, V_1, and V_2 have *literal* subscripts and $Eigen_0$, $Eigen_1$, and $Eigen_2$ have Vector or Array subscripts):

The eigenvectors are:

$$V_0 := eigenvec(\tau, \tau_{Eigen_0}) \qquad V_0 = \begin{bmatrix} -0.948 \\ 0.312 \\ 0.057 \end{bmatrix}$$

$$V_1 := eigenvec(\tau, \tau_{Eigen_1}) \qquad V_1 = \begin{bmatrix} -0.272 \\ -0.709 \\ -0.65 \end{bmatrix}$$

$$V_2 := eigenvec(\tau, \tau_{Eigen_2}) \qquad V_2 = \begin{bmatrix} 0.163 \\ 0.632 \\ -0.758 \end{bmatrix}$$

These are orthogonal:

$V_0 \cdot V_1 = 0 \qquad V_0 \cdot V_1 = 0 \qquad V_0 \cdot V_1 = 0$

What we've done here is find the eigenvector corresponding to each eigenvalue. What these represent are the principal axes mentioned earlier, or, in other words, the orientation of the axes on which the principal stresses exist. As a check, we computed their *scalar products* to verify that they do indeed represent a set of perpendicular axes (in fact, it is known that a symmetric matrix will always have *orthogonal* eigenvectors).

Obviously there is a lot more we could do with linear algebra than we have covered here. If you wish more help on this topic, you can use Mathcad's Help menu and its *Resource Center*.

Exercises

Questions 6.1 to 6.5 involve the following matrices:

$$A = \begin{bmatrix} 1 & 3 & -2 \\ 3 & 5 & 4 \\ -2 & 4 & 2 \end{bmatrix} \qquad b = \begin{bmatrix} -1 \\ 13 \\ 8 \end{bmatrix} \qquad c = \begin{bmatrix} 5 \\ 4 \\ 2 \end{bmatrix} \qquad (6.13)$$

6.1 Find $A - A^T$ (explain why you got the result you got), A^{-1}, and the eigenvalues and eigenvectors of A.

6.2 If $Ax = b$, find x. Check your results by computing Ax.

6.3 Compute $b \times c \times c$ and $c \times c \times b$. Explain your results.

6.4 Compute the scalar product of b and c, and also $|b| |c|$. Using these results, find the angle between the two vectors. Hint: Remember the definition of the dot product.

6.5 Find a *unit vector* perpendicular to both b and c. Hint: Remember what happens when you compute $b \times c$.

6.6 An automobile factory has a limit on how many total vehicles it can produce. It also has only so much steel available, and the total electronics and labor budgets are limited. This data is shown in the table below:

	Amount ($\times 10^3$)
Total vehicle capacity (#)	92
Total available steel (tons)	102
Total electronics budget ($)	54,000
Total labor available (hrs)	8,850

The factory can produce several kinds of vehicles: trucks, minivans, sedans, and compacts. Each of these types of vehicles uses differing amounts of material, as shown in the table below.

	Trucks	Minivans	Sedans	Compacts
Each vehicle	1	1	1	1
Amount of steel (tons)	2	1.2	1	0.9
Electronics ($)	500	450	650	550
Labor to make (hrs)	110	100	95	90

Find how many of each type of vehicle the factory should produce so that the factory runs at maximum efficiency (when all materials are used). Hint: Think of the first table as b and the second as A. The unknown will be $x = A^{-1}b$.

6.7 In a soccer league, each team gets a certain number of points for a win, a loss, or a tie, and for each goal scored. You've forgotten what these points are but have the following table of results:

	Wins	Losses	Ties	Goals Scored	Points
Rovers	10	0	5	20	135
Rangers	8	0	7	15	116
Cavaliers	2	2	11	10	63
Chargers	1	5	9	2	39

Find the number of points for each win, loss, and tie and the points for each goal.

Hint: You should use a similar procedure to that used in Exercise 6.6.

6.8 The amount of paint (in gallons) of black, white, and red paint needed in a living room, bedroom, and kitchen of a house is:

	Black	White	Red
Living Room	3	2	1
Bedroom	1	2	0
Kitchen	0	3	4

After painting the rooms, the cost of the paint used in each was:

	Living Room	Bedroom	Kitchen
Cost ($)	$158	$73	$193

Find the cost of a gallon of each color paint.

Hint: You'll need to use a transpose at some point.

6.9 By defining a matrix A to be the coefficients on the left and a vector b to be the coefficients on the right of the following equation, find $x = A^{-1}b$.

$$3x_1 + 5x_2 - 7x_3 - 5x_4 = 24$$

$$x_1 - 7x_2 \qquad + \quad x_4 = -38 \qquad (6.15)$$

$$x_1 + x_2 + \quad x_3 + x_4 = 2$$

$$5x_1 \qquad\qquad - 7x_4 = -3$$

This is the same set of equations that was solved using Mathcad's Given . . . Find in Exercise 5.8.

6.10 Equations (6.15) can be solved by using matrix inversion or by using Given . . . Find. They can also be solved using Cramer's Rule. Although the previous methods are very convenient, use Cramer's Rule to solve the equations. Cramer's Rule states that the unknown x_1 in Equations (6.15) is given by

$$x_1 = \frac{D_1}{D} = \frac{|A_1|}{|A|} \qquad (6.16)$$

where D is the determinant of A (a matrix of the coefficients on the left sides of the equations), and D_1 is the determinant of a matrix obtained from matrix A except the first column of A is replaced with the coefficients on the right of the equations (one way to do this is by editing a copy of A). For x_2, x_3, and x_4, an equation similar to Equation (6.16) can be written. For x_2, for example, instead of D_1, a determinant D_2 is computed, obtained from matrix A_2, which in turn is matrix A with the *second* column replaced with the coefficients on the right of Equation (6.15).

6.11 A prismatic shape is defined by three three-dimensional vectors that represent the three edges of it. The vectors in (x, y, z) space are:

$$a = \begin{bmatrix} 10 \\ 0 \\ 0 \end{bmatrix} \text{ft}, \ b = \begin{bmatrix} 2 \\ 7 \\ 1 \end{bmatrix} \text{ft}, \ c = \begin{bmatrix} 1 \\ 4 \\ 10 \end{bmatrix} \text{ft} \tag{6.17}$$

See if you can sketch this object by hand. Compute the volume (ft^3) of this prism.

Hint: The volume is given by the scalar triple product (look it up in any good mathematics text).

6.12 A force has components 10, 7, and 3 newtons in (x, y, z) space. It is moving with a velocity which has components 2, 3, and –4 m/sec. Find the magnitude of the force (newton), and the angle (deg) it makes with the x axis, the y axis, and the z axis. Find the magnitude of the velocity (m/s). Find the power (watt) required to move the force at this speed. Find the work done (joule) in one minute.

Hint: To find the angle a vector makes with the x axis, compute the dot product of the vector with a unit vector in the x direction and divide by the magnitude of the vector. This will give the cosine of the angle. Also, recall that power is force times velocity and work is force times distance (what kind of product?).

6.13 Consider again the circuit discussed in Exercise 5.11 (shown in Figure 5.10). The equations for the unknown currents are

$$I_1(R_1 + R_2 + R_3) - I_2R_2 \quad\quad - I_3R_3 \quad\quad\quad\quad\quad = V_1$$
$$-I_1R_2 \quad\quad\quad + I_2(R_2 + R_6) \quad\quad\quad\quad\quad\quad\quad = V_2 - V_3$$
$$I_1R_3 \quad\quad\quad\quad\quad\quad - I_3(R_3 + R_5) + I_4R_5 \quad = -V_3 \tag{6.18}$$
$$\quad\quad\quad\quad\quad\quad\quad I_3R_5 \quad\quad - I_4(R_4 + R_5) = V_4$$

The voltages are 100 volt, and all the resistors are 10 ohm. By defining a matrix A to be the coefficients on the left and a vector b to be the coefficients on the right, with x being the unknown currents, find $x = A^{-1}b$. The values obtained for x will be the four loop currents I_1, I_2, I_3, and I_4 (in amps). This same problem was solved using Mathcad's Given . . . Find in Exercise 5.11.

6.14 The crane mechanism shown in Figure 6.8 has a load $F = 1,000$ lbf suspended from it.

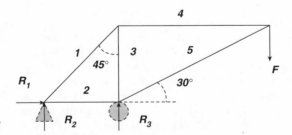

Figure 6.8

We wish to find the loads T_1 through T_5 (tensions or compressions) in the structural members labeled 1 through 5, and the three reaction forces R_1, R_2, and R_3. By summing the horizontal and vertical forces at each joint the following set of equations can be derived (and note that you must type in the unit for degrees when you create this matrix in Mathcad):

$$T_1 \cos(45°) \; + T_2 \qquad\qquad\qquad\qquad + R_1 \qquad\qquad = 0$$

$$T_1 \sin(45°) \qquad\qquad\qquad\qquad\qquad\qquad + R_2 \qquad = 0$$

$$T_1 \cos(45°) \qquad\qquad - T_4 \qquad\qquad\qquad\qquad\qquad = 0$$

$$T_1 \sin(45°) \qquad + T_3 \qquad\qquad\qquad\qquad\qquad = 0 \qquad (6.19)$$

$$T_3 \qquad + T_5 \sin(30°) \qquad\qquad + R_3 = 0$$

$$T_2 \qquad\qquad - T_5 \cos(30°) \qquad\qquad\qquad = 0$$

$$T_4 + T_5 \cos(30°) \qquad\qquad\qquad = 0$$

$$T_5 \sin(30°) \qquad\qquad\qquad = -F$$

By defining a matrix A to be the coefficients on the left and a vector b to be the coefficients on the right of the equations, find $x = A^{-1}b$. The resulting vector x will be the solution to the problem. What does it mean if some of the forces are negative?

6.15 Consider the double glazed window shown in Figure 6.9. It consists of two glass panes each $d = 5$ mm thick separated by a sealed region of width $\delta = 7.5$ mm containing air. The idea is that the trapped air acts as a very good insulator.

Suppose that the room temperature is $T_{room} = 24°C$ (297 K), and the outside temperature is $T_{out} = -5°C$ (268 K). Assume that the convection coefficient for air is approximately $h = 5$ watt/m²-K, the conductivity of the air is $k_{air} = 0.02$ watt/m-K and the conductivity of the glass is $k = 1.5$ watt/m-K. Find how much heat (watt) is leaving the window if its area is $S = 10$ m². One way to do this is to first find, for example, the surface temperature T_1. Then the heat transfer will be given by $Q = Sh(T_{room} - T_1)$. How do we find T_1? We can simultaneously find all the surface temperatures T_1, T_2, T_3, and T_4 by using the concept that the heat transfer is the same at every location. Using this concept leads to

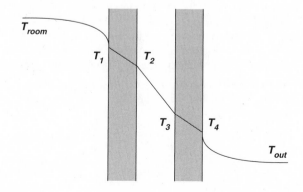

Figure 6.9

$$h(T_{\text{room}} - T_1) = \frac{k}{d}(T_1 - T_2)$$

$$\frac{k}{d}(T_1 - T_2) = \frac{k_{air}}{\delta}(T_2 - T_3)$$

$$\frac{k_{\text{air}}}{\delta}(T_2 - T_3) = \frac{k}{d}(T_3 - T_4)$$

(6.20)

$$\frac{k}{d}(T_3 - T_4) = h(T_4 - T_{\text{out}})$$

Rearrange Equation (6.20) so that you end up with four equations with the four unknowns T_1, T_2, T_3, and T_4 on the left of the equations, and expressions with the known T_{room} and T_{out} on the right (two of the equations will have zero on the right). Then use linear algebra to find the unknown temperatures. Finally, compute the heat transfer (watt). Note that because all of the unknowns have the same units, you can use units in this problem. However, you should express temperatures as degrees Kelvin (if you want your answers in °C, subtract 273 K from your results).

Hint: Be careful in using subscripts here. The best approach is, instead of letting the unknown be a vector x, let it be a column vector whose elements you explicitly set up to be T_1, T_2, T_3, and T_4, using literal subscripts. Remember that Mathcad's default value of ORIGIN is zero, so if you use Vector or Array subscripts there will be an inconsistency: the first element will be T_0 but it should be T_1, according to Figure 6.9, and so on.

6.16 Assume that the double glazed window in Exercise 6.15 is replaced with a single window of thickness d = 1 cm (equivalent to pushing the two panes of glass together to eliminate the air gap). The equations now reduce to

$$h(T_{\text{room}} - T_1) = \frac{k}{d}(T_1 - T_2)$$

(6.21)

$$\frac{k}{d}(T_1 - T_2) = h(T_2 - T_{\text{out}})$$

where now T_2 is the temperature on the outside of the window. Rearrange Equation (6.21) so that you have two equations, with the unknowns T_1 and T_2 on the left of the equations, and expressions with the known T_{room} and T_{out} on the right. Then use matrix algebra to find the unknown temperatures. Finally, compute the heat transfer (watt). If you did Exercise (6.15), compare this heat transfer to that obtained in the previous exercise. Does double glazing significantly reduce the loss of heat through the window? In setting up this problem, review the hint in the previous exercise.

6.17 A mass m_1 = 20 lb is suspended from the ceiling by a spring of stiffness k_1 = 20 lbf/in. Find the natural frequency f (Hz) of this system. The formula for this is

$$f = \frac{1}{2\pi}\sqrt{\frac{k_1}{m_1}} \qquad\qquad (6.22)$$

An additional mass, also of mass $m_2 = 20$ lb, is attached to the first mass using a spring of stiffness $k_2 = 20$ lbf/in, as shown in Figure 6.10.

This system will have two natural frequencies at which the masses will execute purely sinusoidal motion. The low frequency motion will be when the two masses move up and down in phase; the high frequency motion will be when the two masses move up and down exactly out of phase (one is moving up while the other moves down). Find these two natural frequencies. It turns out that the first task is to find the two eigenvalues λ of the following matrix (obtained from studying the equations of motion of the masses):

$$K = \begin{bmatrix} -\dfrac{k_1 + k_2}{m_1} & \dfrac{k_2}{m_1} \\[2mm] \dfrac{k_2}{m_2} & -\dfrac{k_2}{m_2} \end{bmatrix} \qquad\qquad (6.23)$$

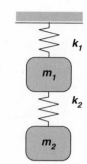

Figure 6.10

Then the natural frequencies will be given by

$$f = \frac{1}{2\pi}\sqrt{-\lambda} \qquad\qquad (6.24)$$

Note that because λ is a vector with two components, you should use Mathcad's vectorize feature when using Equation (6.24) (you can't directly take the square root of a vector). How do the two frequencies compare to the frequency of vibration of the single mass? If you now make the second spring extremely stiff (for example $k_2 = 20,000$ lbf/in), what will the two frequencies of vibration be? Compare this last result to the frequency obtained for a single mass $m = m_1 + m_2$ (modify Equation (6.22) for this). Can you explain the results you get?

6.18 Consider the system shown in Figure 6.11, consisting of three masses and five springs contained between two walls. Each of the masses has mass 20 lb, and each spring has a stiffness of 20 lbf/in. The system has three natural frequencies. Using a similar procedure to Exercise 6.17, find these natural frequencies.

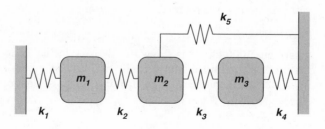

Figure 6.11

It turns out that the matrix obtained from studying the equations of motion for these masses is

$$
K = \begin{bmatrix} \dfrac{-(k_1 + k_2)}{m_1} & \dfrac{k_2}{m_1} & 0 \\[2em] \dfrac{k_2}{m_2} & \dfrac{-(k_2 + k_3 + k_5)}{m_2} & \dfrac{k_3}{m_2} \\[2em] 0 & \dfrac{k_3}{m_3} & \dfrac{-(k_3 + k_4)}{m_3} \end{bmatrix}
\tag{6.25}
$$

What values should be chosen for the spring constants so that this system will reduce to the system shown in Figure 6.10? If you did Exercise 6.17, see if your choice of spring constants does in fact generate the same frequencies as the previous exercise.

6.19 When the stresses in an object are plane stresses, *Mohr's Circle* can be used to find the two principal stresses σ_1 and σ_2. This leads to

$$
\sigma_{1,2} = \frac{1}{2}(\sigma_{xx} + \sigma_{yy}) \pm \sqrt{\frac{1}{4}(\sigma_{xx} - \sigma_{yy})^2 + \tau_{xy}^2}
\tag{6.26}
$$

where σ_{xx} and σ_{yy} are the normal stresses and τ_{xy} is the shear stress. Find the principal stresses using Equation (6.26) if $\sigma_{xx} = 20$ psi, $\sigma_{yy} = 40$ psi, and $\tau_{xy} = 10$ psi. Compare these results with those obtained by applying the eigenvalue method to

$$
\tau = \begin{bmatrix} \sigma_{xx} & \tau_{xx} \\[1em] \tau_{yx} & \sigma_{yy} \end{bmatrix}
\tag{6.27}
$$

where $\tau_{yx} = \tau_{xy}$.

6.20 The plastic lens in a scuba diving mask has been incorrectly installed so that it has a built-in shear stress of 60×10^3 Pa. Normally such a lens can withstand a pressure (a compressive stress) corresponding to 20 m of water before it will crack, but the additional built-in stress will cause this faulty lens to break at a shallower depth. What is the pressure p_{max} (atm) (and note that Mathcad knows the unit "atm") corresponding to $h_{max} = 20$ m, at which a perfect lens will break? To find p_{max} you need to use the hydrostatic equation

$$
p_{max} = \rho g h_{max}
\tag{6.28}
$$

where $\rho = 1000$ kg/m^3 is the water density. At what depth h (within one meter) will the faulty lens actually break? To find the effect of the built-in shear stress, you need to first find the stress tensor at any depth h

$$\tau = \begin{bmatrix} -p & 60 \cdot 10^3 \ \text{Pa} & 0 \\ 60 \cdot 10^3 \ \text{Pa} & -p & 0 \\ 0 & 0 & -p \end{bmatrix}$$ (6.29)

where $p = \rho g h$ is the pressure at any depth h. Then, given a value for h, Mathcad can be used to find the eigenvalues of matrix τ. You recall from Section 6.3 that one of the eigenvalues is the maximum normal stress. In this problem the normal stresses will be pressures (negative stresses). Dividing these eigenvalues by p_{max} will indicate if the maximum pressure is exceeded at the chosen value for h. By starting at $h = 5$ m and increasing its value by one meter at a time, the depth at which the maximum pressure is first exceeded can be obtained (and of course you can set this up as a Given . . . Find problem if you wish).

Solving Ordinary Differential Equations

In this chapter we'll explore Mathcad's capabilities as a differential equation solver. As with the topics of some of the previous chapters, the topic of differential equations is a very large one, so we will not be able to explore it in any detail in this chapter. All we'll do here is provide a quick description of the types of differential equations that commonly occur, and then move on to solving a few example differential equations with Mathcad, so you can see how it's done.

If you haven't worked with differential equations, you may wish to postpone reading this chapter until you have done so, although it *is* fairly self-contained and doesn't expect a great deal of knowledge in the topic.

7.1

Types of Differential Equations

Differential equations arise in many engineering analyses. If you think about it, in engineering we're often looking at the *rate of change* or the *gradient* of something. For example, we might be interested in the velocity or acceleration of an object, or the heat flowing through a body (which is determined by the space derivative, or gradient, of the temperature distribution in the body). In fact, the most common derivatives encountered by engineers are the first and second, although higher-order derivatives do occasionally occur.

There are many different kinds of differential equations, with lots of different properties and features, but the most immediate category for classification is whether an equation is a *partial differential* or an *ordinary differential* equation.

A partial differential equation is one where the *dependent variable* (or unknown) is a function of more than one variable. For example:

$$\frac{\partial^2 T}{\partial x^2} + \frac{\partial^2 T}{\partial y^2} = 0 \tag{7.1}$$

is the well-known *Laplace equation,* in this case representing the steady-state, two-dimensional (2-D) temperature distribution in a body. The temperature T varies in both the x and y directions. Another classic example is the *heat conduction equation* (a form of the more general *diffusion equation*):

$$\alpha\frac{\partial^2 T}{\partial x^2} = \frac{\partial T}{\partial t} \tag{7.2}$$

describing the 1-D (x direction) temperature distribution as a function of time t due to heat diffusion.

Partial differential equations themselves can be broken down into many more categories (for example, what are called *elliptic, parabolic,* and *hyperbolic* equations). We will not look at partial differential equations, because Mathcad 7, in both the Standard and Student editions, does not have a built-in partial differential equation solving capability, so that to use Mathcad to study them would involve developing fairly sophisticated worksheets. It should be noted, however, that Mathcad 7 Professional version has some built-in partial differential equation capabilities.

Ordinary differential equations (ODEs) are equations in which the unknown depends on one variable (usually a space dimension, say x) or time t. There are many such equations that come up in engineering analysis. The simplest are *first order* (ones with only the first derivative present). An example of this is

$$R\frac{dQ}{dt} + \frac{1}{C}Q = V(t) \tag{7.3}$$

Equation (7.3) is the equation for Q, the instantaneous charge in a capacitor C that is in series with a resistor R, due to an applied known voltage V. This equation is *linear* because the dependent variable (including its derivative) appears only to the first power.

To integrate Equation (7.3) we would need an *initial condition*.

How do we solve such an equation? Preferably *analytically,* using any of a large number of techniques that have been developed over the years, such as possibly *separating variables,* using an *integrating factor,* developing a *series solution,* and so on. If you're interested in analytic solutions, refer to any good analysis text, such as *Advanced Engineering Mathematics,* by Kreyszig (New York: Wiley, 1993).

Many times a first-order equation (especially *nonlinear* ones, in which the unknown or its derivative, for instance, is present to some power other than unity or is an argument of a trigonometric function) cannot be analytically solved. For these equations a *numerical* method must be used. Many of these methods can be classified as forms of the well-known *Runge-Kutta (RK)* method. These methods essentially involve representing the first-order derivative as some kind of difference formula. For example, in the first-order Runge-Kutta method (also known as the *Euler method*), the derivative in Equation (7.3) is represented as the change in Q over an increment of time (in other words, it's approximated as the first term of a Taylor series). Applying this to the derivative in Equation (7.3), we get

$$\frac{dQ}{dt} \approx \frac{Q_{i+1} - Q_i}{h} = \frac{V(t)}{R} - \frac{1}{RC}Q_i \Rightarrow Q_{i+1} \approx Q_i + h\left(\frac{V(t_i)}{R} - \frac{1}{RC}Q_i\right) \quad (7.4)$$

In this equation, h is the time step chosen (e.g., 0.01 s), Q_i is the charge at t_i (the ith time step), and Q_{i+1} is the charge at the $(i + 1)$th time step. Hence, given the initial value Q_0, Equation (7.4) can be used to obtain Q_1, then Q_2, and so on.

This is a pretty crude and inaccurate method of numerically solving an ODE of the first order. So-called higher-order Runge-Kutta methods have been developed in which more complicated, but more accurate, numerical representations of the derivative are created. The most commonly used one is the *Fourth-Order Runge-Kutta method* (called the *RK4 Method,* or sometimes, confusingly, simply the Runge-Kutta method).

These numerical procedures are usually programmed in, say, BASIC, Fortran, or C. In recent years, spreadsheets such as Microsoft Excel have also been used for their implementation.

Many texts are available on using the various Runge-Kutta methods (and other numerical methods). For example, see *Numerical Methods for Engineers,* by Chapra and Canale (New York: McGraw-Hill, 1988).

In this chapter we'll see that to solve a first-order ordinary differential equation, whether it's linear or nonlinear, we don't need to dig into these numerical methods (although Mathcad could easily be made to handle them if we used Vector or Array subscripts). The reason for this is that Mathcad has a built-in function for solving such equations.

Let's first see how to use Mathcad to solve a first-order equation.

7.2

Integrating First-Order Equations Using Mathcad

What we'll see is that this simply involves understanding how to use the built-in function *rkfixed(v,x1,x2,n,F)*. It will take a little bit of effort to fully understand this, but you'll be rewarded with the ability to solve many first- or higher-order equations, and even sets of such equations.

Instead of simply listing the steps involved in using Mathcad to solve a first-order equation, let's do so while solving an engineering problem. You should start a new worksheet (call it "Example 7.1"), in which we'll solve the following example.

Example 7.1   Draining of a tank   A storage tank of floor area $A = 1 \text{ m}^2$ contains water to a level $y_0 = 50$ m. It springs a leak. The leak consists of a small hole of area $a = 0.05 \text{ m}^2$ at the bottom of the tank. Plot the height y (m) of the water level for the first 60 seconds.

It can be shown that the equation for this problem is

$$A\frac{dy}{dt} = -a\sqrt{2gy} \tag{7.5}$$

This equation is based on the fact that the rate of decrease of the volume of water in the tank (the left-hand side of the equation) is equal to the rate at which water is leaving through the hole (the velocity of the water is given by the root expression, where g is the acceleration of gravity). This equation can actually be analytically solved, but here we'll pretend otherwise.

The steps required to solve this, or any other first-order ODE, follow:

1. Enter the *given data* and *initial condition*. The initial condition must be entered assuming it's a *vector* with only one element. To do this, you recall, you use the Vector or Array subscript ([). If you're not sure about this, see Chapter 6. Unless otherwise defined, the default value of ORIGIN = 0 is assumed.

As we'll see, it turns out that the solution method generates a matrix containing values of the *independent* variable (in this example t) in the *first* column and corresponding values of the *dependent* variable (in this example y) in the *second* column. You recall that all the elements of a matrix *must* have the same units, or no units. Because of this, you *cannot use units when using this solution method*. It's up to you to set up your equations so that *you've* taken care of the units.

For Example 7.1, then, in Mathcad, do the following:

Draining of a Tank

By (Your Name)

The initial condition and data are: $y_0 := 50 \quad A := 1 \quad a := 0.05 \quad g := 9.81$

Note that we've defined g because we *don't* want Mathcad to use its built-in value, which has units!

2. Define a *differential function* of the dependent and independent variables. This is so-called because it is equal to the differential. What you must do is rearrange the engineering equation, as necessary, so that the differential is on the left and *everything else* is on the right. For example, Equation (7.5) can be rearranged easily. Doing this in Mathcad:

The right-hand side of the equation is: $D(t, y) := -\dfrac{a}{A} \cdot \sqrt{2 \cdot g \cdot y_0}$

The variable y_0 represents the depth (y_1 will eventually be created representing the first derivative of depth).

In this equation we have chosen to call this function D, but we could have used any name we wished. However, using D is a good idea, because it reminds you that the function is equal to the differential. Note that the *independent* variable (here t) *must* be the *first* argument and the *dependent* variable (here y) *must* be the *second* argument.

3. Define an *integration variable* using the built-in Mathcad function rkfixed. In our example we'll call this Z. The built-in function is described by Mathcad's Insert Function window (obtained by clicking on the Insert Function icon, using the menu item *Insert . . . Function*, or typing **Ctrl + F**) as rkfixed($v,x1,x2,n,F$). This function is actually a Runge-Kutta procedure, executed in the background by Mathcad.

The arguments of this function are

a. A vector v, containing the initial condition. In our example we will call this y_0.

b. The beginning and ending values $x1$ and $x2$ of the independent variable. In our example these will be 0 and T (which we'll define to be equal to 60).

c. The number n, indicating the number of points to be computed (the number of points will actually equal $n + 1$). In our example this will be N = 100.

d. The function F, equal to the first derivative. In our example we've called this D.

In Mathcad:

Set up the range: $T := 60$ $N := 100$

The solution vector is then: $Z := \text{rkfixed}(y, 0, T, N, D)$

Note that instead of defining $x1$ we simply inserted the value 0. We could have also inserted the values 60 and 100 (our choice for the number of data points) for $x2$ and n, but we get slightly more flexibility by defining them as T and N, where these terms have been previously defined.

The last expression generates a matrix Z. The first column will always contain the independent variable values (in our example t values); the second column will contain the corresponding dependent variable values (in our example y values); and the third column will contain the corresponding values of the first derivative. This is the solution to the differential equation!

You could ask Mathcad to give you this matrix:

The final solution is: $Z =$

	0	1
0	0	50
1	0.6	49.065
2	1.2	48.138
3	1.8	47.221
4	2.4	46.312
5	3	45.412
6	3.6	44.521
7	4.2	43.639
8	4.8	42.766
9	5.4	41.901
10	6	41.045
11	6.6	40.198
12	7.2	39.36
13	7.8	38.531

As we predicted, the first column contains the times (the independent variable) and the second the water depths (the dependent variable).

It's not in a very useful format is it? This is because, first of all, the matrix is large and is thus displayed in the spreadsheet format. This format can be overridden, of course, so that the normal matrix format is produced, but we'll still have a large, confusing-looking matrix. Instead of this matrix, we need to do a bit of work to *interpret* our results.

4. Format the results. In our example, it will be convenient to define two new vector variables, t and y_{num} (the subscript should be created using the literal subscript). We can then plot the dependent vector against the independent vector. We don't *have* to define these new variables, because we could just plot the second column of Z against the first column, but doing so might be a bit confusing to someone reading your worksheet. Define the time vector t_i to be equal to the first column of Z, namely $Z_{i,0}$ (remember we're counting starting with zero), and the water depth vector to be equal to the second column. In Mathcad:

Define some solution variables: $i := 0 .. N$ $t_i := Z_{i,0}$ $y_{num_i} := Z_{i,1}$

Notice that we needed to define a new range i in order to define the vectors, and also that the graph was resized.

The problem of the leaking tank has been *numerically* solved. The solution makes sense: the level falls rapidly at first, and then slows down as it empties because the exit velocity will have decreased.

Before doing another example, let's compare this result to the exact analytic solution. As we pointed out, Equation (7.5) *can* be solved (by using the *separation of variables* technique), so, strictly speaking, we didn't have to solve it numerically. We did it this way so that you could see how the method is used. The analytic solution to Example 7.1 is

$$y_{exact}(t) = \left(\sqrt{y_0} - \frac{a}{A} \sqrt{\frac{g}{2}} t \right)^2 \tag{7.6}$$

(Can you derive it? Try using Mathcad's *symbolic integration* after you've separated variables!)

Let's plot this with the numerical solution. To do so we need to create a vector corresponding to the exact solution. The simplest way to do this is by using the time vector as the argument of the solution given in Equation (7.6). Be careful with your subscripts! In the graph below the *exact* subscript is literal [using the period (.)] and the i subscript is a Vector or Array subscript [using the left square bracket ([)].

We can then modify the graph by adding this new variable:

The analytic solution is:
$$y_{exact}(t) := \left(\sqrt{y_0} - \frac{a}{A} \cdot \sqrt{\frac{g}{2}} \cdot t \right)^2$$

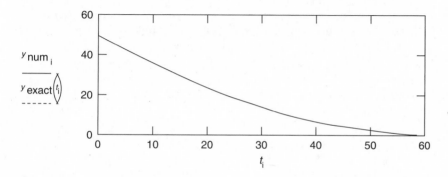

As you can see, for *this* particular problem, the numerical solution is essentially indistinguishable from the exact. In fact, we can create a new vector evaluating the error at each point and use the max Mathcad function (look it up in Mathcad's Help if you're not sure about it) to find the maximum error:

The error is: $\quad E_i := \left| \dfrac{y_{exact}(t_i) - y_{num_i}}{y_{exact}(t_i)} \right|$

The maximum error is: $\quad max(E) = 0.0011 \cdot \%$

It turns out that this extremely low maximum error occurs at the last time step. The solution is extremely accurate because this particular problem happens to have a very smooth and monotonic behavior, which will of course not be true in general.

There are a couple of points we can make about the function rkfixed($v, x1, x2, n, F$):

1. You cannot use units when solving a differential equation, because in solving it, Mathcad needs to generate a matrix containing both independent and dependent variables. As we've mentioned on several occasions, a matrix cannot have elements with differing units.

2. The solution method, because it *is* numeric, doesn't always work. Whether a solution can be obtained depends not only on the equation being solved, but also on the number of steps chosen and the beginning and ending values of the independent variable. If a solution cannot be obtained, increasing the number of steps, in particular, will make a solution more likely.

Let's do another example.

Example 7.2   Lag in a control system   In a control system the response can often be described by

$$\frac{dy}{dt} = \frac{Af(t)}{\tau} - \frac{y}{\tau} \tag{7.7}$$

In Equation (7.7) y is the *response* of the system to the input function $f(t)$, A is the *gain,* and τ is the system *time constant*. We'd like to find the maximum amplitude of the response of the system to the input function shown in Figure 7.1. To find the maximum amplitude of y we need to

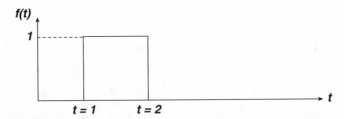

Figure 7.1

first solve Equation (7.7). However, there's one small problem: how do we mathematically define the *discontinuous* function $f(t)$? It turns out to be pretty easy because Mathcad has built into it the *Heaviside step function* $\Phi(x)$. This function is defined such that it has the value *zero* when its argument x is less than or equal to zero and is *unity* otherwise. This is a circuitous way of saying that it is a *unit step function,* where the step occurs at $x = 0$. If you think about it, we can use this function to create the function $f(t)$.

Let's start a new worksheet called "Example 7.2" to solve this problem. Try to do the following (where the step functions are created using the usual procedure for Greek symbols [e.g., F (not f) followed immediately by **Ctrl + G**)]:

Lag in a Control System

By (Your Name)

The constants for the control system are: $A := 2$ $\tau := 0.5$

The input function is: $f(t) := \Phi(t - 1) - \Phi(t - 2)$

The function we've defined may not make sense to you at first. The first term on the right jumps from zero to one when t reaches one; the second term jumps from zero to *minus* one when t reaches two. Hence, when they're combined, the function $f(t)$ is generated (after $t = 2$ the two step functions cancel one another).

We can then follow the procedure rkfixed($v,x1,x2,n,F$) outlined above. This time let's use the name *Solution* rather than Z for the solution matrix. Everything else is pretty much done as in Example 7.1, except that we plot the input function with the response:

The derivative function is: $D(t, y) := \dfrac{A \cdot f(t)}{\tau} - \dfrac{y_0}{\tau}$

The initial value and number of data points are: $y_0 := 0$ $n := 500$

The solution vector is: *Solution* := rkfixed(y, 0, 5, n, D)

We can now construct solution vectors:

$i := 0 .. n$ $t_i := Solution_{i,0}$ $y_{num_i} := Solution_{i,1}$

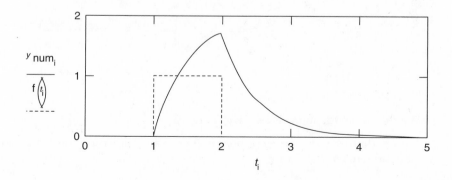

The maximum response is: $y_{max} = 1.725$

The system started to respond to the first step and then died down to zero after the input returned to zero.

Example 7.2, it turns out, can be solved analytically but would involve a bit of work: it would consist of two solutions, one from $t = 1$ to 2 and another for $t > 2$, and they would have to be matched together at $t = 1$.

Once again, we see that performing a relatively sophisticated math operation in Mathcad is not much more difficult than knowing what to type!

There is one thing different about this procedure compared to most other operations in Mathcad: the rkfixed function, and the appearance of a solution matrix, would probably be confusing to someone not familiar with Mathcad who's reading such a worksheet. If you're preparing a worksheet as, say, part of a report, you might want to move these parts of the worksheet past the right margin and replace them with some explanatory text. Then you would just print to the right margin (to do this use menu item *File . . . Page Setup* and in the Page Setup window check the Print single page width check box).

For example, the Example 7.2 worksheet can be made to look something like

Lag in a Control System

By (Your Name)

The constants for the control system are: $A := 2$ $\tau := 0.5$

The input function is: $f(t) := \Phi(t-1) - \Phi(t-2)$

The initial value and number of data points are: $y_0 := 0$ $n := 500$

The solution to the control system problem, using Mathcad's built-in numerical ordinary differential equation solver, is:

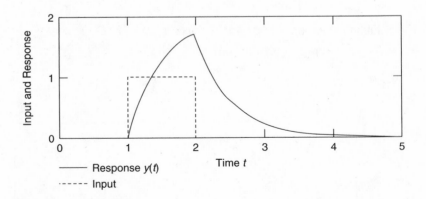

The maximum response is: $y_{max} = 1.725$

Note that we did some work here in formatting the graph (see Chapter 3 for help on this).

Exercises

7.1 Consider a resistor-inductor (RL) circuit. The resistance is $R = 10$ ohm and the inductance is $L = 5$ henry. The voltage applied to it, shown in Figure 7.2, is given by $V(t) = V_0 \sin(\pi t)$, where $V_0 = 100$ volt for 1 second, after which it is zero. Find the current in the circuit as a function of time. The equation for this is

$$L\frac{dI}{dt} + RI = V(t) \qquad (7.8)$$

Hint: Use a product of a sine wave and a Heaviside step function to create $V(t)$.

7.2 A robot cat is designed to chase a mouse, keeping away from the mouse a constant distance of $a = 13$ ft. The cat runs directly toward the mouse at each instant. The initial positions of the cat and mouse are as shown in Figure 7.3. If the mouse moves to the right along the x axis, find and plot the path $y(x)$ that the mouse takes. The equation for this is

$$\frac{dy}{dx} = -\frac{y}{\sqrt{a^2 - y^2}} \qquad (7.9)$$

7.3 The blood sugar level S in a patient is given by

$$\frac{dS}{dt} = I(t) - kS \qquad (7.10)$$

where $I(t)$ is the sugar intake over 24 hours and $k = 0.2$ is a measure of the patient's natural sugar secretion. If the sugar intake over 24 hours

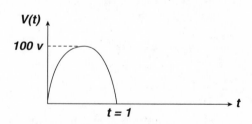

Figure 7.2

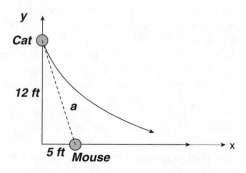

Figure 7.3

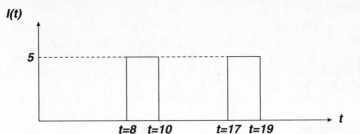

Figure 7.4

is given by Figure 7.4, plot the sugar level over the same period. The initial sugar level is 5 units.

7.3

Integrating a Set of First-Order Equations

Now that we've learned how to solve a single equation, let's do an example involving *coupled* ordinary differential equations, meaning equations that cannot be separated into separate equations, so they must be solved *simultaneously*.

Example 7.3   Predator and prey populations   Consider an island populated only with wolves and deer. The wolves live off the deer, and the deer off the natural vegetation, which is abundant. There are 100 deer and 5 wolves, but we wish to predict the populations of both species 50 years into the future, and in particular what the minimum and maximum populations of each species will be.

The interaction of the two species can be modeled using the Lotka-Volterra equations:

$$\frac{dD}{dt} = g_D D - d_D DW$$

$$\frac{dW}{dt} = g_W WD - d_W W$$

(7.11)

In these equations D and W are the populations of deer and wolves at any time t. The constants $g_D = 0.2$ and $g_W = 0.005$ are the natural growth rates of the species, and the constants $d_D = 0.015$ and $d_W = 0.15$ are the natural death rates of the species. What does all this mean? The first equation states that the growth rate of the deer population increases as the population itself gets large. For instance, 10 deer will have more births than natural deaths at the rate of 2 offspring per year, but 20 would have a rate of 4 per year. The equation also indicates that the deer population will tend to decrease (the growth rate will be made negative) as both the deer and wolf populations become large, because the more wolves and deer that are present, the larger the number of deer kills. A similar logic explains the equation for the wolf population.

How do we solve such a set of coupled equations? It turns out that all the traditional programming techniques we discussed (e.g., the Euler method or other Runge-Kutta methods) can be employed. However, it's much easier to still use Mathcad's rkfixed($v,x1,x2,n,F$) method. Let's learn how to solve sets of equations by solving Example 7.3 (you can start a new worksheet with this name and replicate what follows):

1. Enter the given data and initial conditions. The initial conditions must be entered assuming they are a *vector* with the elements being the initial conditions (in this example, there are two). Unless otherwise defined, the default value of ORIGIN = 0 is assumed. You must be *very* careful with your subscripts: in this first part, all the subscripts are *literal* [i.e., created using the period (.)]. For example, in Mathcad:

<u>Predator and Prey Populations</u>

By (Your Name)

The growth and death rates are:

$g_D := 0.2 \qquad d_D := 0.015 \qquad g_W := 0.005 \qquad d_W := 0.15$

The initial populations are: $D_{init} := 100 \qquad W_{init} := 5$

We can then define the vector of initial conditions: $\quad y := \begin{bmatrix} D_{init} \\ W_{init} \end{bmatrix}$

2. Define a *differential vector function* equal to the differentials. In this example, these are the two right-hand sides of Equations (7.11). Note that the initial condition vector y determines the order of everything else that follows: in this example *deer* quantities come first and *wolf* quantities second. This means that in translating Equation (7.11) into this vector form, y_0 represents the deer and y_1 represents the wolves, where both subscripts are *vector* [created with the left square bracket ([)]. Doing this in Mathcad:

The vector representing the derivatives is:

$$M(t, y) := \begin{bmatrix} g_D \cdot y_0 - d_D \cdot y_0 \cdot y_1 \\ g_W \cdot y_1 \cdot y_0 - d_W \cdot y_1 \end{bmatrix}$$

In this equation we have chosen to call this function M, but we could have used any name we wished. Note that as before the independent variable (here t) must be the first argument and the dependent variable (here y) must be the second argument.

3. Define an *integration variable* to be equal to the Mathcad rkfixed function. In our example we'll call this *Solution*. Rather than enter numbers as arguments, we've defined some new variables:

The time period and number of data points are: $\quad T := 50 \qquad N := 500$

The solution matrix is then: $\qquad Solution := \text{rkfixed}(y, 0, T, N, M)$

The last expression generates the matrix *Solution*. The first column will contain the independent variable values (t values); the second column will contain the corresponding first dependent variable values

(*D* values); the third column will contain the corresponding values of the second dependent variable values (*W* values).

In Example 7.3 we only have *two* first-order equations for *two* unknowns. In general, if we have *n* first-order equations in *n* unknowns, the solution matrix will contain in each of its columns the independent variable, then the first, second, third, and so on, dependent variables. The number of rows will be determined by the number of data points chosen.

4. Format the results. The matrix contains the solution to the differential equations. As in the previous examples, this matrix is a bit unwieldy, so we can define new variables (using the vector subscript) and plot the results. In Mathcad:

The results are:

$$i := 0 \ .. \ N \qquad t_i := Solution_{i,0} \qquad D_i := Solution_{i,1} \qquad W_i := Solution_{i,2}$$

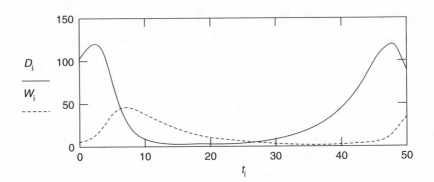

Once we have the solution, we can ask Mathcad to find the minimum and maximum values of the deer and wolf vectors:

$$\min(D) = 2 \qquad \max(D) = 120 \qquad \min(W) = 2 \qquad \max(W) = 46$$

These results are fascinating: initially the deer population increases because there are so few wolves, but this large amount of deer quickly allows the wolf population to explode, until after 10 years there are actually more wolves than deer. This in turn causes an imbalance, and wolves die of starvation, allowing the deer population to recover after about 40 years. The cycle then repeats itself over about a 50-year cycle. Note that the cycle is quite precarious, because at various times, each population falls as low as two!

Once you have the worksheet, Mathcad's live nature allows you to perform all kinds of what-if's. For example, what happens if there are *no* wolves? If you change W_{init} to zero, you'll see that the deer population explodes. On the other hand, if there are wolves but no deer, the wolf population vanishes. Finally, see what happens if you start with 30 deer and 13 wolves. You should get something like

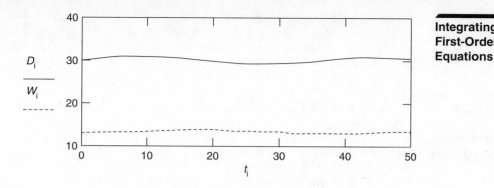

$$\min(D) = 29 \qquad \max(D) = 31 \qquad \min(W) = 13 \qquad \max(W) = 14$$

This indicates that these numbers constitute the natural stable populations on the island.

Exercises

7.4 Solve the set of equations shown below:

$$10\frac{dx}{dt} = y$$

$$10\frac{dy}{dt} = -|y|y - 100x \tag{7.12}$$

The initial conditions are $x(0) = 2$, $y(0) = 0$. Find the values of y and x at $t = 20$.

7.5 A viscous fluid coupling connects an automobile engine to the car wheels, as shown schematically in Figure 7.5. What this essentially does is provide some damping (or slip) between the engine and wheels, so that sudden changes in the speed of the wheels are not transmitted to the engine, and vice versa.

The vehicle is moving such that the rotation speed of the wheels is $\omega_w = 290$. The speed of the coupling is $\omega = 300$, and the power being provided by the engine is $P = 100$. The power reaching the wheels is $P_w = 90$. If the brakes are now applied, plot the speeds of the coupling and the wheels for time $t = 0$ to 30. The equations for this are

$$I\frac{d\omega}{dt} = \frac{P}{\omega} - k(\omega - \omega_w)$$

$$I_w\frac{d\omega_w}{dt} = k(\omega - \omega_w) - 2\omega_w - \frac{P_w}{\omega_w} \tag{7.13}$$

Fluid Coupling

Figure 7.5

Here $k = 1.5$ is a factor allowing for the viscous coupling effects, and $I = 10$ and $I_w = 2$ are the coupling and wheel inertias. Note that the question has been set up so that no units are used, to make solution of the problem easier.

7.4

Integrating a Higher-Order Equation Using Mathcad

In engineering we frequently encounter second-order derivatives (and occasionally higher-order ones). For example, in mechanics the acceleration of a body is given by the second time derivative of position, and the net heat flux through a point in a body is determined by the second spatial derivative of the temperature.

Now that we know how to solve a set of first-order equations, we can solve a single ODE of any order! To illustrate this, let's look at an example of a second-order ODE.

Example 7.4 Forced damped vibration Consider the system shown in Figure 7.6. It shows a *mass M* = 1 kg, which is connected to a *spring* with a spring constant $k = 0.75$ N/m, and a *dashpot* (a friction device) with a friction coefficient $c = 0.1$ N-s/m. It will move with motion $x(t)$ in response to the applied force $F(t)$ shown in the figure. The mass is initially at rest at its equilibrium location.

The equation for this is

$$M\frac{d^2 x}{dt^2} + c\frac{dx}{dt} + kx = F(t) \tag{7.14}$$

This is a second-order, linear ordinary differential equation for x. To integrate Equation (7.14) we need two initial conditions (in general, the number of initial conditions needed equals the order of the equation).

How do we solve a second- (or higher) order equation? As for the first-order equations, an analytic solution should first be attempted. Once again, many approaches have been developed, depending on the equation properties, such as whether it's linear or nonlinear, or homogeneous, and so forth. Some classic approaches involve using variation of parameters, the method of undetermined coefficients, the power series method, as well as transforms such as Laplace transforms.

If such an equation cannot be solved analytically, a numerical approach must be used. Some advanced ad hoc techniques have been developed, but the most common approach is to break the equation down

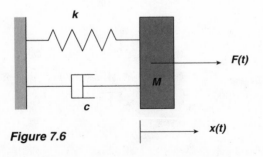

Figure 7.6

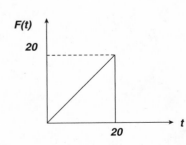

into a set of first-order equations. For example, Equation (7.14) could be represented as

$$\frac{dx}{dt} = v$$

$$M\frac{dy}{dt} + cv + kx = F(t)$$

$$(7.15)$$

where v is the velocity. Equations (7.15) can then be arranged in the following way:

$$\frac{dx}{dt} = v$$

$$\frac{dv}{dt} = \frac{1}{M}[F(t) - cv - kx]$$

$$(7.16)$$

These equations represent two coupled equations for the two new dependent variables (unknowns), position x and velocity v. Note that each equation is a first-order equation. Techniques based on a Runge-Kutta method, either involving writing code or using a spreadsheet, could now be used on this set.

On the other hand, we can solve this set of equations using Mathcad, just as we did in Section 7.2. Let's do this by starting a new worksheet (call it "Example 7.5"). First do the following:

Forced Damped Vibration

By (Your Name)

The data for the problem are: $M := 1$ $c := .1$ $k := .75$

The steps involved in solving a second-order (or higher) equation are:

1. Restructure the second-order equation into two first-order equations. In this example Equation (7.14) leads to Equations (7.16). For a third-order equation we would end up with three first-order equations, and so on.

2. Enter the initial condition vector and other given data. In this example we have two initial conditions and the force function. Once again, be careful to distinguish between literal and vector subscripts:

Forced Damped Vibration

By (Your Name)

The data for the problem is: $M := 1$ $c := .1$ $k := .75$

The initial conditions are: $x_{init} := 0$ $y_{init} := 0$ $y := \begin{bmatrix} x_{init} \\ v_{init} \end{bmatrix}$

The force function is: $F(t) := \Phi(20 - t) \cdot t$

The expression for $F(t)$ may be a bit confusing: the Heaviside step function will be unity until $t > 20$, when it drops to zero.

3. Set up the differential vector function:

The derivative vector is then:
$$D(t, y) := \begin{bmatrix} y_1 \\ \dfrac{1}{M} \cdot (F(t) - c \cdot y_1 - k \cdot y_0) \end{bmatrix}$$

In this example, this vector will have two rows, but if we had three first-order equations, it would have three rows, and so on.

There is an important point here: the initial condition vector and the differential vector must have the same ordering of elements. In this example, the first element refers to position x and the second to the velocity v. The notation here is that y_0 represents position and (perhaps confusingly) y_1 represents velocity. This is because we're building a solution vector Z whose elements are y. Note that the expression for $D(t,y)$ comes directly from Equations (7.16).

4. Set up the integration variable using rkfixed. The solution vector in this example contains in its columns data on t, x, and v. If we were solving a third-order ODE, the three first-order equations would eventually lead to a solution matrix in which the first column contained the independent variable, the second the dependent variable, the third the first derivative of the dependent variable, and the fourth the second derivative. This pattern would be repeated for a fourth-order ODE (the fourth column would contain data on the third derivative).

In Mathcad, continuing Example 7.5:

The time period and number of steps are: $T := 40$ $N := 500$

The solution matrix is then: $Z := \text{rkfixed}(y, 0, T, N, D)$

5. Finally, we can extract a formatted solution:

The results are: $i := 0 .. N$ $t_i := Z_{i,0}$ $x_i := Z_{i,1}$

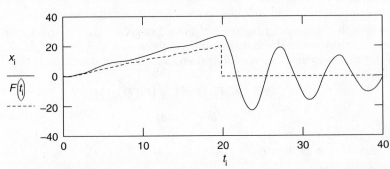

The results are largely as expected. The applied force merely pulls the mass out. When the force drops to zero, the system then undergoes damped oscillations.

As we mentioned, the columns of Z contain, in order, time, position, and velocity data. Hence, if we wish, we can plot the velocity data:

The velocity is: $\qquad v_i := Z_{i,2}$

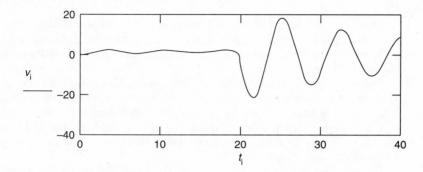

The velocity becomes large *after* the force has pulled the mass out to its maximum amplitude and released it.

Once you have this worksheet, you can do all kinds of what-if's. For instance, try changing the force function:

The force function is now: $\qquad F(t) := 1 - e^{-0.2 \cdot t}$

The results will then update:

The solution is:

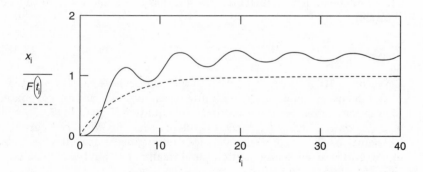

You could then see what happens if you change, say, the mass, the spring, and so forth.

This method, of breaking a second-order differential equation into two first-order equations, can be generalized to an *ODE* of any order. Let's practice what we've learned so far by doing another second-order problem.

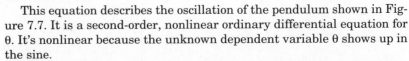

Example 7.5   Large amplitude pendulum   Consider the

following equation:

$$\frac{d^2\theta}{dt^2} = -\frac{g}{l}\sin(\theta) \tag{7.17}$$

This equation describes the oscillation of the pendulum shown in Figure 7.7. It is a second-order, nonlinear ordinary differential equation for θ. It's nonlinear because the unknown dependent variable θ shows up in the sine.

Once again, two initial conditions are needed to obtain a solution. With this example we can see a common-sense reason why two initial conditions are needed: once it's moving, the pendulum will always execute an approximately sinusoidal motion, but it could be started by either providing it an initial displacement or giving it an initial velocity, or a combination of both.

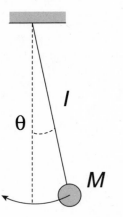

Figure 7.7

Let's assume the pendulum is started from rest and that it has an initial displacement of $\theta_{in} = 45°$. When the pendulum is released, it will oscillate. We'd like to examine this oscillation for the first few cycles.

Even this simple-looking equation is tricky to solve analytically (can you do it?). One way to get a solution is to assume the maximum amplitude (in this case θ_{in}) is small (but how small is small?). With this approximation, the term $\sin(\theta)$ can be approximated as θ, so that the equation becomes linear:

$$\frac{d^2\theta}{dt^2} \approx -\frac{g}{l}\theta \tag{7.18}$$

This makes a solution much easier. It turns out that using the method of undetermined coefficients, the solution to Equation (7.18) can be obtained:

$$\theta_{lin}(t) = \theta_0 \cos\left(\sqrt{\frac{g}{l}}\,t\right) \tag{7.19}$$

Equation (7.19) is an *exact* solution to the *approximate* Equation (7.18).

On the other hand, because all numerical methods are approximate, the rkfixed method we'll use on the *exact* equation [Equation (7.17)] will be *approximate* (albeit to a good degree of accuracy). We'll compare the two solutions. This represents a choice that engineers are often forced to make: either to solve an equation numerically or to analytically solve a simplified approximation of the original equation.

The first step in the numerical method is to break Equation (7.17) into two first-order equations:

$$\frac{d\theta}{dt} = \omega$$

$$\frac{d\omega}{dt} = -\frac{g}{l}\sin(\theta) \tag{7.20}$$

Here ω is the derivative of θ with respect to time, our second unknown.

In Mathcad, let's start a new worksheet (call it "Example 7.5") and enter the given data:

<u>Large Amplitude Pendulum</u>

By (Your Name)

The data is: $g := 32.2$ $l := 2$

Remember that we have to explicitly define g so that Mathcad doesn't use its built-in value, which has units. We can then define the initial condition and differential function vectors.

The initial conditions are: $\theta_{init} := 45 \cdot deg$ $\omega_{init} := 0$ $y := \begin{bmatrix} \theta_{init} \\ \omega_{init} \end{bmatrix}$

The differential function is: $D(t, y) := \begin{bmatrix} y_1 \\ -\dfrac{g}{l} \cdot \sin(y_0) \end{bmatrix}$

Here y_0 represents θ and y_1 represents ω. The number of points to compute and the integration variable come next:

We will compute N points: $N := 100$

The integration variable is: $Sol := rkfixed(y, 0, 3, N, D)$

Finally, we can look at the results:

$i := 0 .. N$ $t_i := Sol_{i,0}$ $\theta_{num_i} := Sol_{i,1}$

$$\theta_{anal}(t) := \theta_{init} \cdot \cos\left(\sqrt{\frac{g}{l}} \cdot t\right)$$

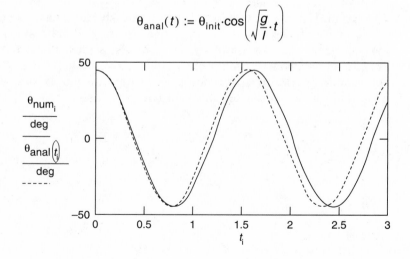

Which of these curves is correct, and what's the cause of the discrepancy between the two solutions? It turns out that, although both the numerical solution to the exact Equation (7.17) and the approximate analytic solution given by Equation (7.19) are in error, the latter is more so. If you remember, the analytic solution assumes that $\sin(\theta_{in}) = \sin(45°) = 0.707$ is close to $\theta_{in} = 45° = \pi/4 = 0.785$, which it is clearly not.

Hence we can conclude that the pendulum will have a slightly longer period than the pure sinusoidal oscillation if the amplitude of the motion is large. You might want to try using Zoom and Trace (see Chapter 3 for details on these) to find the period of this oscillation. If you then change the value of θ_{in} to, say, 5°, you can find the period for the pure oscillation case, and you'll also see that the two curves agree.

Exercises

7.6 Consider again the system shown in Figure 7.6, except now the mass $M = 1$ kg, the spring constant $k = 0.4$ N/m, and the friction coefficient $c = 1$ N-s/m. It will move with motion $x(t)$ in response to the applied force $F(t)$, shown in Figure 7.8, which is sinusoidal from $t = 0$ s to 1 s, and then zero. The mass is initially at rest at its equilibrium location. Find the response of the system for the first 10 seconds.

7.7 Some physical systems have the property that for small oscillations, energy is fed into them, but for larger amplitudes energy is removed. Such systems tend to seek a periodic behavior, although it will not be in any way sinusoidal. These systems can be modeled using the van der Pol equation:

$$\frac{d^2x}{dt^2} - \mu\left(1 - x^2\right)\frac{dx}{dt} + x = 0 \tag{7.21}$$

where x is the position at time t and $\mu = 2$. Find the behavior of the system over the time range $t = 0$ to 20 if it starts from rest at position $x = 2$.

Additional Exercises

In all of these exercises, use Mathcad's rkfixed function to obtain a solution. When you plot the solution you should choose N, the number of data points, to be large enough to produce a smooth-looking graph (depending on your computer's power and memory). In some cases you must choose a large value of N to get the solution to work. In order not to get computation errors, you should use a separate worksheet for each exercise.

7.8 Solve

$$y' = x + \frac{y}{5} \tag{7.22}$$

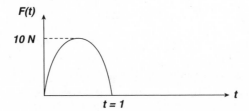

Figure 7.8

with initial condition $y(0) = 0$, from $x = 0$ to 25. Compare this to the exact solution

$$y_{exact}(x) = 25e^{\frac{x}{5}} - 5x - 25 \tag{7.23}$$

by plotting both on the same graph. Compute the maximum error (%).

7.9 Solve

$$y' = \frac{1}{4}(x + y)^2 \tag{7.24}$$

with initial condition $y(0) = 0$, from $x = 0$ to $\pi/2$. Compare this to the exact solution

$$y_{exact}(x) = 2\tan\left(\frac{x}{2}\right) - x \tag{7.25}$$

by plotting both on the same graph. Compute the maximum error (%).

7.10 Solve

$$y' = y - y^2 \tag{7.26}$$

with initial condition $y(0) = 2$, from $x = 0$ to 5. Compare this to the exact solution

$$y_{exact}(x) = \frac{2e^x}{2\,e^x - 1} \tag{7.27}$$

by plotting both on the same graph. Compute the maximum error (%).

7.11 Solve

$$xy' = (y - x)^3 + y \tag{7.28}$$

with initial condition $y(1) = 1.5$, from $x = 1$ to 2.235. Compare this to the exact solution

$$y_{exact}(x) = \frac{x}{\sqrt{5 - x^2}} + x \tag{7.29}$$

by plotting both on the same graph. Compute the maximum error (%).

7.12 Solve

$$y'' = xy' - 5y \tag{7.30}$$

with initial conditions $y(0) = 0$ and $y'(0) = 1$, from $x = 0$ to 9. Compare this to the exact solution

$$y_{exact}(x) = x - \frac{2}{3}x^3 + \frac{2}{30}x^5 \tag{7.31}$$

by plotting both on the same graph. Compute the maximum error (%). (If you compare these results to those of Exercise 7.13, you can see how a minor change in a coefficient can have a radical effect on the answer.)

7.13 Solve

$$y'' = xy' - 6y \tag{7.32}$$

with initial conditions $y(0) = 1$ and $y'(0) = 0$, from $x = 0$ to 9. Compare this to the exact solution

$$y_{\text{exact}}(x) = 1 - 3x^2 + x^4 - \frac{x^6}{15} \tag{7.33}$$

by plotting both on the same graph. Compute the maximum error (%). (If you compare these results to those of Exercise 7.12 you can see how a minor change in a coefficient can have a radical effect on the answer.)

7.14 Solve

$$(1 - x^2)y'' - 2xy' + 6y = 0 \tag{7.34}$$

with initial conditions $y(0) = -0.5$ and $y'(0) = 0$, from $x = 0$ to 20. Compare this to the exact solution

$$y_{\text{exact}}(x) = \frac{1}{2}(3x^2 - 1) \tag{7.35}$$

by plotting both on the same graph. Compute the maximum error (%).

Hint: When you divide through by $(1-x^2)$ you end up with a function that is singular when $x = \pm 1$. Hence choose an odd value for N (e.g., 201, 501 etc.) so that you never compute at $x = \pm 1$. (The solution is the Legendre polynomial of degree 2.)

7.15 Solve

$$(1 - x^2)y'' - 2xy' + 12y = 0 \tag{7.36}$$

with initial conditions $y(0) = 0$ and $y'(0) = -1.5$, from $x = 0$ to 10. Compare this to the exact solution

$$y_{\text{exact}}(x) = \frac{1}{2}(5x^3 - 3x) \tag{7.37}$$

by plotting both on the same graph. Compute the maximum error (%). Refer to the hint given for Exercise 7.14. (The solution is the Legendre polynomial of degree 3.)

7.16 The tank shown in Figure 7.9 has a cross-sectional area of $A = 2$ m^2 and is initially empty.

Water is poured in at a rate $Q_0 = 2.4$ m^3/sec for a time $T = 90$ sec. There is a hole of area $a = 0.1$ m^2 located at a height $y_{\text{hole}} = 25$ m in the side of the tank. Water will leak out of this hole at a rate dependent on the depth of water above the level of the hole. It can be shown that the equation for $y(t)$, the depth of water, is

$$A\frac{dy}{dt} = Q(t) - a\sqrt{2\,g(y - y_{\text{hole}})}\ \Phi(y - y_{\text{hole}}) \tag{7.38}$$

where $Q(t)$ is the flow rate of water into the tank, and Φ is the Heaviside step function. Plot the water depth in the tank for the first three

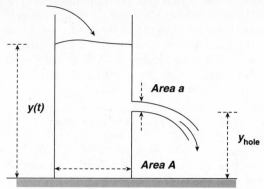

Flow Rate Q(t)

y(t)

Area a

y_{hole}

Area A

Figure 7.9

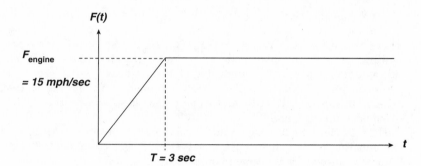

F(t)

F_{engine}

= 15 mph/sec

T = 3 sec

t

Figure 7.10

minutes and find the maximum depth (m). Explain when and why the curve changes. Note that you will have to define the function $Q(t)$ using Q_0 and T and another Heaviside step function.

7.17 Consider the tank problem of Exercise 7.16. Suppose in addition to everything else that a leak of area $a_{leak} = 0.05$ m^2 opens up at the base of the tank at time $T_{leak} = 70$ sec. Plot the water depth in the tank for the first three minutes and find the maximum depth (m). Explain when and why the curve changes. Note that you will have to add an extra term to Equation (7.38) to allow for this additional outflow. It will be similar to the last term in the equation, except the area will be different (there will be no y_{hole}), and you will have to define the Heaviside step function as a function of time and T_{leak}.

7.18 You are sitting in your car, which is in neutral. You change to drive and gradually press the accelerator pedal until you've "floored" it. It turns out that the equation describing the speed v (mph) is

$$\frac{dv}{dt} = F(t) - k_1 v - k_2 v^2 \qquad (7.39)$$

where $k_1 = 0.0075$ sec^{-1} and $k_2 = 0.0015$ 1/mph-sec are drag constants arising due to the rolling resistance of the tires and aerodynamic drag, and $F(t)$ is the thrust (mph/sec) produced by the engine, given by Figure 7.10.

How long does it take you (within a tenth of a second) to reach 60 mph? What is your top speed (mph)?

Hint: Note that Equation (7.39) is written in such a way that you can enter the numerical values as given, and your answers will automatically be in mph. An equation for $F(t)$ can be written, using the Heaviside step function, based on Figure 7.10. To find the time to reach 60 mph, the best approach is to plot the speed for the first 30 sec and then use the Trace feature. You can use Mathcad's max function to find the top speed.

7.19 You are driving the car described in Exercise 7.18 at a steady speed of 60 mph (which requires a constant engine thrust $F_{engine} = 5.85$ mph/sec). After $T = 2$ seconds, you apply the brakes for a total time $\Delta T = 5$ seconds. Find the speed (mph) you slow down to while braking and how long it takes (within a tenth of a second) to speed up again to 55 mph after releasing the brakes. It can be shown that the equation for the car motion is

$$\frac{dv}{dt} = F_{engine} - k_1 v - k_2 v^2 - F_{brake}\Phi(t - T)\Phi(T + \Delta T - t) \qquad (7.40)$$

where k_1 and k_2 are as before, and $F_{brake} = 10$ mph/sec is a factor representing the effect of applying the brakes (note that the product of Heaviside step functions has the effect of applying the brakes for the required period of time). Suppose you had *really* slammed on the brakes so that $F_{brake} = 15$ mph/sec. What would be your lowest speed and the time to speed back up to 55 mph?

Hint: Review the hint given in Exercise 7.18. You can use Mathcad's *min* function to find the lowest speed. Don't forget to subtract $T + \Delta T$ from your answer for the time to pick up speed again!

7.20 Consider the circuit shown in Figure 7.11, consisting of two inductors $L_1 = 50$ henry and $L_2 = 60$ henry, and two resistors $R_1 = 100$ ohm and $R_2 = 100$ ohm, initially with no currents flowing. At time $t = 0$ sec a power surge given by

$$V(t) = V_{max}\sin\left(\frac{2\pi t}{T}\right)\Phi(T - t) \qquad (7.41)$$

where $V_{max} = 10$ volt and $T = 1$ sec is applied (it has a shape similar to that shown in Figure 7.2).

It can be shown that by summing the change in potential in each loop the following equations hold:

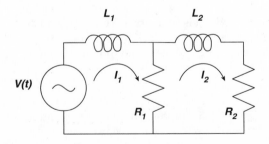

Figure 7.11

$$V(t) = L_1 \frac{dI_1}{dt} + R_1(I_1 - I_2)$$

$$0 = L_2 \frac{dI_2}{dt} + R_2 I_2 - R_1(I_1 - I_2)$$

(7.42)

Plot $I_1(t)$ and $I_2(t)$ (on the same graph) for the first two seconds. Find the maximum currents flowing in each loop.

Hint: In this worksheet, it would be a good idea to set the built-in variable ORIGIN to one so that the differential function $D(t,I)$ can have vector components I_1 and I_2 which will represent currents I_1 and I_2. If you don't do this, vector components I_0 and I_1 will have to be used, which would be a little confusing in the context of Figure 7.11.

7.21 A mass $m = 1$ kg shown in Figure 7.12 is attached to a spring of strength $k = 10$ newton/m.

Initially the spring is relaxed, and the mass is held in place. A magnet is installed at a fixed point $l = 1$ m from the mass, and the mass (which has some iron content) is then released. It is attracted towards the magnet and slides over the surface, compressing the spring, and oscillates until friction brings it to rest. It can be shown using Newton's second law that the equation for the position x (m) of the mass is

$$m \frac{dx}{dt} = -kx + \frac{k_1}{(1-x)^2} - k_2|v|v$$

(7.43)

where $k_1 = 1.45$ newton-m^2 is a force coefficient due to the magnet, $k_2 = 10$ newton-s^2/m^2 is a friction coefficient, and v (m/s) is the instantaneous speed of the mass. Plot (on separate graphs) the position $x(t)$ and speed $v(t)$ over the first ten seconds. What is the closest the mass gets to the magnet? What is the maximum speed?

7.22 Consider the serial chemical reaction of three chemical species A, B, and C:

$$A \xrightarrow{k_1} B \xrightarrow{k_2} C$$

(7.44)

where $k_1 = 0.1$ hr^{-1} and $k_2 = 0.075$ hr^{-1} are the reaction rate constants. It can be shown that the equations for the concentrations (mole/liter) of the species are

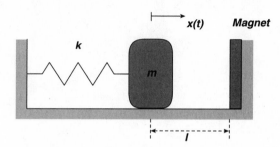

Figure 7.12

Solving Ordinary Differential Equations

$$\frac{dA}{dt} = -k_1 A$$

$$\frac{dB}{dt} = k_1 A - k_2 B \qquad (7.45)$$

$$\frac{dC}{dt} = k_2 B$$

If the initial concentrations are $A_0 = 1$ mole/liter and B_0 and $C_0 = 0$ mole/liter, plot a graph showing all three concentrations over the first 70 hours. Find the maximum concentration (mole/liter) of species B and when this occurs (hrs).

Hint: After solving the differential equations, you can use Mathcad's *max* function to find the maximum of B. One way to find the time is to use the Trace feature (assuming you computed a large enough number of data points to be reasonably accurate).

Doing Statistics with Mathcad

Mathcad is *packed* with built-in statistical features, ranging from such basic things as a function to find the average of a set of numbers, to functions that only a professional statistician would frequently use. As an example, Figure 8.1 shows a list of the probability distributions that Mathcad has built in. (To get to this window, click on the Help icon, and in *Contents* click on *Statistics,* where you'll see a subdirectory called *Density and distribution functions.*)

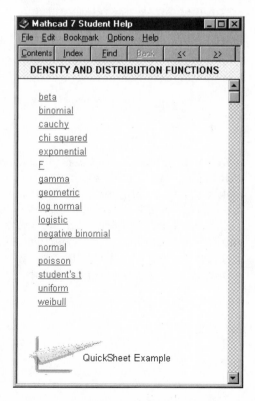

Figure 8.1

Some of these distributions may be familiar to you, and others not, but the point is that they are *available* to you. In this chapter we'll focus in on those statistical features that are most commonly used by engineers. At the conclusion of this chapter we'll indicate where you can find more information on using Mathcad's statistical features.

A common task engineers undertake is obtaining the overall statistical properties of a set of data, so let's look at that first.

8.1

Statistical Properties of Data

To illustrate this, consider a cereal box production line. It's important to know how consistently the cereal boxes are being packed: if the *average* (or *mean*) weight of the boxes falls below a certain limit, the company could be charged with fraud by the government; if the *minimum* box weight is below the value stated on the box, the company may be exposed by a consumer group; if the *maximum* box weight is significantly in excess of the value stated on the box, the company is being inefficient. All of these numbers are *statistical* properties of the production line. Others are the *median* (the weight at which half of the boxes will be lighter and half heavier), the *mode* (the most common weight that occurs), the *variance* and *standard deviation* (both are measures of the amount of spread in the weights of the boxes), and so on. In addition, such data is often plotted in a *histogram,* which is a graph showing the relative frequencies with which, for example, each weight of cereal box occurs.

The only definitions given above with which you may not be familiar are the variance and standard deviation. The variance *s* of a sample is given by

$$s = \frac{1}{n-1} \sum_{i=1}^{n} (x_i - \bar{x})^2 \tag{8.1}$$

where n is the total number of data points x_i (which in our case will be the individual weights) and $\bar{x}$ is the mean. (If you were looking at an entire population rather than a sample, it turns out that you'd use n instead of $n-1$.) As we mentioned, this indicates how much spread there is in the data. For example, if all of the x values were the same (in other words, had no spread), Equation (8.1) gives the correct result that the variance is zero. Note that squaring the deviation of each data point from the mean is done so that a data point *smaller* than the mean does not have the effect of canceling one that is *larger*.

The standard deviation [usually called the *sigma* (σ) value] is simply the square root of the variance. We'll see later when we look at *probability distributions* that the standard deviation has a particular usefulness when computed for a *normal* distribution (the proverbial "bell curve"): 68.3 percent of the data will be between the $\pm\,\sigma$ points, and 99.7 percent of the data will be between the $\pm\,3\sigma$ points.

In many real-world situations a huge amount of data is accumulated. For example, if you were studying the incidence of breast cancer in the northeast United States, you'd probably need to have a sample population of many thousands. In these situations, you would not type data directly into Mathcad but would probably import it from some other source, such as a spreadsheet. In order to make this chapter straightforward, we'll avoid the topic of importing (and exporting) here and only look at small populations. We'll see in Chapter 9 how to import and export data using Mathcad.

To see how to use Mathcad to compute the quantities described above, let's do an example.

Example 8.1 Cereal box production line statistics

A factory produces breakfast cereal in boxes that should weigh at least 1.5 kg (note that we're using the colloquial meaning of "weight," meaning we're using kg, which of course actually measures mass).

A sample of 20 boxes is randomly selected and weighed. Their weights (kg) are

```
1.549  1.552  1.563  1.575  1.562  1.516  1.469  1.621  1.599  1.492
1.557  1.635  1.534  1.448  1.479  1.484  1.524  1.553  1.52   1.533
```

Find the smallest and largest weights and the variance, average, median, and standard deviation of this sample.

Let's start a new worksheet called "Example 8.1." Create a matrix named *Cereal,* with 20 rows and one column, in which you should enter the data. Then you can simply type the names of the statistical entities you want to obtain. Each one of them assumes that the data is in a matrix format. Remember, if you don't know the correct syntax for a built-in function, you can always click on the Insert Function icon for guidance.

See if you can obtain the following:

Cereal Box Production Line Statistics

By (Your Name)

$$
Cereal := \begin{bmatrix} 1.549 \\ 1.552 \\ 1.563 \\ 1.575 \\ 1.562 \\ 1.516 \\ 1.469 \\ 1.621 \\ 1.599 \\ 1.492 \\ 1.557 \\ 1.635 \\ 1.534 \\ 1.448 \\ 1.479 \\ 1.484 \\ 1.524 \\ 1.553 \\ 1.52 \\ 1.533 \end{bmatrix} \cdot kg
$$

The statistics are:

$Smallest := \min(Cereal)$ $Smallest = 1.448 \cdot kg$

$Largest := \max(Cereal)$ $Largest = 1.635 \cdot kg$

$Variance := \mathrm{var}(Cereal)$ $Variance = 0.002 \cdot kg^2$

$Average := \mathrm{mean}(Cereal)$ $Average = 1.538 \cdot kg$

$Median := \mathrm{median}(Cereal)$ $Median = 1.542 \cdot kg$

$Deviation := \mathrm{stdev}(Cereal)$ $Deviation = 0.048 \cdot kg$

Note that Mathcad handles the statistics even though the data has units. We'll see later that we can do a lot more with this data, but for now let's look at the *histogram* of this data. A histogram is a graph that essentially counts the frequencies with which data values in a sample occur. For example, it could be used to indicate how many boxes in the sample weigh between 1.4 kg and 1.425 kg.

To create a histogram we use the built-in function *hist(intervals, data)*, where *intervals* is a vector containing the ranges in which the *data* is sorted. The results of this can then be plotted in a bar graph.

For our example, the smallest (1.448 kg) and largest (1.635 kg) weights help us set up the weight ranges we might want to examine. Let's break this range down so that we find how many boxes have weights between 1.4 and 1.425 kg, 1.425 and 1.45 kg, . . . , through 1.65 kg. The first step is to set up this range (using Vector or Array subscripts) and call it *intervals* (although you could give it any name you wish):

$$N := 10 \qquad i := 0 .. N \qquad intervals_i := 1.4 \cdot kg + \frac{i}{N} \cdot .25 \cdot kg$$

$intervals^T =$

	0	1	2	3	4	5	6	7	8
0	1.4	1.425	1.45	1.475	1.5	1.525	1.55	1.575	1.6

·kg

Note that in order not to take up a lot of space, we've looked at the values generated by the range by evaluating the *transpose* of the *intervals* vector, and have also left it in its default spreadsheet format (you recall that the transpose can be invoked by either using the accelerator keys **Ctrl + 1** or by using the Matrix Transpose icon on the Vector and Matrix palette). If you wish you can double-click on this result to access the Number Format window and change the display to Display as Matrix. You can picture this *intervals* range as a set of "bins" (a terminology used by spreadsheets when they are used for this task) into which the boxes are sorted, much as mail is sorted by the post office. Also, we've used the default value of ORIGIN = 0.

The histogram function can then be invoked and plotted as a function of this range. Let's define a new vector *Weights* to be equal to the histogram results:

Weights := hist(*intervals,Cereal*)

$Weights^T =$

	0	1	2	3	4	5	6	7	8	9
0	0	1	1	3	3	3	5	2	1	1

We need to plot the vector *Weights* against the vector *intervals* (see Chapter 3 if you've forgotten how to do this). The graph will be an *X-Y* plot, with the trace changed to Bar. Try to get something like the graph below (and note that we've done quite a bit of formatting of the graph):

The frequency distribution is:

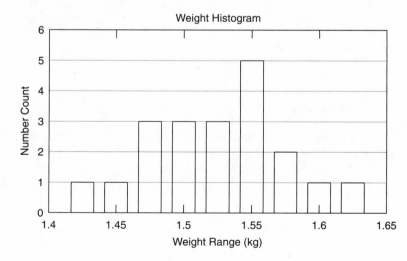

We can interpret this graph as follows: the hist(*intervals,Cereal*) function generates a vector containing the number counts of boxes weighing between *intervals*$_i$ and *intervals*$_{i+1}$. Hence we can see that, for example, there is one box in the range 1.425 kg and 1.45 kg (it weighs 1.448 kg), and there are two boxes between 1.575 kg and 1.6 kg.

Once the histogram is obtained, we can observe, for example, how many boxes weigh less than 1.5 kg (1 + 1 + 3 = 5) and what the *mode* is. The mode is the most commonly occurring weight range. In this example, this is the range 1.55 to 1.575 kg, for which there is a count of five boxes.

Extracting information (such as that discussed in the previous paragraph) from the histogram is really an example of using a *database*. Although Mathcad can be made to extract this information using, for example, the If function to set criteria, it is not really convenient for this. For extensive database work, it's best to use a database computer application such as Microsoft Access or a spreadsheet such as Microsoft Excel.

8.2

Fitting Equations to Data: Linear Regression

In Section 8.1 we looked at a single set of data. Although it's common for an engineer to have to deal with such data when involved in any kind of manufacturing process, engineers encounter *paired* data whenever any kind of research or experimentation is done. As an example of this, consider the following.

Example 8.2 Pressure and temperature of a gas

An engineer is attempting to find the molecular weight M of an ideal gas of *mass* = 1 kg contained in a rigid tank of volume *vol* = 2.5 m^3. This will be done by heating the gas and measuring the temperature and pressure data. As the gas is heated at constant volume, the following data are obtained:

T (K)	600	625	650	675	700	725	750	775	800	825
p (kPa)	50.2	52	54.5	55.5	57.5	60.3	61.4	63.5	67.7	69.2

This data should conform to the ideal gas equation, which can be written as

$$p \, vol = mass \frac{R_u}{M} T \tag{8.2}$$

where p is the pressure at temperature T and R_u = 8.314 J/mol-K is the universal gas constant.

An estimate for the value of M could be made using Equation (8.2) by using *one* measurement of the temperature and pressure (for example

600 K and 50.2 kPa), so that everything is known except M. However, the data point chosen might happen to have a large experimental error, so the computation of M would also have a large error. A better approach is to use *all* of the temperature–pressure data points and perform a *linear regression*. This has the advantage that it will compute M based not only on one data point, but on all of them, so it will be more accurate. What is a linear regression? This is a technique for finding the "best" straight line to represent the data.

This technique obviously can be used only when the data has a linear behavior, which means the two variables (the independent variable and the dependent variable) are directly proportional to one another. In general, there are two ways to determine if data are linear: (1) there may be a theoretical model that predicts linearity; (2) the data, when plotted, may *look* linear. In our example, both apply.

First, Equation (8.2) can be rearranged:

$$p(T) = \frac{mass\ R_u}{vol\ M}\ T \qquad\qquad (8.3)$$

This indicates that, *theoretically,* for the constant volume process, we should expect the pressure and temperature to have a *linear* relationship (the pressure should be directly proportional to the temperature).

Second, we can plot the data to *see* if it is indeed linear. Start a new worksheet called "Example 8.2," enter the data as two vectors, and plot the pressure against temperature (format the trace to be only symbols):

<u>Pressure and Temperature of a Gas</u>

By (Your Name)

The data are: $T :=$
$\begin{bmatrix} 600 \\ 625 \\ 650 \\ 675 \\ 700 \\ 725 \\ 750 \\ 775 \\ 800 \\ 825 \end{bmatrix}$ ·K $p :=$ $\begin{bmatrix} 50.2 \\ 52.0 \\ 54.5 \\ 55.5 \\ 57.5 \\ 60.3 \\ 61.4 \\ 63.5 \\ 67.7 \\ 69.2 \end{bmatrix}$ ·10^3·Pa

It can be plotted:

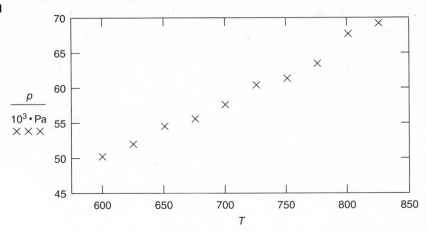

The data *does* look approximately linear, but because each data point has experimental error, the data has *scatter*. If we can find the best line representing the data, we should be able to obtain a and b in

$$p(T) = aT + b \tag{8.4}$$

Comparing Equations (8.3) and (8.4), we can see that if the data agrees with the theory, it should yield the result that $b = 0$, and the value determined for a can be used in the following formula to obtain the unknown molecular weight M:

$$M = \frac{a\ mass\ R_u}{vol} \tag{8.5}$$

Now that we've established that the data for this experiment are linear, let's pause in our solution of Example 8.2 (now would be a good time to save it) and turn to the question of how to do a linear regression.

As we've already mentioned, a linear regression (sometimes called the *method of least squares* or simply a *regression analysis*) is a mathematical technique for obtaining the "best" straight line through a set of data. It turns out that Mathcad can automatically do this for us, but before doing this let's discuss the overall concept. If you wish, you can skip this section.

The Regression Concept

Suppose we have the set of data shown in Figure 8.2. If we picture each point as a nail in a wall, we could imagine hanging a small rubber band over each nail and then slotting a steel rod through each rubber band. When we let go of the rod (and ignore gravity), the tight rubber bands will pull the rod into an *equilibrium* position. If we manually displace the rod, it will always return to this equilibrium (or best) position. This is illustrated in Figure 8.3.

Figure 8.2

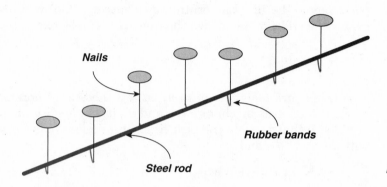

Nails

Rubber bands

Steel rod

Figure 8.3

This unique position is the one where the *energy* stored in the stretched rubber bands is lowest. Note that this means that some bands will be stretched a lot and others only a little, but the *total* stretch in *all* the bands is at a minimum. The energy stored in a band is proportional to the square of the amount it is stretched. Hence, the equilibrium position occurs when the total stored energy is minimized, or when the *sum of the squares* of all the stretches of the rubber bands is at a minimum. This leads to the expression *least squares fit*.

Of course, this best-fit procedure can be described mathematically. To do this consider a set of (x_i, y_i) data such as that in Figure 8.2 (where i counts the data points). Assume that we draw an arbitrary straight line. It will have the mathematical form $y_{lin} = ax + b$, where the slope of the line is a and intercept b. If we choose another line, the values of a and b change. The goal of a linear regression is to find the values of a and b so that the line chosen best represents the data. To do this, first let's compute the disagreement, or error, between the value of y obtained from such a line, and from a data point. This difference is $y_i - (ax_i + b)$. This term, graphically illustrated in Figure 8.4, is the mathematical equivalent of the amount of stretch of a rubber band in the previous description.

Hence, computing this term for each data point, and adding them together, will give a measure of how much the line and the

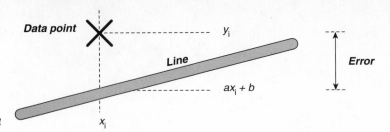

Figure 8.4

data points as a whole disagree. There's one extra point here: Before adding these terms, we need to square each one, so that a point below the line (generating a negative value) will not just cancel the effect of one above the line. This can be expressed as

$$S = \sum_i [y_i - (ax_i + b)]^2 \tag{8.6}$$

If this expression S is *minimized*, by choosing different lines (or in other words by changing a and b), it will lead to the values of a and b that provide the best fit. To minimize we differentiate with respect to a and c:

$$\frac{\partial S}{\partial a} = -2 \sum_i x_i [y_i - (ax_i + b)] = 0$$

$$\frac{\partial S}{\partial b} = -2 \sum_i [y_i - (ax_i + b)] = 0 \tag{8.7}$$

Manipulating these two equations, we obtain two equations for the values of a and b that will minimize S:

$$a(\Sigma x_i) + bn = \Sigma y_i$$

$$a\left(\Sigma x_i^2\right) + b(\Sigma x_i) = \Sigma x_i y_i \tag{8.8}$$

where n is the number of data points. Equations (8.8) can easily be solved for a and b (using, for example, Cramer's rule):

$$a = \frac{(\Sigma x_i)(\Sigma y_i) - n(\Sigma x_i y_i)}{(\Sigma x_i)^2 - n(\Sigma x_i^2)}$$

$$b = \frac{(\Sigma x_i)(\Sigma x_i y_i) - (\Sigma y_i)(\Sigma x_i^2)}{(\Sigma x_i)^2 - n(\Sigma x_i^2)} \tag{8.9}$$

These formulas look very complicated, but they are actually straightforward to compute. The right-hand sides consist of sums of x's and y's, as well as sums of their squares and cross products. The result will be the coefficients in the equation

$$y = ax + b \qquad (8.10)$$

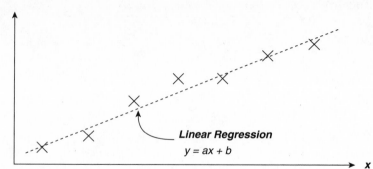

Linear Regression
$y = ax + b$

Figure 8.5

Finally, this line could be plotted with the original data, as shown in Figure 8.5.

This rather tedious process is automated and built into most calculators, as well as spreadsheets. Obviously, it is easier to use these to generate the best-fit line than to do all the above calculations by hand, or even by programming the equations (using, for example, Fortran).

Doing a Linear Regression Using Mathcad

To see how to use Mathcad for performing all these calculations for us, let's return to our Example 8.2 worksheet. All we need to do is use Mathcad's built-in functions slope(x,y) and intercept(x,y). These can be applied to a set of (x,y) data, and they will find for us the values of a and b in Equation (8.10). The only thing to remember is that x and y must both be *vectors* of data.

In Example 8.2, instead of (x,y), we have (T,p) data. Continuing in the worksheet, do the following (where we've added units on the outputs):

The regression analysis leads to: $\quad a := \text{slope}(T,p) \qquad a = 83.98 \cdot \dfrac{\text{Pa}}{\text{K}}$

$b := \text{intercept}(T,p) \qquad b = -652.73 \cdot \text{Pa}$

These coefficients are used in: $\quad p_{\text{regr}}(T) := a \cdot T + b$

Mathcad has done all of the math of Equations (8.9) for us. As you recall, theoretically b should be zero, but for this data it is −0.65 kPa, which *is* small compared to the pressures in the data. The value of a will enable us to use Equation (8.5) to obtain a value for the gas molecular weight M. However, first let's plot the original pressure data and the regression line against the gas temperature. To do this we generate a vector of values from the function p_{regr} by using a vector argument T_i where $i = 0$ to 10. See if you can do the following:

We can then plot the results: $i := 1.. 10$

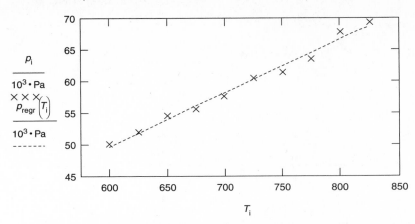

As you can see, the line seems to be a pretty good fit to the data. How good is it? More specifically, to what degree is the data linear? We can ask Mathcad to compute the *correlation coefficient,* which is given by Mathcad's built-in function *corr(x,y)*:

The correlation coefficient is: $corr(T, p) = 0.994$

It turns out that the closer this is to unity, the closer the data is to a perfect straight line, so that for our data the correlation is very good.

We've now finished our description of using Mathcad's linear regression feature. To complete Example 8.2, we can now compute the unknown molecular weight M using Equation (8.5) (you can look up the value of the universal gas constant R_u in any thermodynamics text):

The given data are: $R_u := 8.314 \cdot \dfrac{J}{mol \cdot K}$ $mass := 1 \text{ kg}$ $vol := 2.5 \text{ m}^3$

The molecular weight is then: $M := \dfrac{mass \cdot R_u}{vol \cdot a}$ $M = 39.602 \cdot \dfrac{kg}{10^3 \cdot mol}$

Note that Mathcad is familiar with *moles.*

It's interesting to look in the *Resource Center* under Reference Tables, where you should eventually find the window shown in Figure 8.6. This shows that the molecular weight of our mystery gas is close to that of argon. Hence, our experiment leads to the conclusion that the gas is probably argon, and in addition, that it does behave as an ideal gas (because p and T are proportional when the volume is constant).

The purpose of the linear regression that we performed in solving Example 8.2 was to find the slope of the (T,p) line, so that the molecular weight M of the gas could be determined. More typically, linear regressions are performed in order to *interpolate* or *extrapolate*. Interpolation is when the regression line is used to

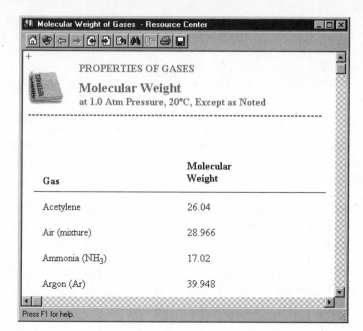

Figure 8.6

predict the value of the dependent variable at some new value of the independent variable that is *within* the range of the original data. Extrapolation is when the new value of the independent variable is *outside* the range of the original data.

To illustrate this, consider again Example 8.2. The range of temperatures was 600 K to 825 K, in steps of 25 K. The pressure at, say, 727 K (inside the range) is found by interpolating:

The pressure at 727 K is: $p_{regr}(727 \cdot K) = 60.4 \cdot 10^3 \cdot Pa$

On the other hand, the pressure at, say, 1000 K (outside the range) is found by extrapolating:

The pressure at 1000 K is: $p_{regr}(1000 \cdot K) = 83.3 \cdot 10^3 \cdot Pa$

The basic difference between these procedures is that you should be careful in extrapolating, because you're essentially *predicting* what happens in a region where no data are available. Generally speaking, you should not extrapolate too far outside the original range. This is a judgment call. In our example, extrapolating out to 1000 K does not seem too dangerous, but extrapolating out to 2000 K would be. This is because, first of all, the regression slope *is* an approximation to what the data are "really" doing, and any small change in the slope will produce large changes far away from the original data, and, second, in any experiment you can never be sure whether or not the underlying physics of the problem change for extreme values (so that, for example, the data may no longer be linear).

Fitting Equations to Data: Nonlinear Regression

This leads us to the next level of difficulty in analyzing data: in many cases, the data being analyzed will *not* be linear.

Data may have an underlying pattern to it, but sometimes it will not. For example, the plot of an individual stock of the Dow Jones Industrial Average versus time may often appear to conform approximately to an exponential curve, but sometimes (as most stocks did in 1987) it can abruptly drop in value. There is no permanent discernible pattern to this data (and if there was, anyone with sufficient math skills could make future predictions about stock prices and make a fortune!).

In most engineering data, however, there *will* be a pattern, because after all we're usually interested in finding how one variable is affected by another (in other words, the dependent variable y will be some function of the independent variable x). This dependency may be known from theory (for example, the radiation q leaving a body is known to depend on T^4, where T is the body temperature), or it may become evident when the data are plotted.

The relationship between a given x and y set of data could have any mathematical form, but a surprisingly large number of experimental curves fall into one of only a few simple forms:

1. Linear: $y = ax + b$
2. Power: $y = Ax^n$
3. Exponential: $y = ce^{\lambda x}$

These curves are illustrated in Figure 8.7. Note that a *power* curve is a special case of a *polynomial* curve, which we'll discuss in detail shortly.

There are subtle differences between exponential and power curves: The exponential curves (positive or negative) have a *finite* value for y at the origin, whereas the power curves are either zero or shoot off to infinity at the origin.

How do you know which curve to apply to experimental data? Sometimes a graph of the data will suggest which of these curves is the best representation of the data; at other times, the engineer has a theoretical model that suggests a choice of curve. For instance, we've already looked at an example of linear behavior; on the other hand, radiation from a body, as we just mentioned, should have *power* behavior; and radioactive decay will have *exponential* behavior [where, in terms of Figure 8.7, y will be the level of radioactivity, x the time, c the initial radiation level, and λ will lead to a (negative) time constant].

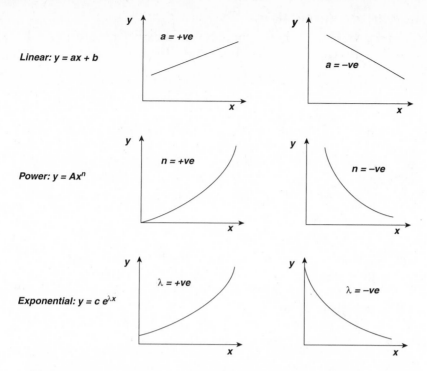

Figure 8.7

If the data itself does not suggest which type of curve to use, and there is no theory to act as a guide, the only alternative is to fit the data to all three types of curves to see which has the best fit (the correlation coefficients of each must be compared).

In any event, the goal of performing an experiment is usually to find, from the data, the values of the constants in one of these expressions. We've already seen how to perform a linear regression to find a and b. How do we perform a regression on power or exponential data?

The answer is that we could perform the same kind of error minimization analysis (although the details will be different) as was used for linear data [see Equations (8.6) through (8.10)]. Instead of a and b, the constants obtained would be A and n, or c and λ. We won't do this here, but details on this approach can be found in any good engineering numerical methods book, such as Chapra and Canale's *Numerical Methods for Engineers, with Personal Computer Applications* (New York: McGraw-Hill, 1988). In addition, current spreadsheets such as Microsoft Excel have a built-in feature for fitting data to one of these (and other) curves, so if you need to perform a nonlinear regression analysis, you might want to try one of these.

There *is* an approach in Mathcad to tackle these problems.

Linearized Analysis

The trick here is to make the power and exponential forms take on a linear form. To do this, simply take the logarithms:

$$y = Ax^n \quad \Rightarrow \quad Y \equiv \ln(y) = n\ln(x) + \ln(A) \equiv aX + b$$
$$y = ce^{\lambda x} \qquad Y \equiv \ln(y) = \lambda x + \ln(c) \qquad \equiv aX + b \tag{8.11}$$

Equations (8.11) show that a power equation can be transformed into a linear equation if $Y = \ln(y)$ is plotted against $X = \ln(x)$, and an exponential equation can be transformed if $Y = \ln(y)$ is plotted against x. The slope a and the intercept b of the regression line will give the coefficients of the original equations:

$$\begin{aligned} n &= a \quad \text{and} \quad A = e^b \\ \lambda &= a \quad \text{and} \quad c = e^b \end{aligned} \tag{8.12}$$

There's only one thing to be careful about when doing this in Mathcad: Because you cannot take the logarithm of anything with units, it's best *not* to use units here. This is not really a big disadvantage, because after all we're looking for correlations between sets of numbers, regardless of their units.

To illustrate this approach, consider the following.

Example 8.3   Viscosity of motor oil   An engineer wishes to know if the motor oil she plans to use in a snowmobile motor is of the correct viscosity. The oil will have to work at a temperature as low as $-10°C$ and as high as $100°C$. The viscosity μ of all oils (all liquids, in fact) depends on the temperature T of the oil: the hotter the oil, the "thinner" it gets. If the oil viscosity becomes too high (when it's at $-10°C$) or too low (when it's at $100°C$), the engine will be damaged. The upper and lower limits on the viscosity for this engine are 0.500 N-s/m^2 and 0.001 N-s/m^2. The data available on the oil are:

$T\,(°C)$	0	20	60	70	80
μ (N-s/m^2)	0.415	0.103	0.015	0.010	0.007

Will the oil have acceptable viscosities at $-10°C$ and $100°C$? Because we don't have data at these temperatures, we need to do a regression analysis on the data so we can extrapolate to these temperatures. It is known that the dependency of viscosity on temperature can be expressed by

$$\mu(T) = Ae^{\frac{B}{T}} \tag{8.13}$$

where A and B are physical constants of the particular oil. The temperature in Equation (8.13) is *absolute,* but if the temperature range is not very large, the equation can be approximated by

$$\mu(T) \approx \alpha e^{-\beta T} \qquad (8.14)$$

where T is now in degrees Celsius (°C) and α and β are new physical constants.

The goal here is to use *linear* regression on this *exponential* data, using the logic of Equations (8.11) and (8.12). The first step is to enter the data into Mathcad. Start a new worksheet, which we'll save as "Example 8.3." After providing a title, let's enter the temperature and viscosity data as vectors (and remember, because we'll be taking logarithms, we will not be using units):

Viscosity of Motor Oil

By (Your Name)

The data are
$$T := \begin{bmatrix} 0 \\ 20 \\ 60 \\ 70 \\ 80 \end{bmatrix} \qquad \mu := \begin{bmatrix} 0.415 \\ 0.103 \\ 0.015 \\ 0.010 \\ 0.007 \end{bmatrix}$$

The next step is to graph the data to see if we can see any kind of trend:

The data looks like:

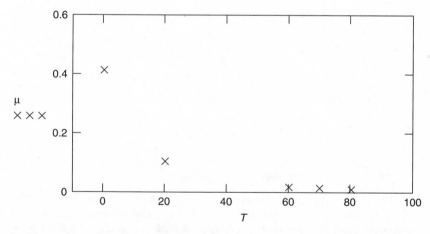

We can see that the data are certainly not linear: as the theory predicted, it appears to have an exponential behavior. Usually engineers plot data in such a way that the data *appears* linear. For the same basic reason as was used in discussing the linearizing of an exponential, it turns out that exponential curves become linear on a *semi-log* graph. Try to customize the graph by changing the Y axis to log scale and by displaying grids on both axes:

The data looks like:

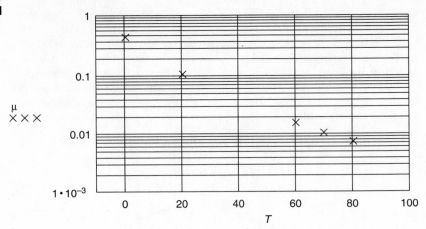

The data does appear linear, again supporting the belief that the original data are exponential. What we need to do now is perform a regression analysis on T and $\ln(\mu)$ (not T and μ!). One way to do this would be to define a new vector, say Y, by using a range i from 1 to 5 (assuming ORIGIN = 1) and computing Y_i to be $\ln(\mu_i)$. The linear regression could then be performed on this (T,Y) data. Instead of this, let's save a step and be a little more elegant by doing the following:

The regression analysis leads to: $\quad a := slope\left(T, \overrightarrow{\ln(\mu)}\right) \quad a = -0.051$

$$b := intercept\left(T, \overrightarrow{\ln(\mu)}\right) \quad b = -1.06$$

The correlation coefficient is: $\quad corr\left(T, \overrightarrow{\ln(\mu)}\right) = -0.996$

Hence the coefficients are: $\quad \lambda := a \qquad \lambda = -0.051$

$$c := e^b \qquad c = 0.347$$

These coefficients are used in: $\quad \mu_{regr}(T) := c \cdot e^{\lambda \cdot T}$

What we've done here is *vectorize*, taking the logarithm of the μ vector (you recall you invoke this by using either the accelerator keys **Ctrl + -** or the relevant icon on the Vector and Matrix palette). We need to do this because in Mathcad you can't take the logarithm of a vector μ, only its components, *unless* you vectorize the operation.

Notice that the correlation coefficient is close to one, one more time giving us confidence that the data are exponential. We should point out here that this procedure, of doing a linear regression on the logarithm of data, means that each data point is not given equal weight (or significance). In terms of our rubber band and nails analogy, it's as if the first few rubber bands were stronger than the last few. Hence, this fit will not in fact be the "best" exponential fit. It will, however, be close enough for most engineering applications.

We can now create a new graph with the original data and regression curve:

We can then plot the results: $T' := -10, -9 \ldots 100$

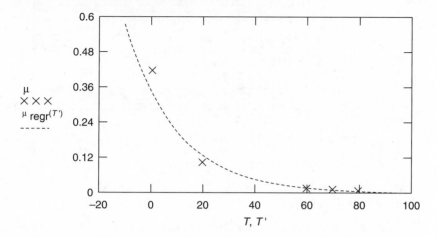

Note that here we defined a new variable T' (remember that the ′ is obtained by using the alternate prime key ‵) so that we get a smooth curve for the function $\mu_{regr}(T')$. (We graphed a function versus a time range and a vector against a vector.) If we had plotted both μ_i and $\mu_{regr}(T_i)$ versus T_i, we would end up with a graph in which Mathcad computed the regression at only the original data points and connected these with a straight line. If you were to do this (you don't need to actually do it now), you'd get

The results look like:

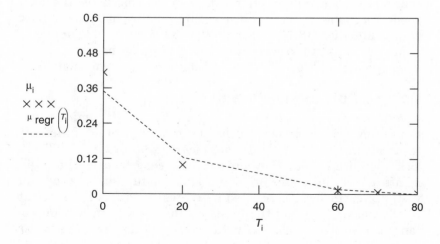

Not a very pretty sight! The graph previous to this, while perhaps nice looking, is not how an engineer would present the final data. He or she would present it on a semi-log graph:

The final graph is:

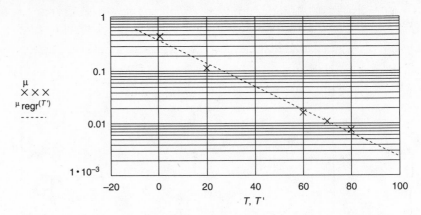

The analysis is almost complete. You remember we wanted the viscosity at −10°C and 100°C:

The viscosity at −10°C is: $\mu_{regr}(-10) = 0.574$

The viscosity at 100°C is: $\mu_{regr}(100) = 0.002$

We have to add the units ourselves, because the regression just works with numbers. Our criterion was that μ should not be less than 0.001 N-s/m^2 or greater than 0.5 N-s/m^2. According to the regression analysis, this oil is not suitable (it becomes too "thick" when it's cold). You can now close this worksheet.

This example showed how to manipulate exponential data so that a linear regression could be performed on it. A similar procedure could be done with power data, except that the regression is done on the logarithm of both the dependent variable *and* the independent variable. We won't do an example of this, but you can refer back to Equations (8.11) as a starting point if you need to do one.

Mathcad has two special features for finding the best-fit curve for other specific kinds of data. The first one involves polynomial fit.

Doing a Polynomial Fit with Mathcad

If you know or suspect that your data fits a *polynomial* equation, then you can use Mathcad's built-in set of functions *regress(xdata,ydata,n)* and *interp(curve,xdata,ydata,x)*. These look complicated but they are actually easy to use. The arguments *xdata* and *ydata* are the original data points, *curve* is a vector of coefficients generated by regress, and *x* is the point at which you wish to find the "best" *y* value. The term *n* is important: it is *not* the number of data points, but denotes what *order* polynomial you'd like to fit:

$$y(x) = a_0 + a_1x + a_2x^2 + \cdots + a_nx^n \tag{8.15}$$

It's up to the engineer to decide what order polynomial to use to fit the data, although in most situations n will be less than 5.

To see how this works, let's start a new worksheet called "Example 8.4," so we can solve the following problem.

Example 8.4 Truck horsepower curve

An engineer has the following data on the engine horsepower needed by a truck to cruise at certain speeds:

P (hp)	13	25	39	63	101
V (mph)	20	35	50	60	75

He wishes to determine the horsepower required to cruise at 55 mph and at 100 mph.

First let's enter the data:

Truck Horsepower Curve

By (Your Name)

The data are:
$$V := \begin{bmatrix} 20 \\ 35 \\ 50 \\ 60 \\ 75 \end{bmatrix} \qquad P := \begin{bmatrix} 13 \\ 25 \\ 39 \\ 63 \\ 101 \end{bmatrix}$$

Next, let's plot the data to see if any trend is discernible:

It can be plotted:

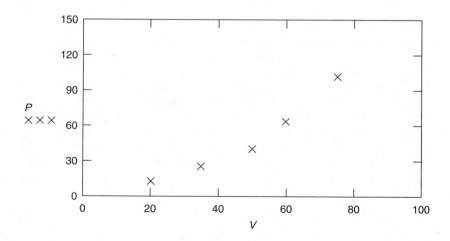

Comparing this to Figure 8.7, it appears that the data may be some kind of power curve (and not because we're plotting *horsepower*!), or, more generally, a *polynomial* curve. In fact, it's known from theory that we should in fact expect the curve to be given by

$$P(V) = aV^2 + bV^3 \tag{8.16}$$

where a and b are constants that are determined by such things as the friction in the drivetrain and aerodynamic drag. Hence, in this case we can feel confident in using Mathcad's polynomial feature. Let's define a vector called *fit* (you can in general give it any name you wish), which will contain the results of the regression. We expect the polynomial to be third order, so we type

The regression analysis leads to: $fit := \text{regress}(V, P, 3)$

We don't need to look at the values contained in *fit*. It is now used in building a new function that will be our best-fit cubic function. You *must* follow the correct order of interp's arguments: the first is the result of the regress function (in our example, *fit*); the second is the independent data (V), the third is the dependent data (P); and the fourth is the *new* independent variable (v):

The polynomial curve is: $P_{\text{poly}}(v) := \text{interp}(fit, V, P, v)$

The new variable P_{poly} is a function of the new variable v. The way this works is that when you give a value for v (say, 55), the interp function computes the best value of the horsepower, which will be $P_{\text{poly}}(55)$. Let's do this to find the horsepower required for this speed as well as for a speed of 100 mph:

Interpolating the horsepower required for a speed of 55 mph:

$P_{\text{poly}}(55) = 50.6$

Extrapolating the horsepower required for a speed of 100 mph:

$P_{\text{poly}}(100) = 212$

We've called the first calculation an interpolation because we've estimated the power for a speed *between* two data points, and the second an extrapolation because we've estimated the power for a speed *outside* the range of the original data.

The results are that for 55 mph we need about 51 hp, and for 100 mph we need about 212 hp. Note that for the 55-mph horsepower requirement, just taking the average of the power required for 50 mph and 60 mph gives the same result, so we didn't really need to do this regression. However, in general, such an averaging might not work. In any event, we *had* to do the polynomial regression to extrapolate out to 100 mph.

We can plot the original data and the regression curve:

We can then plot the results: $v := 0, 1 .. 100$

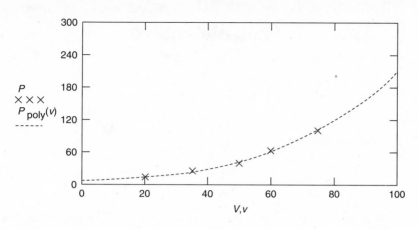

It looks like we obtained a pretty good fit to the data.

This completes our introduction to Mathcad's polynomial curve fitting. The final basic kind of curve fitting we can do with Mathcad is a generalized regression.

Doing a Generalized Regression with Mathcad

Occasionally, engineers encounter situations where some kind of theory has led to a mathematical model, and this model is to be fitted to experimental data. If the mathematical model is of the form

$$y(x) = a_0 f_0(x) + a_1 f_1(x) + a_2 f_2(x) + \cdots + a_n f_n(x) \tag{8.17}$$

where the terms $f_i(x)$ are known functions, Mathcad can be used to find the coefficients a_i that best fit the data, using the built-in function linfit(x,y,F).

To see how to do this, consider the following example.

Example 8.5 Drug absorption A bioengineer has developed a theory on the rate of drug absorption through the skin. The theory results in

$$C(t) = a_0 t e^{-3t} + a_1 \sqrt{t} \tag{8.18}$$

where C is the amount of absorption in time t. The constants a_0 and a_1 are to be determined by using the following data:

t (hr)	0.2	0.4	0.6	0.8	1
C (μm)	1.2	1.6	1.8	2	2.1

In a new worksheet, do the following (using literal subscripts):

Drug Absorption

By (Your Name)

The data are: $t_{data} := \begin{bmatrix} 0.2 \\ 0.4 \\ 0.6 \\ 0.8 \\ 1.0 \end{bmatrix}$ $C_{data} := \begin{bmatrix} 1.2 \\ 1.6 \\ 1.8 \\ 2.0 \\ 2.1 \end{bmatrix}$

Next, we need to define a vector function (in this example, a function of t), containing the functions we wish to model (here we have two functions, but we could have any number). Let's call this $F(t)$ (but in general you can give it any name you wish):

The assumed functions are: $F(t) := \begin{bmatrix} t \cdot e^{-3 \cdot t} \\ \sqrt{t} \end{bmatrix}$

Note that these are the two given functions in Equation (8.18). Finally, to generate the best values of coefficients a_0 and a_1 in this equation to fit the data, simply type the special function $linfit(x,y,F)$. The first argument *must* be the independent data, the second the dependent data, and the third the vector function:

The coefficient function is:

$Coeffs := linfit(t_{data}, C_{data}, F) \qquad Coeffs = \begin{bmatrix} 2.924 \\ 1.968 \end{bmatrix}$

Again, this could be given any name, but here we've called it *Coeffs*.

We're all done here. The result is that Equation (8.18) becomes (after rounding down the coefficients)

$$C(t) = 2.9 \, te^{-3t} + 1.9\sqrt{t} \qquad\qquad (8.19)$$

Once again, the only trick in accomplishing this rather tricky task is knowing how to type in the particular functions used.

Finally, as a check, let's plot the original data and the results of the generalized regression. Instead of typing Equation (8.19) into Mathcad, all we need to do is a dot-product of *Coeffs* and $F(t)$:

Hence the combined function is: $C(t) := Coeffs \cdot F(t)$

$t := 0, .01 .. 1.1$

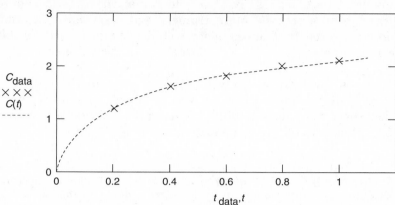

As you can see, the fit works very well. This generalized regression feature is a very powerful feature that enables you to fit pretty much any kind of mathematical expression to a set of data.

Instead of regression curves, engineers sometimes wish to plot not just a curve that gives the "best fit" to the data, but rather a curve that actually passes *through* each data point. The most common approach to this is the *cubic spline interpolation,* which is built in to Mathcad. In this method, a cubic equation is used to represent the behavior of the curve between each pair of data points (x_i, y_i) and (x_{i+1}, y_{i+1}). Why a cubic? The answer is that it turns out that if we used a linear function, we'd end up with a series of straight lines connecting the data points, and if we used a quadratic function, we'd end up with parabolas between each set of points, but the slopes of the parabolas might not match at the connection points. A cubic between each set of data points, it turns out, allows enough flexibility that we end up with a smooth, continuous final curve passing through all the data points. An example of a linear and a cubic fit is shown in Figure 8.8.

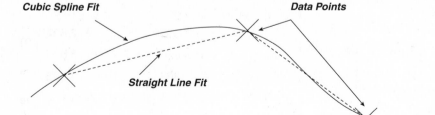

Figure 8.8

Why call it a *spline*? Because this was the name of a drawing instrument that was used, before the advent of technical drawing applications (such as *AutoCad*), for *manually* drawing curves through data points. The instrument was essentially a flexible, spine-like rod that an engineer would bend to follow the data points on a drawing. He or she would then draw the curve using the spline as a guide.

We've obviously moved well beyond this manual procedure. In fact, Mathcad has both linear and cubic splines built in, so we don't even need to go into the mathematical details of how these are constructed. Let's do an example to illustrate this.

Example 8.6   Airfoil profile   A new airfoil profile has been designed. The upper and lower surfaces are given by the following data:

x (ft)	0	1	2	3	4	5	6	7	8	9	10
y_u (in)	0.000	3.878	5.663	6.669	7.063	6.925	6.308	5.258	3.816	2.031	0.000
y_l (in)	0.000	−0.278	0.737	1.731	2.537	3.075	3.292	3.142	2.584	1.569	0.000

Here x is the distance horizontally from the leading edge of the wing, and y_u and y_l are the vertical coordinates of the two surfaces. We wish to find the cross-sectional area of the profile.

To accomplish this task, we need to derive expressions for the two surfaces using splines, and then we can integrate them to find the area. We'll use Mathcad's cubic splines for this (but we should point out that Mathcad also has a function linterp for linear interpolations).

Starting a new worksheet called "Example 8.6," let's enter the data first:

Airfoil Profile

By (Your Name)

$$\text{The data are: } x := \begin{bmatrix} 0 \\ 1 \\ 2 \\ 3 \\ 4 \\ 5 \\ 6 \\ 7 \\ 8 \\ 9 \\ 10 \end{bmatrix} \cdot ft \quad y_u := \begin{bmatrix} 0 \\ 3.878 \\ 5.663 \\ 6.669 \\ 7.063 \\ 6.925 \\ 6.308 \\ 5.258 \\ 3.816 \\ 2.031 \\ 0 \end{bmatrix} \cdot in \quad y_l := \begin{bmatrix} 0 \\ -.278 \\ .737 \\ 1.731 \\ 2.537 \\ 3.075 \\ 3.292 \\ 3.142 \\ 2.584 \\ 1.569 \\ 0 \end{bmatrix} \cdot in$$

We can now plot the two y vectors against the x vector. The graph below has been formatted by, among other things, plotting each y divided by in., adding titles, hiding arguments, and so on:

The airfoil looks like:

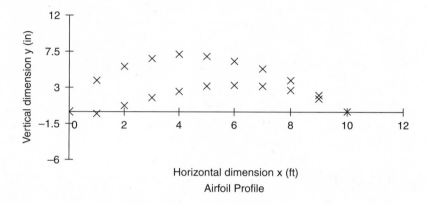

Horizontal dimension x (ft)

Airfoil Profile

In this example we'll be doing two separate cubic splines: one for each surface. The special Mathcad function for this is *cspline(x,y)*, where x and y are the independent and dependent variables. This function creates a vector of numbers that are used in constructing the spline. (Mathcad actually has two other functions, *pspline* and *lspline,* which are used in the exact same way as cspline. The only difference is how each handles the *ends* of the entire curve: lspline makes the ends of the curve straight, pspline makes them parabolic, and cspline makes them cubic. Which you should use depends on the problem you're solving, but cspline is the most commonly used.)

After using cspline, to generate the function that will plot the spline, you must use the function *interp(v,x,y,x′)*, where v is the vector of coefficients created by cspline, and $x′$ is a new independent variable. Of course, in using both cspline and interp you may use any variable names you wish, as long as you place them in the correct order (for instance, the first argument of interp must be the result of using cspline). You should now do the following (using literal subscripts):

$curve_u := \text{cspline}(x,y_u)$ $Y_u(x′) := \text{interp}(curve_u,x,y_u,x′)$

$curve_l := \text{cspline}(x,y_l)$ $Y_l(x′) := \text{interp}(curve_l,x,y_l,x′)$

Note that the two splines are called $Y_u(x′)$ and $Y_l(x′)$, functions of a *new* independent variable $x′$. We can now plot the results:

The airfoil shape is: $x′ := 0 \cdot ft, .1 \cdot ft .. 10 \cdot ft$

Creating this graph may be a bit of a challenge! To create it, on the vertical axis you should plot y_u, y_l, $Y_u(x')$ and $Y_l(x')$, and on the horizontal x, x, x', and x'. In addition, you should not display numbers or axes, and you should impose limits on the vertical axis so that the airfoil is not distorted. Finally, the original data points are markers only, and the two splines are formatted as dashed lines.

We've now finished generating the splines. As you can see, once you understand how to use the cspline and interp functions, it's a pretty straightforward procedure.

We can now compute the cross-sectional area. This is obtained by integrating the width of the wing from the leading edge to the trailing edge:

The cross-sectional area of the foil is:

$$A := \int_{0 \cdot ft}^{10 \cdot ft} (Y_u(x) - Y_l(x))\,dx \qquad A = 2.485 \cdot ft^2$$

Note that we don't have to use the new variable x' when we do this integral.

This completes our discussion of the general topic of fitting a curve to data by using either a regression or analysis or a spline.

8.5

Probability Distributions

As we saw in Figure 8.1, Mathcad has most of the common probability distributions built in. Let's immediately do an example to see what these are about.

Example 8.7 Space shuttle height requirement

Suppose NASA is developing a new space shuttle cabin which has the severe height constraint that the height of an astronaut must be between 5' 10½" and 6'. What percentage of the astronauts will this include? Also, NASA will have to reduce the number of astronauts by 10 percent. Because height can be a disadvantage in some space missions, they have decided to set a new maximum height requirement for all astronauts. At what height will 10 percent of the current astronaut population be excluded? It's known that the astronaut population, which is *normally* distributed, has a mean of 5'9" and a standard deviation of 4".

First, if you're not sure about the meaning of *mean* and *standard deviation,* refer back to Section 8.1. Let's now start a new worksheet called "Example 8.7" and enter the basic data (in inches):

Space Shuttle Height Requirement

By (Your Name)

The population data are: $\mu := 69$ $\sigma := 4$

Note that we haven't used units here because Mathcad's probability distributions don't allow them. We can now use the built-in *normal probability density distribution* function called $dnorm(x,\mu,\sigma)$. The first argument in this function is x, the value of the distribution at which the probability density is evaluated (in our case we'll call this h for height). The quickest way to see how this works is to use it and plot the results. Do the following:

The probability density distribution is: $\quad$ *Number*(h) := dnorm(h, μ, σ)

$$h \ := 60, 60.1 .. 80$$

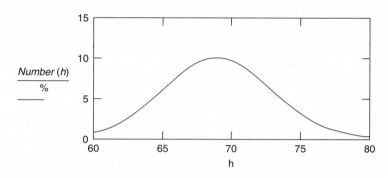

This is, of course, the famous "bell curve" of statistics, describing the distribution of many kinds of random phenomena, including the height distribution of a population. As we mentioned in Section 8.1, for a normal distribution, 68.3 percent of a population is between the ± σ points (and 99.7 percent will be between the ± 3σ points). In our case the ± σ points are the heights $69'' - 4'' = 5'5''$ and $69'' + 4'' = 6'1''$.

We can check these numbers by looking at the *cumulative probability distribution,* which is the integral of the density distribution. Mathcad has the cumulative probability distribution built in for many distributions. For the normal distribution, the function is *pnorm*($x,μ,σ$). Again, to get a sense of what it means, let's plot this for our data:

The cumulative probability distribution is: $\quad$ *Total*(h) := pnorm(h, μ, σ)

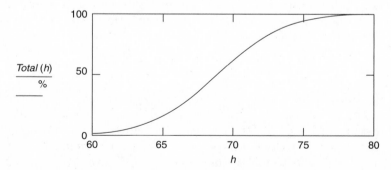

As you can see, what this does is compute the total percentage of the population that is shorter than a given height h. For example, essentially 100 percent of the population is shorter than $80'' = 6'8''$. Of course, we don't have to use the graph to get percentages: we can just evaluate our function *Total*(h) at any height h. For instance, we can find the percentage of the population with heights less than or equal to $5'10\frac{1}{2}''$ (70.5 in.)(where we added the "unit" for %):

The percentage less than or equal to 70.5″ is: *Total*(70.5) = 64.6·%

We're now ready to answer the question about what percentage of astronauts are between 5′ 10½″ and 6′:

The percentage between 5′ 10½″ and 6′ is:

Total(72) − *Total*(70.5) = 12.7·%

Hence we conclude that 12.7 percent of the astronauts will qualify for working in the new space shuttle cabin.

We can also verify the statement that 68.3 percent of the population is between the ± σ points and 99.7 percent is between the ± 3σ points:

Total(μ + σ) − *Total*(μ − σ) = 68.3·%

Total(μ + 3·σ) − *Total*(μ − 3·σ) = 99.7·%

The last question we wish to answer is, what maximum height requirement will eliminate 10 percent of the astronauts? To answer this, we use the *third* kind of built-in probability function: the *inverse cumulative probability distribution*. For the normal distribution, this is *qnorm*(*p*,μ,σ), where *p* is the percentage of the population we wish to select. To see this, let's ask Mathcad to tell us the height at which 90 percent of the population is too short:

The height that is too high for 90% of the population is:

qnorm(90·%, μ, σ) = 74.1

Hence 90 percent of the population is less than 74.1″ = 6′2.1″, so if NASA sets a maximum height for astronauts of 6′2″, they will eliminate 10 percent of the astronauts from the program.

In Example 8.7 we've seen that we can obtain lots of information on a normal distribution by using the dnorm, pnorm, and qnorm functions built in to Mathcad. There are similar functions for the other distributions listed in Figure 8.1. For example, the corresponding *binomial distribution* functions are dbinom, pbinom, and qbinom.

8.6

Where to Find More

If you wish to find more details on these statistical features, and many others such as *smoothing* of data, you can use Mathcad's extensive Help, or, for even more specific details and examples, the *Resource Center*, where you can click on *Practical Statistics*. This will lead to the window shown in Figure 8.9. This window lists some of the large body of information on statistics available within Mathcad.

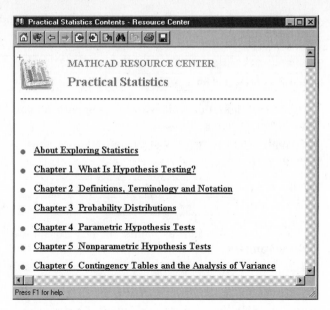

Figure 8.9

Exercises

8.1 The following data shows the test scores (%) of 22 students in a course *Using Mathcad in Engineering*.

70	45	67	99	99	94	95	45	52	65	90
94	60	60	65	40	80	97	90	65	85	30

By defining a vector *Grades* with this data as cell values, obtain the lowest and highest grades, the median grade, and the average score, and generate a frequency distribution histogram plotted as a bar graph. After you do this, you realize that there's an error: all grades above 90% were incorrectly given an extra 5%. Correct this error and re-compute the average grade. You then discover another error: all grades less than 50% were accidentally penalized 10%. Correct this error and re-compute the average grade. Finally, generate a second graph showing the new distribution.

Hint: So that you don't have a large column vector (which is cumbersome to work with), define *Grades* initially as a matrix with one row and 22 columns, and then immediately compute $Grades = Grades^T$ (where ^{T} denotes the transpose). Also, to re-compute the grades, try using the if statement $Grades_i = \text{if} (Grades_i > 90\%, Grades_i - 5\%, Grades_i)$, (where i is defined as a range from zero to 21) to subtract 5% from grades over 90%, and then a similar expression to correct the second error.

8.2 Apply a linear regression to the following data and find the slope and intercept.

x	1	2	3	4	5	6	7	8	9	10
y	1.9	1.8	1.45	1.25	1.1	0.9	0.89	0.6	0.51	0.31

Plot the original data as points, along with a dotted line (no points) representing the regression line.

8.3 Apply a linear regression to the following data and find the slope and intercept.

x	0	1	2	3	4	5	6	7	8	9	10
y	3.1	−1.1	−5	−9.2	−13	−17.5	−21	−24	−30	−35	−37

Plot the original data as points, along with a dotted line (no points) representing the regression line.

8.4 A marketing manager for a sneaker manufacturer approaches you and asks for help. She asks you to consider the data shown in the table below, which indicates that for the last few months the amount of advertising strongly influences the number of units sold each month (it appears to be a linear relationship).

Month	1	2	3	4	5
Advertising Budget ($)	25,060	12,920	14,140	9,840	20,208
Sales	26,107	10,615	17,875	9,942	21,501

She wants to know approximately how much she should spend ($) on advertising next month if she wants to sell 23,000 units. How much should she spend? After you tell her, she comes back to you and says she was only given a budget of $17,000. Approximately how many units should she expect to sell with this budget? Are these results very reliable, or is the data too scattered? To determine this, plot the original data and the regression line so you can make a visual determination, (you can also compute Mathcad's corr function).

Hint: Although there are several ways to solve this problem, first you must do the linear regression to find the slope and intercept of the Sales − Budget line. Then one way to find the budget for 23,000 in sales is to try using Given . . . Find with an equation representing the regression line. You can use another Given . . . Find to find the sales due to a budget of $17,000. Alternatively, you can generate a range of Budget values, plot the Sales − Budget linear regression line and pick off the two data points you want using the Trace function. Note that because the data values rise and fall in step, you can safely use Mathcad's sort function to make the data uniformly increase.

8.5 You wish to find out of what material a wire of diameter $d = 1$ mm and length $l = 1$ m is made. To do so, you decide to measure Young's modulus E (Pa) of the material, which is given by

$$E = \frac{\sigma}{\varepsilon} \qquad\qquad (8.20)$$

where σ (psi) is the stress and ε is the strain in the wire when you hang a weight from the end of it. The stress is given by

$$\sigma = \frac{W}{\pi \frac{d^2}{4}} \qquad\qquad (8.21)$$

where W (lbf) is the weight. The strain ε is given by the amount of stretch δ (in) produced by the weight, divided by the original length l (in other words, ε is the fractional change in length of the wire). Instead of just adding one weight and measuring one amount of stretch, a series of measurements is taken so that any measurement errors in one individual test will not produce an erroneous result. Taking a set of measurements will also show that the stress-strain curve is a straight line, as Equation (8.20) predicts. Suppose you obtain the following data:

W (lbf)	10	25	40	60	100	125	155	180	225	250
δ (mm)	0.1	0.3	0.5	0.7	1.2	1.5	2	2.3	2.7	2.9

Use this data to compute the corresponding stresses and strains. Perform a linear regression on this stress-strain data and plot the data along with a straight line based on the regression results. The slope of the regression line will be the experimental value of E. Compare this to tabulated data available in the *Resource Center* (look up *Modulus of Elasticity*) and determine the material of the wire.

8.6 Consider the following data:

x	0.2	0.4	0.6	0.8	1	1.2	1.4	1.6	1.8	2
y	1.2	2.1	2.5	2.9	3	3.4	3.6	3.8	4	4.2

It approximately conforms to the equation

$$y(x) = Ax^n \qquad\qquad (8.22)$$

By doing a linear regression find the best values of A and n. Plot on the same graph the data as points and a smooth dotted curve (for $x = 0$ to 2.25) representing Equation (8.22). In addition, plot on either a log-log or semi-log graph as appropriate (with $x = 0.1$ to 5, and limits on the vertical axis as necessary to get a good plot) to obtain a straight line.

8.7 Consider the following data:

x	1	2	3	4	5	6	7	8	9	10
y	90	76	66	63	60	58	54	54	52	50

It approximately conforms to Equation (8.22). By doing a linear regression find the best values of A and n. Plot on the same graph the data as points and a smooth dotted curve (for $x = 1$ to 10) representing Equation (8.22). In addition, plot on either a log-log or semi-log graph as appropriate to obtain a straight line.

8.8 A car is tested in the wind tunnel to obtain data on the aerodynamic drag F (lbf) at various speeds V (mph). The data are shown below.

V (mph)	30	35	40	45	50	55	60	65	70	75
F (lbf)	10	13.5	17.5	22	27.5	33	40	47	52	63.5

This data approxiately conforms to the following equation:

$$F(V) = A\, V^n \tag{8.23}$$

where A and n are constants. Using a linear regression find the values of A and n (and note that you should not use units here because you will have to take logarithms of data, and you can only do this with pure numbers). Use these results to obtain a value for the car's drag coefficient C_d. The drag coefficient is a measure of how streamlined a body is: a well-streamlined car will have a low drag coefficient, usually less than about 0.3 for modern cars. The drag on the car is given by

$$F = \frac{1}{2}\, \rho\, A_{fr} C_d\, V^2 \tag{8.24}$$

where $\rho = 1.2$ kg/m^3 and $A_{fr} = 1.5$ m^2 is the frontal area (the area of the car directly facing the air flow). By comparing Equations (8.23) and (8.24) you can verify whether the data is a good fit by checking the value obtained for n. Is it close to two? You can also use the value obtained for A to solve for C_d:

$$C_d = \frac{A}{\dfrac{1}{2}\, \rho\, A_{fr}} \tag{8.25}$$

Find the drag coefficient for this car.

Hint: The drag coefficient is dimensionless. To get the correct result from Equation (8.25) you must assign the units lbf/mph^2 to the value of A obtained by doing the regression analysis. To do this, just set A equal to itself times these units.

8.9 Consider the following data:

x	0.2	0.4	0.6	0.8	1	1.2	1.4	1.6	1.8	2
y	8.1	6.6	5.3	4.3	3.5	2.8	2.3	1.9	1.5	1.2

It approximately conforms to the equation

$$y(x) = c\, e^{\lambda x} \tag{8.26}$$

By doing a linear regression find the best values of c and λ. Plot on the same graph the data as points and a smooth dotted curve representing Equation (8.26). In addition, plot on either a log-log or semi-log graph as appropriate (with limits on the vertical axis as necessary to get a good plot) to obtain a straight line.

8.10 An engineer is measuring the cooling of a hot body in air. He obtains the following data on the temperature ΔT (°F):

t (min)	0	12	24	36	48	60	72	84	96	108	120
ΔT (°F)	200	160	135	110	90	75	60	50	40	35	25

These data should conform to the following equation:

$$\Delta T(t) = \Delta T_0 \, e^{-\frac{t}{\tau}} \tag{8.27}$$

where τ (sec) is the cooling time constant. Using a linear regression, estimate the value of τ. Plot the data and a smooth regression curve on either a log-log or semi-log graph as appropriate (with limits on the vertical axis as necessary to get a good plot) to obtain a straight line. Finally, using a Given . . . Find technique, estimate how long it will take (sec) for ΔT to drop to 20°F.

8.11 Consider the fourth order polynomial

$$y(x) = a_0 + a_1 x + a_2 x^2 + a_3 x^3 + a_4 x^4 \tag{8.28}$$

If the following data are obtained from it:

x	1	2	3	4	5
y	6.1	6	7.3	5.2	−7.5

find the values of the coefficients a_0, a_1, a_2, a_3 and a_4. Plot the data points and the polynomial curve. Find the area under the curve from $x = 0$ to 5. Note that the values generated by Mathcad's regress function include the coefficients. You can ignore the first three values and the remainder will be the coefficients.

8.12 Consider the following data:

x	0	1	2	3	4	5	6	7	8	9	10
y	2	1.65	1.54	1.54	1.65	2.01	2.4	3	3.55	4.39	5.3

Assume the data conforms to the following trend:

$$y(x) = a\,x^2 + b\,e^{-0.2\,x} \tag{8.29}$$

Find the best values for a and b using a generalized regression. Plot the original data and a smooth regression curve on the same graph.

8.13 Consider the following data:

x	1	2	3	4	5	6	7	8	9	10
y	2.17	1.91	1.35	1.21	0.87	0.93	0.79	0.60	0.51	0.47

Assume the data conforms to the following trend:

$$y(x) = \frac{a}{x} + \frac{b}{x^3} \tag{8.30}$$

Find the best values for a and b using a generalized regression. Plot the original data and a smooth regression curve on the same graph.

8.14 Consider the following data:

x	0	1	2	3	4	5	6	7	8	9	10
y	5.2	2.5	2.5	2.5	2.5	3	3.5	4.5	5	6	7

Assume the data follows the trend given by

$$y(x) = a\, x^{1.5} + \frac{b}{x+1} \tag{8.31}$$

Find the best values for a and b using a generalized regression. Plot the original data and a smooth regression curve on the same graph. By using a Given . . . Find on the derivative of the fitted curve equation, find the minimum value of $y(x)$, and its location.

8.15 Consider the following data:

x	0	1	2	3	4	5	6	7	8	9	10
y	0	2	7	6	12	6	13	10	8	10	19

Fit a cubic spline to this data (using cubic ends) and plot the original data (as points) and the cubic spline (as a smooth dotted line). Find the area under the spline from $x = 0$ to 10.

8.16 Consider the following data:

x	0	1	2	3	4	5	6	7	8	9
y	0	12	21	20	37	51	75	47	79	108

Fit three cubic splines to this data (using linear, parabolic, and cubic ends) and plot the original data (as points) and the cubic splines (as smooth curves with differing line types) from $x = 0$ to 10. In addition, plot two additional graphs from $x = -1.5$ to 1, and $x = 8$ to 12.

8.17 The normal probability density distribution is given by

$$f(x) = \frac{1}{\sigma\sqrt{2\pi}} e^{-\frac{1}{2}\left(\frac{x-\mu}{\sigma}\right)^2} \tag{8.32}$$

where σ is the standard deviation and μ is the mean. This is the function computed by Mathcad's dnorm function. The cumulative distribution (given by Mathcad's pnorm function) is then

$$F(x) = \int_{-\infty}^{x} f(x)dx \tag{8.33}$$

To find the percentage of the data between any two values a and b, Equation (8.33) can be used with these values as lower and upper limits. Consider data for which $\mu = 10$ and $\sigma = 1$. To test these expressions, use Equations (8.32) and (8.33), and dnorm and pnorm to find the probability density of the distribution at $x = 10$ and find the percentage between $x = 8$ and $x = 12$.

8.18 On a construction site, rivets are required which have a length of 28.0 ± 0.2 cm. The supplier says the supply of rivets is normally distributed with $\mu = 27.9$ cm and $\sigma = 0.1$ cm. What percentage of rivets will meet the specification? If the specification is changed to 28.0 ± 0.1 cm, what percentage of rivets will meet this specification?

8.19 Due to variations in manufacturing, the average storage space on floppy disks is 1.44 MB, with a standard deviation of 0.20 MB. If they are to be used to store files of size 1.4 MB, what percentage of disks are likely to be usable? If they are to be used to store programs of size 1 MB, what percentage of disks are likely to be usable?

Hint: The percentage larger than a particular value is 100% minus the percentage smaller than the value.

8.20 The breaking strength of a company's wire product has a normal distribution with a mean of 2500 lbf and a standard deviation of 55 lbf. What is the maximum load such that no more than 5% of the wires can be expected to snap? Do this two ways: using Mathcad's qnorm function, and by using a Given . . . Find in conjunction with pnorm.

8.21 Airmail envelopes have a mean weight of 1.950 gm, with a standard deviation of 0.025 gm. In a lot of 1000 envelopes, how many will weigh more than 2 gm?

8.22 If the lifetime T of automobile batteries is normally distributed with a mean of 4 years, a standard deviation of 1 year, and the manufacturer wishes to guarantee the battery for 3 years, what percentage of batteries will she have to replace under the warranty?

8.23 Consider a normal distribution with $\mu = 100$ and $\sigma = 10$. Find the percentages of the distribution between 90 and 110, 80 and 120, and 70 and 130 (these are the ± σ, ± 2σ and ± 3σ points).

8.24 Consider a normal distribution with $\mu = 0$ and $\sigma = 10$. Find the values of ± x for which 5%, 25%, 50%, and 75% of the distribution is selected.

Hint: To do this use Given . . . Find with expressions like pnorm(x,μ,σ) − pnorm($-x,\mu,\sigma$) = 5%.

Importing and Exporting, the Web, and Some Advanced Concepts

In this final chapter, we'll review how to use Mathcad to read and write data in various formats and how to make it communicate with other computer applications. To wrap up, we'll then explore a couple of more advanced mathematics topics, so you can get a better feel for the power available in Mathcad version 7: *complex notation* to study *potential theory,* and *Laplace transforms.* If you're not familiar with either complex mathematics or Laplace transforms, you can skip that material, although it's fairly self-contained and doesn't demand too much of you. If you are familiar with these, you'll probably be impressed with how Mathcad handles them.

9.1
Importing and Exporting Data

Mathcad has several ways to either import or export data. Which you use depends on the form of the data (in other words, whether the data are in a word processor document, in a data file, or in a spreadsheet worksheet, for example), and to some degree on your personal preferences. Let's look at each method in turn.

Copying and Pasting Data

If you don't have a lot of data, a convenient way to copy it into or out of Mathcad is to use Windows' copy and paste technique. In any Windows application, you'll find menu items and icons for copying and pasting, and you also have the accelerator keys **Ctrl + C** (for copying) and **Ctrl + V** (for pasting). In addition, all Windows 95 applications have a feature where you can select what you wish to copy and then press the *right mouse button* to get access to a menu, which includes copy and paste options. When you use any of these methods to copy an object or objects, Windows temporarily stores the information on its *clipboard*. To paste something you've copied, simply click at the location you wish to paste and use any of the techniques just listed. However, you have to be a little bit careful in using pasting: depending on what you're copying and pasting, and where you're pasting it, Windows will give different results.

To see this let's try copying objects from a file created with Microsoft Word. This file is shown in Figure 9.1. (So that you can follow what we're doing, you should reproduce this file in Word or in your favorite word processor.) Notice that this document has several parts: four paragraphs of text, a drawing, and a table. You can select any of these, or all of the document.

In this example, let's select the numerical data in the table by, for example, wiping over it using the mouse. Then use one of the copying techniques to copy the objects to the clipboard. Finally, you need to switch to Mathcad (or open it if it's not currently running) and on a blank worksheet use one of the techniques to paste the clipboard contents.

If you do all this, you should get something like Figure 9.2. We've obtained an *object* that is *embedded*. What this means is that the object has been pasted in such a way that Mathcad remembers what application was used to create it (in this case Word), and the object is controlled by the *original* application.

If you wish to edit the object you must *double-click* on it. Doing this will temporarily change Mathcad's menu and icons to those of the original application, as shown in Figure 9.3, so you can edit the object. When you click outside the object, you'll revert to the Mathcad menu and icons.

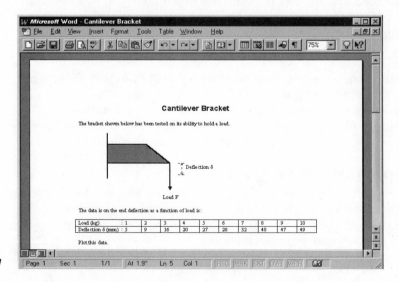

Figure 9.1

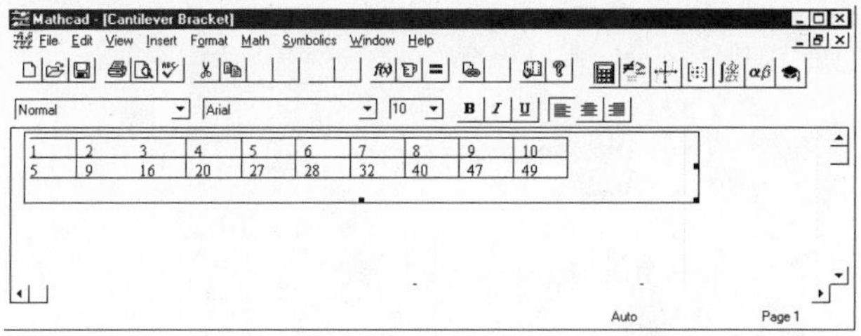

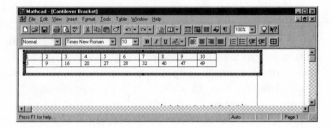

Figure 9.2

Figure 9.3

This method of pasting is sometimes convenient, and at other times very much inconvenient (and we'll see shortly that there is another way to paste that produces a different result). This procedure *is* useful when you're copying and pasting a *graphic,* because Mathcad doesn't have its own drawing module. On the other hand, it is not really useful when you're copying and pasting either text or numerical data, because with these you probably want to use Mathcad to edit copied text or use the numerical data in a computation. The object shown in Figure 9.2 appears to be numerical data, but as far as Mathcad is concerned, it's a graphic!

Let's delete this object and instead copy and paste the drawing from the Word document. If you do so you'll have an image of the drawing in Mathcad. If you ever need to edit this image in Mathcad, you simply double-click on it and Word's drawing icons would become available for you to use. [The only time this won't work is if you open the Mathcad file you've created using a computer that does not have the original application (in this case Word) installed.]

What we've been doing here is copying and pasting using *OLE* (*O*bject *L*inking and *E*mbedding), a built-in feature of Windows 95. With OLE, when you copy and paste an object from one application to another, the object is *embedded* when it's pasted. This means just what we've discovered: the pasted object can be edited using the original application. What's *linking?* It's the same as embedding, with one major difference: when you double-click on the pasted object and edit it, not only is the pasted object changed, but so is the *original* in the original application. We won't look at linking in this text, but for guidance on linking in Mathcad, use its *Help . . . Index* to search for *Linking.*

274

**Importing and
Exporting, the
Web, and Some
Advanced
Concepts**

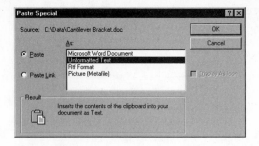

Figure 9.4

The copy and paste method we've used so far is obviously quick, but as we already mentioned, most of the time when you're copying text or numerical data from an application into Mathcad you want to paste them *not* as an *object* but as a *text region* or a *math region*, so that you can work with them using Mathcad itself. How do we do this? The answer depends on what you're pasting and where you're pasting it in Mathcad.

First let's see how to paste text from a word processor as a *text region* into Mathcad. Select the title paragraph (although, of course, in reality you wouldn't bother copying and pasting just a few words) and copy it to the clipboard. Then switch to Mathcad, and instead of using any of the paste options we've described, use the menu item *Edit . . . Paste Special*. This will present the window shown in Figure 9.4, in which several options for pasting are presented. Note that the first option listed would paste the title as a Word (or your word processor's) object, which is what we've been doing up to now. Also, depending on what you're pasting, the options in the window will vary. Finally, note that there is an option for linking, if desired. We want to paste it as Unformatted Text so that we can work with it in Mathcad.

If you do this you'll end up with a text block, which you can edit or format as you wish (for example, make it 16-point Helvetica Bold). Your worksheet should now look something like

Cantilever Bracket

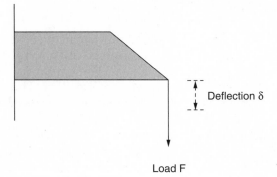

What about pasting numerical data? As we saw in Figure 9.2, regular pasting creates just an object. To paste numerical data into Mathcad *as* numerical data, there are two approaches: you can use the menu item *Edit . . . Paste Special* just as we did for the title text, or you can simply paste the numerical data (using any of the techniques we've described, such as using **Ctrl + V**) *directly* into a math placeholder. When you paste into a math placeholder, Mathcad understands that you're *not* pasting an object and instead creates a matrix containing the data.

Let's try both methods for the numerical data in the table (to create the math placeholder, start defining a variable M using the assignment equals). You should get for the two pastings

1	2	3	4	5
6	7	8	9	10
5	9	16	20	27
28	32	40	47	49

$$M := \begin{bmatrix} 1 & 2 & 3 & 4 & 5 & 6 & 7 & 8 & 9 & 10 \\ 5 & 9 & 16 & 20 & 27 & 28 & 32 & 40 & 47 & 49 \end{bmatrix}$$

Actually, the first pasting didn't *really* create numerical data after all: it gave us a text region. It's not useless, however, because you could now, within Mathcad, select one or more of the data values and copy and paste each one to a variable assignment. Note that the second method created a matrix, into which it poured the numerical data, making it immediately useful.

These concepts of pasting, using either one of the regular pasting techniques or *Paste Special,* apply for pasting into Mathcad from other applications, such as spreadsheets, as well as from Mathcad to other applications. The results of using these pasting techniques don't always appear as expected, so sometimes you have to just try both to obtain the desired results.

Finally, Mathcad version 7 has implemented *OLE2,* which means that if you wish to copy data between it and another OLE2 application, you can simply drag and drop from one to the other directly. For details on this see Mathcad's *Help.*

You can now discard this practice worksheet and start a new blank one for the next topic. The second major way Mathcad can be made to communicate with other applications or with data files is with its Components feature.

276

**Importing and
Exporting, the
Web, and Some
Advanced
Concepts**

Using Mathcad's Components Feature

To invoke this method, either to import or export data, you use the menu item *Insert . . . Component* (or click on the Component Wizard icon on the toolbar). This will invoke the window shown in Figure 9.5, which shows the components that can be inserted with the Student edition of Mathcad.

What happens next depends on what choice you make for the component to insert, but there will always be guidance provided by the Component Wizard. Suppose we have a Microsoft Excel file from which we'd like to extract data, as shown in Figure 9.6 [you should produce two columns of data like this (your data does not need to be as detailed) in Excel or in your favorite spreadsheet].

Although Excel is not listed as a choice in Figure 9.5, we can click on *File Read or Write* and press the Next button. In the next window that appears, select *Read from a data source* and move on to the next window (shown in Figure 9.7), where you can select the file type that contains the data (all of the common spreadsheets are listed).

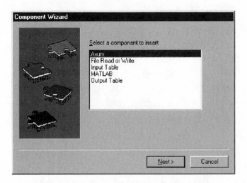

Figure 9.5

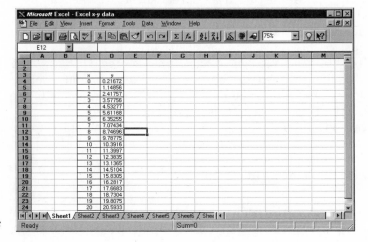

Figure 9.6

Figure 9.7

Finally, you can browse to find the file and click on the Finish button. You should end up with something like

■ :=

C:\.\Excel x-y data.xls

We've successfully inserted the data from the Excel spreadsheet. The only thing left to do is assign it a variable name, for example, *M,* in the placeholder. We can then evaluate *M* to see how everything worked out:

The data are: $M =$

	0	1	2	3
0	0	0	0	0
1	0	0	0	0
2	0	0	0	0
3	0	0	0	0.217
4	0	0	1	1.149
5	0	0	2	2.418
6	0	0	3	3.578
7	0	0	4	4.533
8	0	0	5	5.612
9	0	0	6	6.353
10	0	0	7	7.074
11	0	0	8	8.747
12	0	0	9	9.788
13	0	0	10	10.392

Note that we've used the default value of ORIGIN = 0. Comparing this to the spreadsheet shown in Figure 9.6, we can see that *too much* data was imported! It turns out that we need to change the properties of the component, so it will only read the spreadsheet data we want and not include as data the blank

278

**Importing and
Exporting, the
Web, and Some
Advanced
Concepts**

spreadsheet cells above and to the left. To change the properties of a component, right-click on it to get access to a pop-up menu, which includes a *Properties . . .* option. With this option you can tell Mathcad *where* on the spreadsheet to start (and end) reading data. Using this, see if you can get

The data are: $M =$

	0	1
0	0	0.217
1	1	1.149
2	2	2.418
3	3	3.578
4	4	4.533
5	5	5.612
6	6	6.353
7	7	7.074
8	8	8.747
9	9	9.788
10	10	10.392
11	11	11.4
12	12	12.384
13	13	13.137

We're finally all done. Of course, if you wish, you can choose to display this as a matrix.

One of the most useful things about using Component to import data is that each time you open the Mathcad file, it will re-read the data file. Also, if you wish to *force* Mathcad to re-read the data, all you need to do is click once on the component and press **F9.**

Although the specific details will vary, you can use the same basic Component procedure to insert or import data from any of a wide variety of file formats. To see this, as an exercise let's take the square roots of all the *y* values and save these new *y* values with the original *x* values in a new file called "Exported X-Y data." To do this, we must first find out how many values of *x* or *y* we have. Then we can compute each new value of *y*. Finally click on *Insert . . . Component . . . File Read or Write* (or use the Component Wizard icon on the toolbar) and choose the file write option to get access to a window where you can choose the type of file to save. Select the *Tab Delimited Text* option (which will save the data with *x* and *y* data pairs in rows, with each *x* and *y* value separated by a tab) and type the data filename and the location of your choice. After completing the File Read or Write Wizard windows, you'll have the component inserted on the worksheet, and all you will need to do is type in the placeholder the matrix you wish to export.

If you do all this you should have something like

$$N := \text{length}(M^{<1>}) \qquad N = 21 \qquad i := 0 .. N \qquad M_{i,1} := \sqrt{M_{i,1}}$$

Exported X-Y data

M

(If you're rusty on working with matrices, refer back to Chapter 6.)

You will now have a saved data file, which you could open using any of a number of applications. Here let's use the Windows accessory WordPad (you should set the *files of type* to All Documents). You'll get results similar to those shown in Figure 9.8 (although your numbers will be different). Note that the *y* column contains numbers that are the square roots of our original *y*'s.

We've finished our introduction to Mathcad's Component feature. You'll find this to be a very useful feature if you work with lots of data in various formats. We only looked at using it to import Excel data and export tab-delimited text, but of course there are many import and export formats available.

One final point about the Component feature: you can use it to create an input table or an output table. These are simply alternative ways for you to either type in data in Mathcad or have it present results. You recall that to enter a matrix of data into Mathcad, you first create a matrix by starting with, for example, the accelerator keys **Ctrl + M**. Instead of this, you can use the menu item *Insert . . . Component . . . Input Table*. On the other hand, if you want to see the values in a matrix you've previously defined, you can just type the matrix name with the evaluation equals, or instead you can use the menu item *Insert . . . Component . . . Output Table*. Why use these table modes instead of the matrix mode? It's basically a matter of personal preference: they have the same effect but present the data in slightly different formats. For details on using these table modes, see Mathcad's *Help*.

The final method for importing and exporting data is by reading and writing ASCII files.

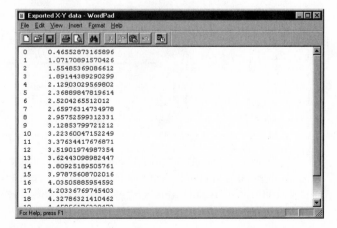

Figure 9.8

280

Importing and
Exporting, the
Web, and Some
Advanced
Concepts

Reading and Writing ASCII Files

This method, which is a carryover from previous versions of Mathcad, is not quite as elegant as the previous methods but is often convenient because it's very simple and quick, when you're using the right type of files.

The most important thing you need to remember about this method is that there are two different functions for reading a file, namely, READ(*file*) and READPRN(*file*), and two for writing to a file, namely, WRITE(*file*) and WRITEPRN(*file*). Let's look at READPRN(*file*) and WRITEPRN(*file*) first. These are for reading from and writing to a file that has data in a *structured* format: that is, each line of the file has the same number of data values. For instance, the file called "Exported X-Y data" shown in Figure 9.8 is structured data in which each line of the file contains one *x, y* pair. The only tricks here are that you must type in the file name starting with the double-quote ("), and you must specify where the file is located. The data you read must be assigned to a variable.

To practice this, let's read the file Exported X-Y data into our worksheet as a new variable $Data_{Read}$ using the READPRN(*file*) function. See if you can obtain something like

$Data_{Read} := $ READPRN("C:\Data\Exported X-Y data")

$Data_{Read} = $

	0	1
0	0	0.466
1	1	1.072
2	2	1.555
3	3	1.891
4	4	2.129
5	5	2.369
6	6	2.52
7	7	2.66
8	8	2.958
9	9	3.129
10	10	3.224
11	11	3.376
12	12	3.519
13	13	3.624

The function WRITEPRN(*file*) is used in a similar way, except a previously defined variable is assigned to it, rather than the other way around.

Try creating the new matrix $Data_{Write}$ shown below and saving it as a file called "Write Test" in a location of your choice:

$$Data_{Write} := \begin{bmatrix} 1 & 3 & 7 \\ -2 & 0 & 6 \\ -5 & 4 & 4 \end{bmatrix} \qquad \text{WRITEPRN}("\text{C:\textbackslash Data\textbackslash Write Test}") := Data_{Write}$$

You'll now have a structured ASCII file, with each row of the original matrix assigned to a new line (and each data value in a line will be separated by a tab). The contents of the file are:

1	3	7
-2	0	6
-5	4	4

You can customize how Mathcad writes to a data file by changing the built-in variables PRNCOLWIDTH and PRNPRECISION. When you use WRITEPRN(*file*) Mathcad creates a new file, and *if a file of that name already exists, it writes over it*. You can ask Mathcad to simply add extra data values to the end of an existing file by using APPENDPRN(*file*) instead of WRITEPRN(*file*). For information on each of these functions see Mathcad's *Help*.

Finally, we can mention Mathcad's READ(*file*) and WRITE (*file*) functions. These are used to read and write data in an *unstructured* format. When a data file is read with READ(*file*), the result will be a vector (a matrix with a single column) containing the data, regardless of whether the original file is structured or unstructured. Because each use of READ(*file*) reads one data point, it is usually used in conjunction with a subscripted variable. To see how this works, do the following (where you should use the location of your Write Test file):

$$i := 0 \, .. \, 20 \qquad a_i := \text{READ}("\text{C:\textbackslash Data\textbackslash Write Test}")$$

$$a = \begin{bmatrix} 1 \\ 3 \\ 7 \\ -2 \\ 0 \\ 6 \\ -5 \\ 4 \\ 4 \end{bmatrix}$$

Note that we defined a range of 0 through 20, even though we have only 9 data points, to illustrate what you need to do if you

282

**Importing and
Exporting, the
Web, and Some
Advanced
Concepts**

don't know how many data points a file contains: You should use a fairly large range, and then edit it to increase it as necessary until you're sure you've picked up all the data. Mathcad will stop reading the file when it runs out of data. Notice that the file data, originally three lines of data, was read by READ(*find*) as a single column (in other words, it lost its structure).

Finally, let's practice using WRITE(*file*) by writing the first five values of the vector a to a new file called "Last Test":

$$i := 0 .. 4 \qquad \text{WRITE("C:\textbackslash Data\textbackslash Last Test")} := a_i$$

Mathcad will create an unstructured file with the following data:

$$1 \quad 3 \quad 7 \quad -2 \quad 0$$

This is as far as we'll go in discussing how to import and export data with Mathcad, but as you can see there are many different ways to do this. For more information on all these methods, consult the *Resource Center* and use it to search for *data files,* where you'll find lots more information.

We can now look at the next major communication need you'll probably have with Mathcad: communicating using the World Wide Web (otherwise known simply as the Web).

9.2

**Using the World
Wide Web**

Mathcad has several ways in which to access the Web. First of all, you must obviously have an Internet provider. If you are using Mathcad on a college network, you should have no difficulty in doing what we're about to describe. If you're using a home computer, you can already be attached to the Web before running Mathcad, or Mathcad will dial up for you, as needed.

Probably the most direct way of accessing the Web is by using the Collaboratory. To do this, use the menu item *File . . . Collaboratory,* and the window shown in Figure 9.9 will appear. This window shows information in a format just like Windows 95's own Windows Explorer file manager, except that now you can open files created by other Mathcad users worldwide! In fact, you can even *insert* the contents of a Web worksheet into your own worksheet, so that any variables defined by the Web worksheet will be valid in your worksheet (see *reference* under *Help* for guidance in doing this).

You can also send a worksheet you've created to one of the subdirectories shown, so others can benefit from your work (again, see Mathcad's *Help* for guidance).

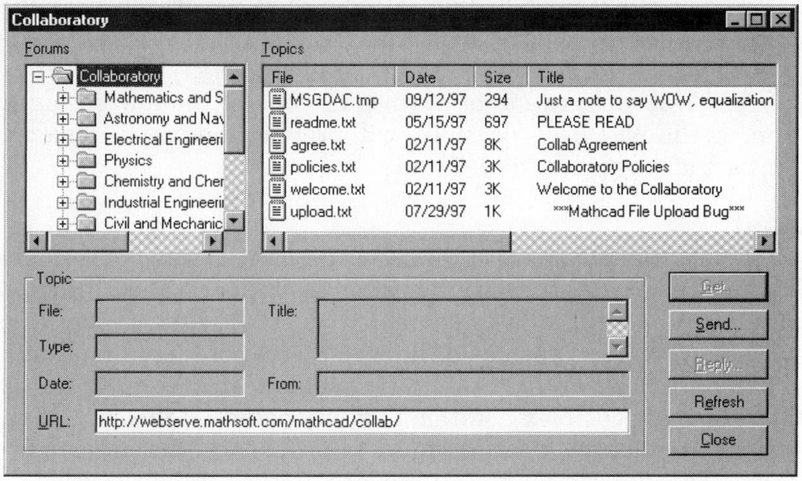

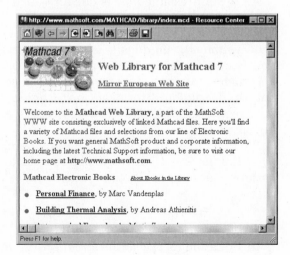

Figure 9.9

In this way Mathsoft (the developers of Mathcad) are encouraging the growth of an international community of users. It's definitely worth your while to examine the files that are available.

The second main method for communicating via the Web is to open the *Resource Center,* where you'll find three jumping-off points: the *Web Library,* shown in Figure 9.10; the Mathsoft home page http://www.mathsoft.com; and the *Web Store,* where you can find information on the latest Mathcad products, such as Mathcad books. The Web Library has lots of information and data free for you to use in developing your own worksheets.

Figure 9.10

284

**Importing and
Exporting, the
Web, and Some
Advanced
Concepts**

We won't comment further on accessing the Web here, but if you're at all experienced in surfing the Web, using these features will be very easy for you.

This Web integration of Mathcad is one of its new strengths and, as the Web itself develops, will probably end up being a major part of why you use Mathcad.

9.3

Some Advanced Topics

In the first few chapters of this text, we covered some of the basic features of Mathcad by studying some simple engineering problems. In some of the later chapters, we studied some more complicated problems, such as differential equations. As a final topic for this text, let's look at two fairly sophisticated areas of mathematics: using complex notation to study potential theory, and the use of Laplace transforms to solve ordinary differential equations. The descriptions of these are fairly straightforward, so even if you're not familiar with them you'll still be able to follow the material, especially as Mathcad will do all the hard work for us. To make things a little simpler, in all of what follows, we will not use units.

Potential Theory Using Complex Notation

Potential theory is the name given to that part of fluid mechanics in which the flow is *steady, incompressible,* and *inviscid* (and it's usually applied to two-dimensional flows). More generally, potential theory also describes gravitational fields, electrostatic fields, and steady-state heat conduction.

An incompressible flow is one for which the density of the fluid particles does not change. Although no fluid is truly incompressible, in a very large number of flows (including much of *aerodynamics*), the density changes are negligible. An inviscid flow is one in which there is no fluid friction. Again, all real fluids (such as air or water) have *viscosity,* so all flows have internal fluid friction. However, once again, in many flows the friction is negligible. Hence, many real flows can be modeled using potential theory.

We don't need to go into the details here, but it turns out that potential flows can be described by Laplace's equation (which has nothing mathematically to do with Laplace transforms!):

$$\frac{\partial^2 \Psi}{\partial x^2} + \frac{\partial^2 \Psi}{\partial y^2} = 0 \tag{9.1}$$

In Equation (9.1) ψ is the *stream function,* which is a function of the coordinates x and y. Solutions of this equation lead to curves representing the *streamlines* of the flow under study.

There is also a variable called the *velocity potential* φ, which is also a solution of Laplace's equation:

$$\frac{\partial^2 \varphi}{\partial x^2} + \frac{\partial^2 \varphi}{\partial y^2} = 0 \tag{9.2}$$

The variables ψ and φ represent what are called an *orthogonal set:* curves of constant ψ are everywhere perpendicular to curves of constant φ. Obviously, solving these two equations for given boundary conditions is not easy. It turns out, however, that complex notation comes to our aid. It can be shown that if we create a new variable *z,* given by

$$z = x + iy \tag{9.3}$$

where *i* is the square root of minus one, then *any* function *F(z)* will generate solutions to Equations (9.1) and (9.2). How do we obtain the functions ψ and φ from *F*? It's easy, because it's known that the following relation holds:

$$F(z) = \varphi + i\psi \tag{9.4}$$

In other words, to create a solution to Equations (9.1) and (9.2), simply write a function of *z* (even make it up!) and we can then obtain the stream function and velocity potential of this flow by computing the following (where Re means take the real part only and Im means take the imaginary part only):

$$\varphi = \text{Re}(F(z))$$
$$\psi = \text{Im}(F(z)) \tag{9.5}$$

Of course, when you just make up a function *F(z)* you have no idea what flow field will be generated. It turns out that there are theories for deriving specific functions to represent specific flows, but just so you can see how this whole system works, let's choose an arbitrary function and see what happens. Let's define

$$F(z) = z^3 \tag{9.6}$$

We have no idea to what flow this will lead, but let's proceed anyway. First, define this function in a new blank worksheet (which you might want to save as, say, "Potential Flow using Complex Notation" in your preferred location):

Potential Flow Using Complex Notation

By (Your Name)

The complex potential is: $F(z) := z^3$

286

**Importing and
Exporting, the
Web, and Some
Advanced
Concepts**

Next, let's define a range of x and y values between zero and one:

Define the number of x and y values to be computed: $N := 100$

$$m := 0 .. N \qquad x_m := \frac{m}{N} \qquad n := 0 .. N \qquad y_n := \frac{n}{N}$$

We're now ready to do our first complex math in Mathcad. To create the imaginary value i you type $1i$ (when you leave the expression the 1 in $1i$ disappears):

The coordinates are: $z(x,y) := x + i \cdot y \qquad z_{m,n} := z(x_m, y_n)$

Note that Mathcad recognizes both conventional notations, of i and j, for the square root of minus one (although you *must* enter them as $1i$ or $1j$).

Mathcad will automatically take care of the complex arithmetic for us, so to get the stream function ψ, all we need to do is type

The stream function is: $\psi_{m,n} := \text{Im}(F(z_{m,n}))$

Note that Mathcad automatically knows what Im means!

Why did we choose to define ψ as a *matrix* rather than a function (which we will do a little later)? Because we want to plot ψ in a contour plot, and you recall from Chapter 3 that you can only use this plot with a matrix. Let's create a contour plot to see what we get:

The plot looks like:

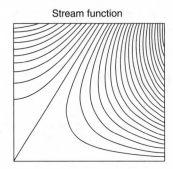

Stream function

ψ

One of the nice concepts in potential theory is that any streamline can be imagined to be a solid boundary. Hence, it appears that the function we chose, $F(z) = z^3$, produces a flow that looks like flow in an acute-angled corner (and we can ignore the streamlines above the straight streamline). We'll see soon that in this example the corner angle is 60°.

Let's see what the corresponding velocity potential φ looks like:

$$\phi_{m,n} := \text{Re}(F(z_{m,n}))$$

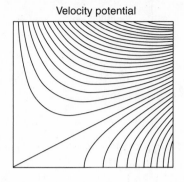

Velocity potential

φ

It turns out that if you were to place these plots one on top of the other, at every point of intersection the streamlines and lines of constant potential would be perpendicular (the orthogonality we mentioned earlier).

Because all of this was so easy to do in Mathcad, you might think that what we've done is trivial. Let's see what mathematics Mathcad in fact had to do for us to generate ψ and φ. First of all, combining Equations (9.3) and (9.6) and simplifying:

$$F(x) = z^3$$
$$= (x + iy)^3$$
$$= x^3 + i3x^2y - 3xy^2 - iy^3 \qquad (9.7)$$
$$= (x^3 - 3xy^2) + i(3x^2y - y^3)$$

Comparing this to Equations (9.5) we finally obtain

$$\varphi = (x^3 - 3xy^2) \qquad (9.8)$$
$$\psi = (3x^2y - y^3)$$

Quite a bit of work for a very simple function $F(z) = z^3$. You can imagine that this process would be extremely cumbersome for more complicated functions. Once we have the stream function, we can then compute the horizontal and vertical components of velocity u and v at any point of the flow, as illustrated in Figure 9.11. It turns out these are obtained from

$$u(x,y) = -\frac{\partial \Psi}{\partial y}$$
$$\qquad (9.9)$$
$$v(x,y) = \frac{\partial \Psi}{\partial x}$$

288

**Importing and
Exporting, the
Web, and Some
Advanced
Concepts**

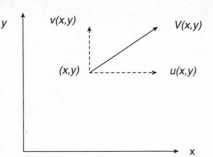

Figure 9.11

To find the velocity components at any point, we would have to use Equations (9.8) in Equations (9.9). Instead, let's have Mathcad do this for us. Although Mathcad cannot display *partial* derivative symbols, its derivative function *does* execute them. To see all this, let's redefine all our variables as functions of x and y, and also compute the total velocity $V(x,y)$, so that we're not working with vectors. Then we can see what we have at, say, point (1,0) (a point on the horizontal axis):

$$z(x,y) := x + i \cdot y \quad F(x,y) := z(x,y)^3 \quad \psi(x,y) := \text{Im}(F(x,y))$$

$$u(x,y) := -\frac{d}{dy}\psi(x,y) \quad v(x,y) := \frac{d}{dx}\psi(x,y) \quad V(x,y) := \sqrt{u(x,y)^2 + v(x,y)^2}$$

$$x := 1 \quad y := 0 \quad u(x,y) = -3 \quad v(x,y) = 0 \quad V(x,y) = 3$$

The velocity at point (0,1) is evidently of magnitude 3, along the horizontal axis. Finally, let's evaluate the magnitude and direction of the velocity at a point on the 60° "wall":

$$x := 1 \quad y := \sqrt{3} \quad u(x,y) = 6 \quad v(x,y) = 10.392$$

$$V(x,y) = 12 \quad \text{atan}\left(\frac{v(x,y)}{u(x,y)}\right) = 60 \cdot \text{deg}$$

The velocity is at an angle of 60° with the horizontal, confirming that the wall is at 60°.

As you can see, the complex notation is a very compact and powerful method for setting up potential flow fields.

As a second example, let's choose a more general function $F(z)$ than that used in Equation (9.6):

$$F(z) = z^k \tag{9.10}$$

where we will define k to be different values to see what happens (and from now on we'll just plot streamlines).

Let's work with this new function. You can either edit the previous Mathcad calculations on this worksheet or delete them and start over, because we're essentially redoing the problem in a more general way.

Try to do the following (where we have chosen a wider range for x and have selected k to be 2):

Set up the computation of x and y values: $\qquad N := 100$

$$m := 0 .. N \qquad x_m := \frac{2 \cdot m}{N} - 1$$

$$n := 0 .. N \qquad y_n := \frac{n}{N}$$

The coordinates are: $\qquad z(x,y) := x + i \cdot y \qquad z_{m,n} := z(x_m, y_n)$

The coefficient k is: $\qquad k := 2$

The complex potential is: $\qquad F(z) := z^k$

The stream function is: $\qquad \psi_{m,n} := \text{Im}(F(z_{m,n}))$

Stream function

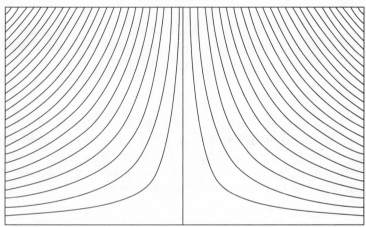

ψ

We appear to have generated flow that can be interpreted as flow down onto an infinite horizontal plane, or, in terms of our previous discussion, if you just look at the right part of the plot, flow in a 90° corner. We're beginning to see a pattern: when $k = 3$ (our previous example) the corner angle was 60°, and with $k = 2$ we get a 90° angle.

Next, try changing the value of k to 5:

The coefficient k is: $\qquad k := 5$

The complex potential is: $\qquad F(z) := z^k$

The stream function is: $\qquad \psi_{m,n} := \text{Im}(F(z_{m,n}))$

Stream function

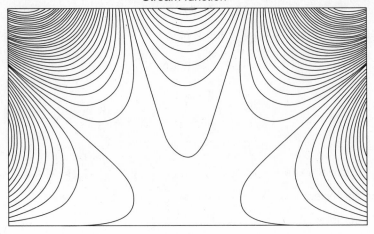

ψ

This complicated flow can be interpreted as including flow in a 36° corner. The pattern is now pretty obvious: Equation (9.10) describes flow in a corner of angle α, given by

$$\alpha = \frac{\pi}{k} \tag{9.11}$$

Let's look at two more potential flows (and we'll skip a lot of the Mathcad details from now on). First let's look at uniform flow of speed U over a cylinder of radius a. This is the same flow we studied in Example 3.6 without using complex notation. It can be shown that the appropriate function is

$$F(z) = U\left(z + \frac{a^2}{z}\right) \tag{9.12}$$

Mathcad gives the following results (where $U = 1$ and $a = 1$ for simplicity):

The flow of speed U over a cylinder of radius a is given by the complex potential:

$$a := 1 \qquad U := 1 \qquad F(z) := U \cdot \left(z + \frac{a^2}{z}\right)$$

The coordinates are specified by: $\qquad z(x,y) := x + i \cdot y$

Set up the computation of x and y values: $\qquad N := 101$

$$x_l := -5 \cdot a \qquad x_u := 5 \cdot a \qquad m := 0 .. N \qquad x_m := x_l + \frac{(x_u - x_l)}{N} \cdot m$$

$y_l := -3 \cdot a \qquad y_u := 3 \cdot a \qquad n := 0 .. N \qquad y_n := y_l + \dfrac{(y_u - y_l)}{N} \cdot n$

and: $\qquad z_{m,n} := z(x_m, y_n)$

The stream function is: $\qquad \psi_{m,n} := \text{Im}(F(z_{m,n}))$

Stream function

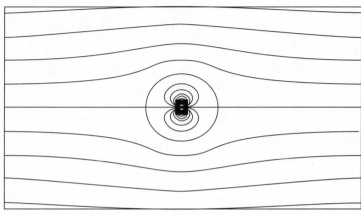

ψ

Note that we set the odd number of data points $N = 101$ so that the x and y values we compute will not include $(0,0)$ $[F(z)$ is singular when $z = 0]$. Once again we see that some simple complex arithmetic can generate fairly complicated flow patterns.

As a final example, let's consider a *source* of unit strength in the vicinity of a wall located along the x axis. A source is a flow in which fluid emanates from a central point, so that all the streamlines are radial from that point. It's known that the function that produces a source at a point z_0 [in other words the point (x_0, y_0)] is

$$F(z) = \frac{1}{2\pi} \ln(z - z_0) \tag{9.13}$$

What we need to do is modify this to allow for the fact that we want the x axis to be a streamline. If you think about it, if you put another source at the mirror-image point to the first one with respect to the x axis, you'll end up with a flow that is symmetric about that axis. Hence, we modify Equation (9.13) to be

$$F(z) = \frac{1}{2\pi} \ln(z - z_0) + \frac{1}{2\pi} \ln(z - \bar{z}_0) \tag{9.14}$$

where

$$\bar{z}_0 = x - iy \qquad (9.15)$$

is the *complex conjugate* of z_0 (and Mathcad will do this for us!).

To work with these equations, let's first redefine our x and y values:

Set up the computation of x and y values: $N := 101$

$$m := 0 .. N \qquad x_m := \frac{2 \cdot m}{N} \qquad n := 0 .. N \qquad y_n := \frac{3 \cdot n}{N}$$

The coordinates are: $z(x,y) := x + i \cdot y \qquad z_{m,n} := z(x_m, y_n)$

Next, try to do the following in Mathcad [use the double-quote (") to generate the complex conjugate]:

The source is located at: $z_0 := 1 + i$

The complex potential is: $F(z) := \dfrac{1}{2 \cdot \pi} \cdot \ln(z - z_0) + \dfrac{1}{2 \cdot \pi} \cdot \ln\left(z - \bar{z}_0\right)$

The stream function is: $\psi_{m,n} := \text{Im}(F(z_{m,n}))$

Stream function

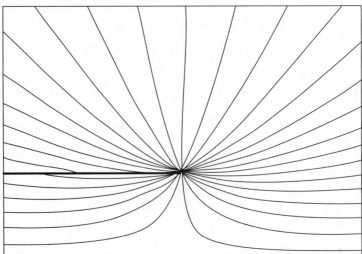

ψ

As you can see, we get what appears to be the flow due to having a source near a wall. (The dark horizontal line has to do with the way Mathcad evaluates logarithms with complex arguments.)

Could you figure out what to do to generate the flow due to a source near a 90° corner? To do this you'd have to place three sources at appropriate mirror-image points.

If you're interested in learning more about potential theory and complex notation for studying fluid flows, one of the classic works is *Theoretical Hydrodynamics*, by Milne-Thomson (New York: Macmillan, 1968).

This completes our introduction to using Mathcad to do complex notation. As our last project in Mathcad, let's look at Mathcad's built-in Laplace transforms.

Using Laplace Transforms

Engineers, after applying a mathematical model to an engineering problem, often end up with a differential equation, and sometimes an integral equation, that they then need to solve. There are many ways to go about tackling the solution of such an equation, but if it's *linear,* we can often use *Laplace transforms* to convert the *differential* or *integral* equation into an *algebraic* equation.

As with the discussion of potential theory and complex notation in the previous section, we won't go into a lot of the details of Laplace transform theory here, but just introduce it and then move on to using Mathcad to perform the transforms.

The basic idea is that we can transform a time-domain function $f(t)$ into an s-domain function $F(s)$ by using the following formula:

$$F(s) = \mathscr{L}(f) = \int_0^\infty e^{-st} f(t) \, dt \tag{9.16}$$

Here $\mathscr{L}(f)$ means "the Laplace transform of f."

This seems an odd thing to do, until you realize that it can be shown that the Laplace transform of the derivative of f, namely f', is

$$\mathscr{L}(f') = s\mathscr{L}(f) - f(0) \tag{9.17}$$

This equation states that the Laplace transform of the derivative is equal to s times the *original* Laplace transform of the function, minus the function's initial condition. In other words, a derivative in the t domain becomes a simple product of terms in the s domain. There are similar expressions for higher-order derivatives.

We can also write an expression for the Laplace transform of an integral in terms of $\mathscr{L}(f)$:

$$\mathscr{L}\left(\int_0^t f(\tau) \, d\tau \right) = \frac{1}{s} \, \mathscr{L}(f(t)) \tag{9.18}$$

What these equations mean is that you can take a differential or integral equation for an unknown $f(t)$ in the time domain t and convert it into an algebraic equation for an unknown $F(s)$ in the s domain. Why do this? Because an algebraic equation can usually be solved for the unknown, so an explicit expression for $F(s)$ can

294
Importing and
Exporting, the
Web, and Some
Advanced
Concepts

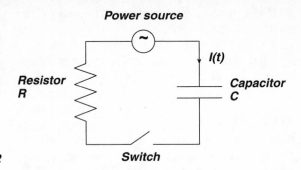

Figure 9.12

be found. The only tricky part is then finding the *inverse* transformation back to the time domain. This may seem a little abstract, but by using Mathcad we'll see how easy the method is.

Suppose you have the circuit shown in Figure 9.12. Initially the circuit is open and there is no charge in the capacitor. At time $t = 0$ s the switch is closed and the following voltage is applied:

$$V(t) = V_0 \cos(\omega t) \tag{9.19}$$

where V_0 is the maximum voltage and ω is its frequency.

By summing the potential changes around the circuit, it can be shown that at any instant of time

$$RI(t) + \frac{1}{C}\int_0^t I(t) = V_0 \cos(\omega t) \tag{9.20}$$

Let's type this into a new worksheet in Mathcad, using the Boolean equals so that we can conveniently do some symbolic mathematics (under which category Laplace transforms can be found):

Using Laplace Transforms

By (Your Name)

$$R \cdot I(t) + \frac{1}{C} \cdot \int_0^t I(\tau)d\tau = V_0 \cdot \cos(\omega \cdot t)$$

Next, all we need to do is select one of the *t*'s in the equation and use the menu item *Symbolics . . . Transform . . . Laplace* (or instead of this, you could open the Symbolic Keyword palette and use the Laplace button). You should get:

has Laplace transform

$$R \cdot \text{laplace}(I(t), t, s) + \frac{1}{(C \cdot s)} \cdot \text{laplace}(I(t), t, s) = V_0 \cdot \frac{s}{\left(s^2 + \omega^2\right)}$$

(Here, before doing the transform, we used the menu item *Symbolics . . . Evaluation Style* to tell Mathcad to automatically show comment lines.)

Mathcad has converted the integral equation in *t* space to an algebraic expression in *s* space. If you look it up in a table of transforms [for example, in *Advanced Engineering Mathematics,* by Kreyszig (New York: Wiley, 1993)], you'll see that the Laplace transform of a cosine is indeed the expression shown on the right. Notice that Mathcad also gave us the correct expression for the transform of the integral.

Unfortunately, as you can see, the symbolic processor gave the transform of *I(t)* an ugly, unusable name laplace(*I(t),t,s*) (which means "the Laplace transform of *I* from *t* space to *s* space"). This leads to an important point about symbolic processing (in Mathcad or in any other mathematics application with this feature): the technology behind symbolic math is still relatively new, so symbolic manipulators sometimes give results that are not in a compact form; in other words, they are not quite as good (yet!) as a well-trained human, in symbolic manipulations. Fortunately, we'll soon see that the processor can be asked to simplify, or clean up, an expression that it has produced for us. However, even then it often doesn't do as good a job as a human would (see the example at the end of Section 2.8). In practice, you'll find that you often need to do some manual manipulations to get answers in just the form you want.

In this particular case, let's manually edit the equation to replace *laplace(I(t),t,s)* with simply *I*. We can then select one of these *I*'s and use the menu item *Symbolics . . . Variable . . . Solve* to find *I*:

$$R{\cdot}I + \frac{1}{(C{\cdot}s)}{\cdot}I = V_0{\cdot}\frac{s}{\left(s^2 + \omega^2\right)}$$

has solution(s)

$$V_0{\cdot}\frac{s}{\left[(s^2 + \omega^2){\cdot}\left[R + \frac{1}{(C{\cdot}s)}\right]\right]}$$

Finally, how do we transform back from *s* space to *t* space? One method is to use a published table of transforms to see if you can find the one shown above (and you'd probably have to manually expand the expression into its factors first). A more convenient method is to ask Mathcad to do it for us. For example, we can use the menu item *Symbolics . . . Transform . . . Inverse Laplace* (after selecting one of the *s*'s) to do the conversion:

296

**Importing and
Exporting, the
Web, and Some
Advanced
Concepts**

$$V_0 \cdot \frac{s}{\left[(s^2 + \omega^2) \cdot \left[R + \frac{1}{(C \cdot s)} \right] \right]}$$

has inverse Laplace transform

$$-V_0 \cdot C \cdot \omega \cdot \frac{\sin(\omega \cdot t)}{\left(1 + R^2 \cdot C^2 \cdot \omega^2\right)} + V_0 \cdot C^2 \cdot \omega^2 \cdot R \cdot \frac{\cos(\omega \cdot t)}{\left(1 + R^2 \cdot C^2 \cdot \omega^2\right)} + V_0 \cdot C \cdot \frac{\exp\left[\frac{-1}{(R \cdot C)} \cdot t\right]}{\left(R \cdot C + R^3 \cdot C^3 \cdot \omega^2\right)}$$

Mathcad has saved us a lot of inconvenience by doing the transform. However, it didn't provide the result in the most convenient form. Let's now select the entire expression and use the menu item *Symbolics . . . Simplify* to get

simplifies to

$$V_0 \cdot \frac{\left[-C \cdot \omega \cdot \sin(\omega \cdot t) \cdot R + C^2 \cdot \omega^2 \cdot R^2 \cdot \cos(\omega \cdot t) + \exp\left[\frac{-1}{(R \cdot C)} t\right] \right]}{\left[R \cdot \left(1 + R^2 \cdot C^2 \cdot \omega^2\right) \right]}$$

We've gone as far as we can with the symbolic processor. We can now manually simplify a bit by dividing throughout by R and by replacing the exp notation with the e notation (depending on personal preference), and then assign this function of time t to the variable $I(t)$. Before doing all of this, we can assign some values to the various quantities:

$$V_0 := 120 \cdot \text{volt} \quad R := 5 \cdot \text{ohm} \quad C := 150 \cdot \mu\text{F} \quad f := 60 \cdot \text{Hz} \quad \omega := 2 \cdot \pi \cdot f \quad T := \frac{1}{f}$$

$$I(t) := V_0 \cdot \frac{\left(-C \cdot \omega \cdot \sin(\omega \cdot t) + C^2 \cdot \omega^2 \cdot R \cdot \cos(\omega \cdot t) + \frac{e^{\frac{-t}{R \cdot C}}}{R} \right)}{\left(1 + R^2 \cdot C^2 \cdot \omega^2\right)}$$

Note that f is the frequency in cycles per second and ω is the frequency in radians per second (T is the voltage period).

We've finished solving the integral equation! All that remains is to plot the current and voltage versus time:

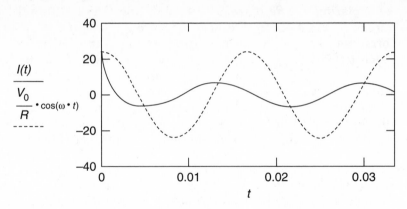

In this graph we plotted the voltage divided by the resistance so that both plotted functions have the units of amps [you recall that you can only plot functions together if they have the same (or no) units]. It turns out that the dashed curve is the result if you had just a resistor in the circuit (to eliminate the capacitor, would you make its capacitance zero or very large? . . . try both!). Notice that the solution consists of an initial transient effect and then a steady-state solution.

We've now finished our very brief introduction to Mathcad's Laplace transforms. For more information, a good place to start is the *Resource Center,* where under *Quicksheets* you'll find a path to *Calculus and Differential Equations.* Finally, under this topic you'll find *Symbolic transforms,* where you'll find information not only on Laplace transforms but also on *Fourier transforms* and *Z transforms.*

A Final Comment

We've seen in this chapter that Mathcad can do some quite advanced and sophisticated mathematics. However, even here we've barely scratched the surface of Mathcad's power. There are lots of terrific features we haven't covered at all, or have just touched upon. We haven't focused, for example, on Mathcad's ability to handle huge amounts of data: up to 8 million data points, depending on your computer's memory. We did not do very much work with *iterative* calculations using range variables, a very useful procedure in numerical methods such as the Finite Difference method. We only briefly touched on Mathcad's extensive statistical features. We haven't mentioned at all its Animation feature. Finally, we only briefly mentioned one of Mathcad's great strengths: its flexibility in formatting worksheets.

All of these topics can be investigated either by using *Help* or by exploring the *Resource Center* (and a particularly useful feature of this is its *Reference Tables,* where you can find a lot of information on topics such as properties of materials, useful calculus formulas, and so on). The *User's Guide* furnished with Mathcad 7 is also a fairly complete manual on Mathcad's features.

Finally, if you need even more power, such as more extensive differential equation solvers, or the ability to explicitly program functions, you can turn to the Professional edition of Mathcad 7.

Answers to Selected Exercises

2.1 M = 18.4 lb.

2.2 A = 0.196 m², V = 8.18 x 10⁻³ m³.

2.3 Bank A yields $1,161,616.78. Bank B yields $1,173,411.40.

2.4 ΔV = −100 ft³.

2.5 a) 95.5°F after 10 minutes; 82.1°F after 60 minutes.

b) 96.7°F after 10 minutes; 88.6°F after 60 minutes.

2.9 The range is $x := 0, 2\cdot\pi \, .. \, 10\cdot\pi$.

2.10 First define x_{start} and x_{end}, then $x := x_{start} \, .. \, x_{end}$.

2.11 $x := 20, 17 \, .. -1$.

2.12 First define x_{start}, x_{end}, and k. Then define $x_{sec} := \dfrac{(x_{end} - x_{start})}{k-1} + x_{start}$. Finally the range is $x := x_{start}, x_{sec} \, .. \, x_{end}$.

2.13 Simplifies to $x - 2$.

2.14 The series around $\theta = 0$ is

$$3\theta - \frac{9}{2}\theta^3 + \frac{81}{40}\theta^5 - \frac{243}{560}\theta^7 + \frac{243}{4480}\theta^9 + O(\theta^{10}).$$

The series around $\theta = \pi/6$ is

$$1 - \frac{9}{2}\left(\theta - \frac{\pi}{6}\right)^2 + \frac{27}{8}\left(\theta - \frac{\pi}{6}\right)^4 - \frac{81}{80}\left(\theta - \frac{\pi}{6}\right)^6 + \frac{729}{4480}\left(\theta - \frac{\pi}{6}\right)^8.$$

2.15 In terms of powers of x: $(1 + y)x^2 + (y^2 - 1)x + y^2$.

2.16 In terms of powers of y: $(1 + x)y^2 + x^2y + x^2 - x$.

2.17 M = 150 lb, 68 kg; W = 667.2 newton; W_{moon} = 25 lbf, 111.2 newton.

2.18 δ = 0.017 in., 0.444 mm.

2.20 Factoring yields $(x + 7)(x^2 - 5)(x^3 - 6)$.

2.22 Expanding and collecting terms yields
$x^4 + (1 - 4y)x^3 + (1 - 3y + 6y^2)x^2 + (1 - 2y + 3y^2 - 4y^3)x + 1 - y + y^2 - y^3 + y^4$.

2.24 The Taylor series of $\tan(\theta)$, after squaring, simplifying, and expanding, is $\theta^2 + \dfrac{2}{3}\theta^4 + \dfrac{17}{45}\theta^6 + \dfrac{4}{45}\theta^8 + \dfrac{4}{225}\theta^{10}$. This is the same as the Taylor series of $\tan^2(\theta)$.

2.26 $M = 6.23$ lb, $X = 41.7$ cm, $Y = 25.9$ cm.

2.28 $P = 0.98$ kW, 1.31 hp.

2.30 $p_{op} = 21.69$ psi, $p_{act} = 24.79$ psi. At Denver: $m_W = 40$ gm.

2.32 $k = 8.78 \times 10^4$ newton/m, $g_{force} = 24$, $x_{cycle} = 6.94$ ft, g_{force} (cycle)= 69.6.

2.34 $f_{child} = 2$ Hz, $T_{child} = 0.5$ sec, $f_{father} = 1.5$ Hz, $T_{father} = 0.666$ sec.

2.36 $h = 22,247$ miles, $v = 6,858$ mph.

2.38 Bundled: $t_{term} = 40$ sec (approx.), $v_{term} = 175.7$ mph.

Spreadeagled: $t_{term} = 20$ sec (approx.), $v_{term} = 99.8$ mph.

With no drag, after 60 sec the speed would be 1,316 mph.

Chapter 3

3.1 $V_{max} = 6.9$ mph (to one significant figure) and $t_{max} = 8$ to 10 sec approx.

3.10 The roots are approximately at $x = 0.45$, 1.38, 3.54, and 4.21.

3.12 $T_{amp} = 0.02$ sec, $T_{high} = 1.75 \times 10^{-3}$ sec, $f_{amp} = 50$ Hz (the difference in the frequencies of the two sine waves), $f_{high} = 571$ Hz (approx. the average of the frequencies of the two sine waves).

3.16 $A_{max} = 6.69$ (approx.).

3.20 Both speakers are the same at the front, speaker 1 is better at the sides, and speaker 2 is better at the rear. Speaker 1 is better for most people.

Chapter 4

4.1 After manual rearranging: $b_n = \dfrac{2(\sin(n\pi) - n\pi\cos(n\pi))}{\pi n^2}$ (and this could be further simplified, e.g., $\sin(n\pi) = 0$ for all n).

4.2 $A = r^2\pi$.

4.3 $Q = A\tau V$ (Note: if this exercise is done in the same worksheet as Exercise 4.2, instead of A you'll get $r^2\pi$!).

4.4 $T = 0.654$ sec.

4.5 $P = 1,321$ ft.

4.6 $\dfrac{x^{(n+1)}}{(n+1)}$, $\dfrac{-\cos(\omega x)}{\omega}$, $\ln(x)$.

4.10 All integrals are zero *except* when $m = n$, in which case the cos-cos and sin-sin integrals are each equal to π. Note: If you continue in the same worksheet, define m equal to 1000 mm, so that it becomes meters again!

4.12 First derivative: $\dfrac{\cos(x)}{\left(1 + \sin^2(x)\right)}$.

Second derivative (after simplifying and manual rearrangement):

$$\frac{\sin(x)\left(2 + \cos^2(x)\right)}{\left(4\cos^2(x) - \cos^4(x) - 4\right)}.$$

4.14 For $\pm\sigma$: $\text{erf}\left(\frac{1}{2}\sqrt{2}\right) = 68.3\%$.

For $\pm 2\sigma$: $\text{erf}\left(\sqrt{2}\right) = 94.5\%$.

For $\pm 3\sigma$: $\text{erf}\left(\frac{3}{2}\sqrt{2}\right) = 99.7\%$.

4.16 $V = \frac{1}{3}\pi R^2 H$.

4.18 $A = 4\pi R$.

4.22 $m_{\text{friend}} = 168.8$ lb, 76.5 kg, $m_{\text{you}} = 126.6$ lb, 57.4 kg.

Chapter 5

5.2 $t_{2000} = 22.3$ sec.

5.4 a) $v = 0.1465$ m^3/kg, b) $v = 0.1436$ m^3/kg.

5.6 $(-0.225, 2.225)$ and $(2.225, -0.225)$.

5.8 $x_1 = -2$, $x_2 = 5$, $x_3 = 0$, $x_4 = -1$.

5.10 For 95%: 5.1 ft to 6.4 ft, or $\pm 1.96\sigma$.

For 99%: 4.89 ft to 6.61 ft, or $\pm 2.58\sigma$.

For 99.5%: 4.81 ft to 6.69 ft, or $\pm 2.81\sigma$.

5.12 $i = 6.7\%$

5.14 For $y_{\text{end}} = 0$ in., $a = 2.21$ ft.

For $y_{\text{end}} = -1$ in, $a = 1.49$ ft.

For $y_{\text{end}} = 1$ in, $a = 2.79$ ft.

5.16 $x_{\text{max}} = 0.15$ in ($T_{\text{max}} = 880$ R).

5.18 14.3 Hz $< \omega <$ 24.2 Hz.

5.20 $p_2 = 477$ kPa, $V_2 = 243$ m/sec, $\rho_2 = 3.63$ kg/m^3, $T_2 = 462$ K.

Chapter 6

6.2 6.2 $x = \begin{bmatrix} 0 \\ 1 \\ 2 \end{bmatrix}$.

6.4 $b \cdot c = 63$, $|b||c| = 102.6$, $\theta = 52.1$ deg.

6.6 9,333 trucks, 12,667 minivans, 51,333 sedans, and 18,667 compacts.

6.8 Black = $27, white = $23, and red = $31.

6.10 $x_1 = -2$, $x_2 = 5$, $x_3 = 0$, $x_4 = -1$.

6.12 Force magnitude = 12.57 newtons, with angles 37.3 deg, 56.2 deg, and 76.2 deg.

Power = 29 watts, work = 1,740 joules.

6.14 T_1 through T_5 = 2,449, −1,732, −1,732, 1,732, and −2,000 lbf.

R_1, R_2, and R_3 = 0, −1,732, and 2,732 lbf.

6.16 T_1 = 282.7 K = 9.7°C, T_2 = 282.3 K = 9.3°C.

6.18 Natural frequencies: 3.13 Hz, 4.42 Hz, 6.26 Hz.

6.20 p_{max} = 1.94 atm, h = 14 m.

Chapter 7

7.4 $x(2)$ = 0.106, $y(2)$ = −0.404.

7.16 y_{max} = 48.8 m.

7.18 v_{max} = 97.5 mph, t_{60} = 6.2 sec (approx.).

7.20 Maximum I_1 = 44.9 mA, maximum I_2 = 14.8 mA.

7.22 Maximum B = 0.422 mole/liter, at t = 11.55 hr.

Chapter 8

8.4 For 23,000 units the budget should be $21,770.

With a $17,000 budget the sales should be 17,823.

8.6 A = 3.056, n = 0.51.

8.8 A = 0.011, n = 1.999, C_D = 0.273.

8.10 τ = 60 min, t_{20} = 138 min.

8.12 a = 0.05, b = 1.98.

8.14 a = 0.202, b = 5.122, y_{min} = 2.257 (at x = 2.327).

8.18 84% of the rivets are between 28 .0 ± 0.2 cm.

48% of the rivets are between 28 .0 ± 0.1 cm.

8.20 Maximum load = 2410 lbf.

8.22 15.9% of batteries will need to be replaced.

8.24 For 5%: ± 0.627. For 25%: ± 3.186. For 50%: ± 6.745. For 75%: ± 11.503.

Index